how to live a
low-carbon
life

the individual's guide to
stopping climate change

Chris Goodall

London • Sterling, VA

First published by Earthscan in the UK and USA in 2007
Reprinted 2007 (three times)

ISBN: 978-1-84407-426-6

Typeset by Domex e-Data Pvt. Ltd, India
Printed and bound in the UK by Antony Rowe, Chippenham
Cover design by Safehouse Creative

For a full list of publications please contact:

Earthscan
8-12 Camden High Street
London, NW1 0JH, UK
Tel: +44 (0)20 7387 8558
Fax: +44 (0)20 7387 8998
Email: earthinfo@earthscan.co.uk
Web: www.earthscan.co.uk

22883 Quicksilver Drive, Sterling, VA 20166-2012, USA

Earthscan publishes in association with the International Institute for Environment and Development

A catalogue record for this book is available from the British Library

Library of Congress Cataloging-in-Publication Data

Goodall, Chris.
How to live a low carbon life: the individual's guide to stopping climate change/Chris Goodall. p. cm.
ISBN-13: 978-1-84407-426-6 (pbk.)
ISBN-10: 1-84407-426-9 (pbk.)
1. Atmospheric carbon dioxide–Climatic factors. 2. Atmospheric carbon dioxide–Environmental aspects. 3. Climatic changes–Social aspects. 4. Consumers–Environmental aspects. 5. Carbon dioxide–Environmental aspects. I. Title.
QC 879.8.G62 2007
363.738'7–dc22

2006100479

The paper used for this book is FSC-certified and totally chlorine-free. FSC (the Forest Stewardship Council) is an international network to promote responsible management of the world's forests.

how to live a
low-carbon
life

Contents

List of Figures and Tables

FIGURES

TABLES

Sources and Units of Measurement

In this book, I have used information from many sources and often combined this data in a single table. Where I have merged or averaged multiple different sources, I have not credited any single author in order to avoid any misstating or misattribution. Where I just use data from one place, I credit this source beneath the table. When data is merged, the main sources are specified in endnotes.

I have standardized on kilowatt hours (kWh) as the unit of measurement. At various points in the book, conventional analysis might use 'million barrels of oil equivalent', kilocalories or petajoules. I hope it aids comprehensibility to use just one unit. When referring to high values I have sometimes made it clearer by referring to megawatt hours (MWh, equal to a thousand kWh) and gigawatt hours (GWh, equal to a thousand MWh or a million kWh). The huge numbers of noughts in many energy-related figures means that I am almost certain to have slipped up somewhere in making the hundreds of conversions I have calculated in this book. I apologize in advance for any errors.

Throughout the book, I have used the weight of carbon dioxide (CO_2) as the index of global warming effect. Much of the data in the field is actually expressed in terms of just carbon. To get from the weight of carbon to that of carbon dioxide, one multiplies by 3.6667. Thus, 1 tonne of carbon is equivalent to 3.6667 (three and two-thirds) tonnes of carbon dioxide. As explained in the text, other greenhouse gases, such as methane, are expressed in terms of the equivalent global warming effect of carbon dioxide. The weight of methane, for example, is multiplied by 21 to get to a carbon dioxide equivalent. Different international bodies use slightly different multipliers for the various gases, and I have used the official European figures.

When dealing with energy prices to households, I use round numbers for the costs in autumn 2006. Generally I have referred to UK pound sterling prices (denoted by £); if I use $ it means US dollars. By the time the book is published, these numbers will inevitably be wrong and in the event of substantial upward or downward movement readers may have to make some adjustments to the calculations. I am sorry for the inconvenience that this may cause. I suspect all calculations will still be broadly correct. For the most up to date information, check this book's companion website at www.lowcarbonlife.net.

Acknowledgements

This book necessarily contains a huge amount of information and analysis. The original data comes from a very wide spectrum of sources; but I want particularly to acknowledge the importance of information derived from the Market Transformation Programme (MTP), a research body supported by the Department for Environment, Food and Rural Affairs (Defra), the UK government department with principal responsibility for climate change policies. At several points in this book, I cast doubt on the MTP's optimistic projections; but its data is carefully collected and processed and I am very grateful for the painstaking work. I have also extensively used the superb work of Paul Waide of the International Energy Agency on household lighting and electricity use. Substantial amounts of source data are taken from the impressively compendious publications of the Building Research Establishment and the extremely stimulating papers of Oxford University's Environmental Change Institute. Errors of interpretation and analysis of the data are, of course, all mine.

I owe a substantial debt to Paul Klemperer for several stimulating discussions on climate change issues over the last two years. John Coleman gave me very useful advice on many occasions. John Bleach got me interested in the quantification of the effects of household behaviour when he used our house in his postgraduate research. Councillor Craig Simmons, the bedrock of the Oxford Green party, gave me important help for which I am very grateful. Claire Enders was hugely encouraging and helpful in the last phases of the book's preparation. Of course, these individuals don't necessarily agree with the analysis or conclusions in this book.

My wife Charlotte Brewer has been a tower of support and a constant gentle encouragement. Our children, Alice, Miriam and Ursula, have had to put up with both their parents completing books at the same time, and have done so with noisy good humour and appropriate cynicism. The family tolerance for eccentric domestic experiments, such as measuring the energy used in cooking toast, was well beyond the call of domestic duty.

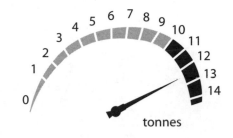

Introduction

• •

getting from 12½ tonnes to 3 tonnes of carbon dioxide per person

T his book tries to show that individuals – rather than governments or companies – are going to have to be the driving force behind reductions in greenhouse gases. We cannot hide behind an unjustified expectation that political or corporate leaders are going to do something for us: the threat from climate change requires each of us to take personal responsibility for reducing our impact on the planet's atmosphere. Individually, of course, we are powerless; but our actions influence those around us. Eventually, private companies will perceive a market for low-carbon products, and governments will come to see that real action on climate change is not electorally disastrous. Individuals must provide the leadership that will eventually galvanize the rest of society.

Very few people know the details of how the activities of our day-to-day lives generate emissions of carbon dioxide (CO_2) and other harmful gases. This book provides information and practical suggestions that will enable concerned individuals to do the best they can to reduce greenhouse gas emissions. It is intended as a reference work to help people make good decisions on how most effectively to reduce their own responsibility for climate change.

Taking international air travel into account, people in the UK are each responsible for about 12.5 tonnes of greenhouse gases a year.[1] This figure is approximately the same as the European Union (EU) average, and other European countries face similar problems of controlling emissions. In most countries, including the UK, the tonnage of carbon dioxide is rising slightly year on year, largely as a result of increasing personal travel. About half of the total comes directly from the way in which we live our lives – running our homes and getting from place to place in car or plane. The share of all emissions coming from homes and personal transport is growing. Increasingly, it is our day-to-day way of life that is causing the continued rise in carbon dioxide and other warming gases.

The other half of the UK's greenhouse gases is emitted indirectly but on our behalf – bringing us our food, heating and cooling our offices, making the steel and plastics for the things we buy, and powering the construction of our new buildings. Just because we have no direct control over fossil fuel use in industry and commerce doesn't mean we can't do anything about it. Individual citizens can, and should, change their purchasing habits and, perhaps, even their place of work in order to help reduce global warming.

If we are to have any hope of meeting our obligations to others on this planet, as well as to unborn generations, we need to slash today's unsustainable and dangerous 12.5 tonnes of greenhouse gas emissions per person, bringing it down to no more than 3 tonnes each. This book shows how.

GOVERNMENTS AND COMPANIES ARE NOT DEALING WITH THE PROBLEM

In 2000, the UK government published its first Climate Change Programme.[2] A barrage of initiatives and new proposals backed up the government's forecast that it would reduce the UK's greenhouse gas emissions in 2005 by about 37 million tonnes below the expected level. It didn't turn out that way: provisional figures for 2005 suggest that the government's many schemes had no impact whatsoever. Reductions in some areas masked substantial increases in others. Absolutely none of the planned reduction in emissions actually happened. UK carbon dioxide emissions rose in 2005 and now stand 4 million tonnes higher than in 2000. Even the notoriously optimistic long-range government forecasts see UK carbon dioxide output rising strongly in the period after 2010. The UK is not unusual; most countries will miss their targets for greenhouse gas emissions.

Speeches and articles contributed by political leaders worldwide conclude that climate change is a serious problem. But the figures reveal that we are as addicted as ever to the consumption of fossil fuels. Society has not yet grasped that reducing greenhouse gas emissions is difficult, even in mature economies. In the newly industrializing states, such as China and India, the problem is even worse.

The global economy, based on free markets, economic competition and international trade, and run by more or less democratic political institutions, will remain wholly reliant on the burning of cheap fossil fuels. Despite the increasing interest in low-carbon technologies, companies the world over face an imperative to continue to use large quantities of oil, gas and coal. The only possible route forward is, therefore, for individual citizens to take action to change their styles of life in order to minimize their own responsibility for emissions. This is what this book is about. As responsible members of prosperous societies, we have a duty to curb our own consumption rather than to rely on ineffectual governments and profit-seeking corporations. I try to show that cutting emissions systematically and substantially is within the easy grasp of everybody.

Why have companies and governments failed to cut emissions so far? The reasons are simple. It is not in the interest of any single government to act to reduce carbon emissions if most of the rest of the world continues to pollute in growing volumes. If, for example, the UK were unilaterally to introduce higher taxes on gas use, and our competitors did not follow, gas-using industries would simply shift abroad. There is no electoral advantage in addressing climate change: applying real restraint on fossil fuel use would lose votes, at little benefit to the global atmosphere, unless every country acted similarly.

Corporations face a similar problem. Their senior executives do genuinely worry about the long-term impact of climate change on the world's peoples. However, in market economies, such as the UK, the role of business is no more and no less than to meet consumer requirements at the cheapest possible price. Companies will therefore use the least expensive source of energy, knowing that failure to do so will mean competitors are able to charge less. Furthermore, business will always be able to lobby successfully for the lowest possible energy prices in order that their prices remain internationally competitive.

Second, companies will always follow consumer tastes. If customers demand appliances with higher energy consumption – such as, for example, larger cars, big-screen TVs or American-style refrigerators – companies will supply the requirement. Any company that did not would consign itself to failure. In the modern economy, successful companies meet consumer demands rather than fight against them. Unfortunately, as this book will repeatedly illustrate, most consumers prefer products and services that contain increasing amounts of fossil fuels.

The upshot is that neither government nor companies have any choice about climate change. They can talk a good story, advertise their green credentials and promise future virtue; but they will remain obdurately set in their ways. They will follow what the voters ask for or what purchasers require. We therefore cannot shift the responsibility for dealing with climate change onto others; the responsibility belongs to individual citizens of the world. In particular, it belongs to the educated members of prosperous societies. We know enough – it is almost undeniable that climate change is going to devastate large areas of the world, particularly the rural South – and we also have the capacity to easily reduce our own impact.

A further point arises. It is not generally understood that it is the wealthiest members of wealthy countries who pollute the most. The heaviest responsibility for addressing the issues of climate change falls upon the economic elite. You may not think of yourself as a member of this club, but you probably are. If you travel abroad for holidays, run a reasonably sized saloon car and have a conventional middle-class lifestyle, your damage to the global environment may be double that of the national average. The hydrocarbon feeding frenzy is led by ordinary people, not by monster corporations or evil governments. Responsible citizens need to change their habits. The good news is that this is not difficult.

Nevertheless, getting people to change their ways is rarely easy. We are lazy and listen to siren voices that say that inertia is a perfectly satisfactory alternative. Just at the moment, the voices urging inaction have three good stories: first, the world is running out of fossil fuels and pollution will eventually fall; second, technology will reduce the demand for hydrocarbons; and, last, increased prosperity brings with it a natural propensity for decreased energy use because of improving efficiency. These are all falsehoods. Do not imagine that the declining availability of oil will reduce carbon emissions at any stage in the near future. More oil is burned each year than is discovered in new fields, and probably 50 per cent of the world's recoverable oil has been extracted. But one estimate suggests that we have access to 180 years of coal at current consumption rates.[3] We are not going to be saved from ourselves by running out of hydrocarbons.

Carbon emissions will not be reduced by the scarcity of fuels. Nor will they be dramatically curtailed by a move to nuclear electricity; easily recoverable uranium deposits will probably run out long before the coal does.[4] The move to the so-called 'hydrogen economy' is also a dangerous mirage. Current technologies to produce hydrogen consume more fossil fuel energy than is generated by the gas when combusted. This is unlikely to change for decades. Also, independent forecasters almost universally see global energy consumption rising by over 50 per cent in the next 20 years.[5] The official forecast for the US sees demand rising by over 30 per cent between now and 2030, and most of this increase will be met by greater use of oil and coal.[6] Prosperity increases the demand for fossil fuel products.

While government waits and wrings its hands, this book shows how a concerned citizen of the world can cut his or her consumption of fossil fuels to a level that is commensurate with the continued existence of normal life on Earth. Of course, the actions of single individuals, even multiplied a million fold, are wholly insignificant. But in acting as examples to others, and showing companies and governments the support for genuine changes in lifestyle, your actions can be powerful. The great movements in social improvement in Western society, such as the end of slavery, the universal franchise, control over child labour and universal primary education, all came after sustained action by small groups of committed individuals. My thesis is that action to address climate change can only happen in the same way.

This book presents a summary of what we need to do to cut our carbon emissions by 75 per cent. This reduction is necessary across the developed world if we are to have any prospect of avoiding temperature increases that make life impossible in large parts of the globe. There are two ways for the concerned citizen to get to the target: spending money or changing lifestyle – both types of action are addressed in the following chapters. Most people will find a combination of these routes most congenial. Low-carbon living isn't necessarily compatible with all aspects of the aspirational Western style of life; but it is surprisingly easy to make huge reductions in carbon emissions.

This book contains detailed accounts of how today's lives generate carbon emissions. For those seeking simple prescriptions as to what to do, a summary of recommendations is contained near the beginning of the later chapters.

THE ELEMENTARY SCIENCE

Almost 30 billion tonnes of carbon dioxide enters the atmosphere as a result of human activities each year.[7] Carbon dioxide is one of the two main products of the combustion of hydrocarbons, such as coal and gas, which fuel the modern economy. This otherwise innocuous gas, the most important contributor to global warming, still only constitutes about 380 parts per million of the world's atmosphere. The concentration is rising by 2 to 3 parts per million every year and, if current trends continue, looks set to exceed 500 parts per million by 2050, or almost twice pre-industrial levels. Other greenhouse gases, such as methane and nitrous oxide, will push the concentrations to the equivalent of more than 550 parts per million.

Visible light from the sun warms the Earth's surface. Like a conventional room radiator, the surface eventually retransmits this energy outwards as heat in the form of infrared radiation and convection. Increasing levels of greenhouse gases render the atmosphere less transparent to outgoing infrared radiation, and the heat is trapped. More carbon dioxide in the atmosphere will, all other things being equal, raise the temperature of the atmosphere at the Earth's surface.[8]

No one can be completely sure about the precise relationship between rising greenhouse gas concentrations and increasing temperatures. The consensus estimate is that a concentration of 550 parts per million is likely to increase temperatures by about 2 to 4 degrees Celsius above today's levels. The increase is likely to vary substantially between different parts of the world. The higher temperatures will have a variety of severe effects, ranging from drought in areas now reliant on the summer melting of rapidly disappearing glaciers to higher sea levels, making life impossible in the coastal areas that are home to a large fraction of the world's population. Some optimists claim we can cope with temperatures 4 degrees higher. In the temperate regions, this is possible. We can build higher sea walls, adjust our agriculture and acclimatize to higher temperatures. In countries living on the margin – stressed already by water shortages, coastal flooding, tropical hurricanes or temperatures too high for good agricultural productivity – this option is not available. In general, it is the poorest countries that are going to find it most difficult to adapt to rising temperatures and disruption of weather patterns. The carbon emissions of the rich world will ruin the lives of the poor.

The mid-point of the range of expected temperature rise – 3 degrees – is about half the difference between the temperatures of the last ice age and the early modern period. It may not seem much; but this increase will totally alter the distribution of animal and insect life, often causing extinction as species fail to adapt in time. Even more worryingly, this increase may not be the maximum possible. Evidence is strongly emerging that the moderate temperature increases already recorded are inducing changes likely to tip the world towards yet greater rises. These changes include the melting of northern tundras – causing the release of greenhouse gases that had been trapped in permafrost – and the reduction of permanent snow cover, which will tend to reduce the reflection of solar energy back into space.

This story, put here in its simplest possible form, is now well understood and generally agreed by scientists, political policy-makers and many concerned citizens around the world. Newspapers devote pages to the problem. Politicians call it the most serious issue facing the globe. Pressure groups campaign ceaselessly to alert the public to particular implications of rising temperatures. There is still disagreement on many matters; but the single fact – universally acknowledged and the subject of no dispute – that carbon dioxide increases the atmosphere's opacity to infrared radiation from the Earth's surface should be enough to convince even the most hard-boiled sceptic that greenhouse gas pollution is a desperately serious problem.

Carbon dioxide is not the only gas to act as a blanket in this way. Other greenhouse gases, such as methane and nitrous oxide, are produced in very much smaller volumes but have a much more virulent warming effect. In the UK, land-based sources of these other gases are tending to decline, except in the case of emissions from agriculture. Nitrous oxide emissions from aircraft engines are growing as the amount of air travel increases.

WHAT WE CAN DO

Despite our increasing levels of knowledge and the expressions of earnest concern, the world has not yet been successful in reducing carbon dioxide emissions. There is no single scapegoat. For example, we should not focus on the scientific sceptics who deny the scale of the problem. Rather, we should see that the problem is so pervasive, so widespread, that there is no single entity that can be blamed. Governments have, indeed, been ineffective. The impact of the protocols, programmes and policies pursued by governments and companies around the world has only been marginally to diminish the rate of increase in the use of fossil fuel. Carbon dioxide emissions are still rising fast almost everywhere, and on current trends will probably continue to do so for at least a generation to come. Historians writing in the next century will marvel at the extraordinary lassitude with which the world's elite faced the high likelihood of catastrophic changes to climate.

Many people blame the US for the lack of progress on holding down greenhouse gas emissions. This finger-pointing is also convenient but unfair. Almost every developed country will fail to meet its obligations under the Kyoto Protocol to reduce greenhouse gas emissions. Even the UK, proud of its early record in reducing emissions, may well miss its target, although this conclusion is still energetically rebuffed by the current administration. But government ministers do admit that on present trends, UK carbon dioxide output will almost certainly rise well above the Kyoto limit during the decade after 2010.

The UK yearly average of 12.5 tonnes of greenhouse gases per person is equivalent to a column of CO_2 1 square metre in extent, extending upwards for 7km. Stated another way, human activities put the equivalent of a blanket of almost 2m thick of carbon dioxide across the entire UK last year. Other countries in the developed world have higher or lower figures, depending partly upon the proportion of their electricity that is generated with carbon-intensive coal, gas or nuclear fission. The US and Canada are worse, at over 20 tonnes per person, and some oil-exporting states are higher still. China's rapid industrialization has pushed its consumption to over 4 tonnes, while India is also rising fast from its current 2 tonnes.[9]

These levels of emissions are not compatible with stable temperatures. To hold carbon dioxide levels to a maximum of 550 parts per million in the global atmosphere, the world can probably afford emissions of no more than about 3 tonnes per person. Any more and temperatures will continue to rise beyond the 3 degree level. As our scientific knowledge improves, even 3 tonnes seems too high, and a figure of 2 tonnes per person looks a better aim. To take the typical European emissions down to this level, we need a reduction of over 80 per cent. Not even the rhetoric of governments and corporations dares to clearly specify this figure. It seems so difficult to attain that it invites sceptical ridicule. However, the science is clear: minor changes to Western emissions are not going to be enough. Stopping climate change is not about shaving a few percentage points here and there, but about substantial behavioural change among billions of people.

The text of this book was submitted to the publishers in late September 2006. Since that date, major work has been published on the topic of climate change. These publications include George Monbiot's book *Heat* and the detailed final report of Sir Nicholas Stern on the economics of climate change. I try very briefly to deal with the new ideas in these documents in a short Afterword at the end of this book.

For ongoing developments, this book has a companion website: www.lowcarbonlife.net. On this site readers will find commentary on the latest advances in low-carbon goods and services, independent analysis of products, and the most recent data on how our lives generate emissions.

1

the extraordinary cheapness of fossil fuels

E ven after the price increases in the last few years, energy remains extremely cheap. Petrol may cost nearly a pound a litre, and electricity may reach 10 pence a kilowatt hour (kWh) in some parts of the UK; but even at these prices fossil fuels are astonishingly good value for money. A strong human male, working at peak efficiency, can sustain an energy output of about 0.8kW for a few hours a day. To employ this muscular individual as a labourer at the minimum wage costs something over £5 an hour. Even when working at his best, and without adding any ancillary costs, this man's work is at least 60 times as expensive as electricity and 200 times the price of gas or petrol. This is the root of all our problems. Fossil fuel energy is so cheap and so convenient that its use permeates every aspect of our lives. And as more and more of the world's people move into the market economy, they will want to replace their labour with petrol or electricity.

The world's advance from subsistence agriculture to the modern post-industrial state is largely due to the use of huge quantities of fossil fuel to replace human labour. Where one man or woman ploughed the field, often but not always aided by a horse or other working animal, the farmer now employs a huge tractor. The tractor's parts took energy to make and each hectare of ploughing uses a few litres of diesel, which is taxed, incidentally, at a lower rate than when used in a passenger car. The world's industries use machines powered by gas or electricity, supervised by tiny numbers of operatives, whose only role is often to monitor the expensive technology that controls the processes. Walk round a modern steelworks and you will see a few employees dotted around in control rooms, their labour entirely replaced by expensive machinery and cheap energy. The increases in our standard of living have very largely come from reducing the labour it takes to make the goods and services we consume. Cheap energy has been a vital ingredient in this change.

Nothing demonstrates the fundamental cheapness of fossil fuels better than the rise of the low-price airline. Starting in the US, these nimble companies have captured a large fraction of Europe's air travel. In making air travel cheaper than any other form of transport, they have made foreign holidays available to most of the population. Last year, more than half of the UK's population made at least one flight.[10] The economics of flying make it easy to see why.

Although aviation fuel rose significantly in price during 2005, and many airlines started to charge supplements to reflect the rising cost, kerosene remains a small portion of an airline's bills. Easyjet, one of the largest low-cost operators, had fuel bills of only £7.50 per passenger in 2005.[11] The average price of a ticket was £48, so even if kerosene were to double in price, Easyjet would need only to add 15 per cent to its almost ridiculously low fares. A doubling of aviation fuel costs might deter a few passengers; but aircraft travel would remain highly attractive.

Because carbon fuels are so cheap in relation to the alternatives, the underlying demand is breathtakingly unresponsive to price changes. Between the first quarters of 2004 and 2006, the price of crude oil almost doubled, from just over $30 a barrel to about $60. In the same period, the total world demand for oil rose from 82.6 million to 85.1 million barrels a day, a rise of about 3 per cent.[12] The resilience in demand is tribute to the absolute reliance of the world economy upon freely available oil products, particularly petroleum. Of course, eventually the demand for oil may fall as the heaviest users begin to improve the efficiency of their energy-using processes. But for most customers, oil is still remarkably good value and weaning them off reliance on fossil fuel energy is a demanding task.

The reason often adduced for the rise in oil consumption is the voracious demand from China and other newly industrializing countries. This is only partly true. In April 2006, the International Energy Agency (IEA) was forecasting that demand from the 'old' industrial countries of the Organisation for Economic Co-operation and Development (OECD), mostly in Europe and North America, would rise by just under 1 per cent during 2006.[13] Almost all industrial countries seem to be sharing in the continued growth of demand for oil. As the IEA says, global economic buoyancy would have increased demand by an even greater extent had the price of oil not surged over the last two years. But the important fact is that even after the sustained price rises of recent years, the world economy shows no signs of reducing its overall reliance on oil and oil-related products, whether through conservation, more efficient technologies or replacement by renewable sources of energy.

Reading the business pages might give us the wrong impression. Companies do often complain of the impact of rising energy prices on their profitability. In the large majority of cases, this grumble is not justified by the figures. One good example of an industry using large quantities of energy is public transport. First Group, the UK's largest bus company, said in May 2006 that its fuel costs had gone up by £15.5 million during the previous year. While the pain of this increase was surely real, the amount is an insignificant fraction – about 1.5 per cent – of its total turnover of about £1 billion a year.[14] First Group blamed the fuel cost increases for its relatively small increase in profit. But at the same time the *Scotsman* newspaper reported that 'as a result of the soaring fuel costs, First Group put up bus fares by an average of 20 pence or 15 per cent during the trading year'.[15] In other words, passengers were asked to bear price rises ten times as much as the true fuel cost inflation. Despite any appearance to the contrary, fuel prices do not really drive financial decisions, even for transport operators with large fuel bills to consider.

Similarly, cheap aviation delivers a higher material standard of living to people in the developed world. For example, air freight and heated glasshouses can put foods on our plates that used to be unavailable for large portions of the year. However, producing 1kg of winter salad takes about 200 times as much energy in heat and light as are contained in the vegetables. Across the rest of Western agriculture, this ratio is far less stark; but it still takes about nine units of energy to put one unit on the British plate. We'll show later in the book that the astonishing wastefulness of agriculture is responsible for almost 20 per cent of all carbon emissions in the UK. The long-run downward trend in food prices in the UK is due, in large measure, to the replacement of expensive labour with cheap inputs of energy.

Even the retailing of food is an energy-intensive business. The massive chilled food cabinets, the high levels of lighting and the heating of what are effectively thin-walled warehouses are all very costly in terms of energy use. Supermarkets probably produce about 5 million tonnes of greenhouse gases a year, or a little less than 1 per cent of total UK emissions. Tesco uses over 100kWh a year of energy just to operate 1 square foot of selling space, costing perhaps £7.[16] But Tesco generates sales of over £1200 each year in that 1 square foot. The energy cost of running shops is little more than 0.5 per cent of the value of the sales. The incentive to improve is certainly there, but it cannot figure large in the company's calculations. Shop managers know that people buy more chilled goods when they are displayed in enormous open-fronted cabinets, spilling cold air into the adjacent isles, and so Tesco will keep it that way, at whatever cost in energy consumption. It would make no financial sense to change.

At least the food chain delivers something useful. By contrast, most appliances in the home use electricity even when apparently switched off. Even when the TV is dark, every Sky digital set-top box in the country uses about 16 watts (W) of electricity, enough to power a small light bulb. Each box consumes about 140kWh a year, at a cost today of about £14. Does anybody protest? No – the price is low enough for nobody to be worried. But a single Sky box puts 60kg of carbon dioxide into the atmosphere a year, more than the total emissions of somebody living in one of the poorest countries in the world. The 8 million or so Sky set-top boxes consume enough energy when not actually in use to keep a small power station running. To the individual homeowner, the energy use is not noticeable; but added together across all UK homes, appliances quietly consuming power when dormant add more than 10 per cent to the domestic use of electricity.

Many of these appliances – though not Sky boxes – we could easily turn off when we are not using them. Very few people do. The energy use is not great enough to warrant the minor inconvenience of reaching down to the plug. Our time is worth more to us than the savings we can possibly make by economizing on energy use. So in the circumstances when fossil fuel energy is a clear substitute for labour, the rational person almost always buys the electricity rather than do manual work. Tumble dryers cost about 25 pence to dry a full load. It might take half an hour to put this load on a washing line and take it in again at the end of the day, so many people use dryers even on a windy dry day.

The big problem with the successful modern economy is that economic growth makes climate change more and more difficult to fight. As society gets richer and its citizens better paid, it becomes more and more obvious that we should choose the tumble dryer rather than wasting our own time and energy. It certainly does not seem to be worthwhile even turning off the lights in office blocks, whether used by private business or even government departments.

The relative cheapness of energy affects our habits across daily life. A good example is the recycling of soft drink cans. Making new aluminium is one of the most energy-intensive processes known to man. Each tonne of aluminium takes 15,000kWh to make, or four times the typical yearly electricity use of a UK home. This is one reason that aluminium smelters are often located close to sources of particularly cheap energy. If fossil fuel energy is used, each can of soft drink, weighing 18 grams (g) when empty, has contributed about 150g of carbon dioxide to the atmosphere, almost ten times as much. Recycling the can makes good sense in energy terms since it takes less than 10 per cent of the initial energy to recreate a new can. So, in some countries, such as Russia and Brazil, the soft drink industry operates a loop: the can is filled, collected and returned, melted down and refashioned, and then taken back to the factory for filling with another drink.[17] But this requires an army of poorer people for whom it is worth collecting cans for a penny or so. Does this system work in countries like the UK? No – there is nobody for whom a penny a can is enough to make it worth collecting the empties. Instead, we have to make or import large quantities of virgin aluminium and, across Europe, less than 50 per cent of new aluminium is reused. The rapid increases in prosperity in countries such as Brazil and Russia – which none of us want to stop – will mean that the labour to collect cans will eventually dry up. It's true that in some rich countries – Sweden and Switzerland come to mind – strong social pressure can prompt high recycling rates; but these countries are still the exception. Almost 5 billion cans a year are not recycled in the UK at a total carbon dioxide cost of about 0.75 million tonnes.

Using fossil fuel energy is almost invariably the quickest, easiest and cheapest way of getting round life's problem, large and small. Whether it is getting the children to school, buying groceries, enjoying a good holiday or keeping warm in winter, the path of least resistance is usually to take the course that uses fossil fuel. The temptation to reach for the solution that uses energy is ever present in Western society and increasingly in other parts of the world, as well. Choosing to avoid carbon-based energy sources is often expensive, time consuming and inconvenient. The bus, for example, can be more expensive than a car, arrival times are unreliable and the journey takes longer. Society is increasingly designed around maximizing the labour and time-saving benefits of fossil fuel use. As a result, personal use of energy is drifting upwards every year and, for example, UK electricity demand is expected to continue rising at just over 1 per cent a year into the next decade.[18]

REPLACING LABOUR WITH ENERGY IS ONE OF THE PRIMARY ENGINES OF ECONOMIC GROWTH

Domestic servants in the 18th century often carried out tasks that are now fulfilled by fossil fuel energy. These people lit the wood fires early in the morning, washed clothes by hand, swept the floors with brooms, made the bread and cleaned the plates. As the 19th and early 20th centuries progressed, the heating was increasingly provided by coal and then town gas. Labour was 'released' to work in the factories. Increasing levels of automation – often facilitated by the use of coal – in those factories enabled increases in productivity that eventually translated into higher wages. Servant wages crept up in parallel, meaning that all but the very richest people shed domestic labour as electricity came into widespread availability in the first third of the 20th century.

Any elementary summary of the economic history of the past 300 years like this must assign great importance to the changing price and availability of fossil fuel energy. Many of the features of the modern national economy are principally due to the widespread use of coal – both in its original form and then, later, as 'town gas' – and, in the 20th century, to the development of an electric power grid and then natural gas pipelines. For example, the primary economic importance of the canal network lay in its impact on the price of coal in the towns and cities of industrial England.[19] Allowing coal to be cheap meant industry could grow. Among other outcomes, this facilitated specialization – focusing on one activity and then trading the goods or services in return for the products of other specialists. Cheap and efficient transport of goods by road freight completed the process in the second half of the 20th century. Having been a large fraction of the costs of a manufactured good, transport costs are now reduced to a very small element. This has been achieved by a substantial and sustained reduction in the price of fossil fuels, particularly in relation to average wages.

In 1930, 50kWh of electricity cost about 16 pence, or about 4 per cent of the weekly wage of an industrial worker.[20] Even after the price rises of the 2004 to 2006 period, the equivalent percentage today is less than 1 per cent. The fall in the underlying price of electricity has been based partly upon the greater availability of natural gas as a fuel for power stations, but also upon greater efficiency in converting gas into the more flexible form of electricity.

THE MODERN ECONOMY IS HEAVILY DEPENDENT UPON CHEAP ENERGY

We'll see throughout the book that the improving efficiency of fossil fuel use – getting more useful work out of a unit of coal, gas or oil – looks at first sight as if it reduces the need for fuels. However, this impact is almost invariably outweighed by increased levels of usage. The airline industry is a good example. The UK flag carrier, British Airways (BA), has improved its fuel efficiency by 25 per cent since 1990. Good news for climate change, it might seem. But passenger volumes have risen by a far greater amount. For the world airline industry, passenger miles are rising at about 5 per cent a year, enough to completely wipe out the impact of improved seat occupancy (increasing at 1 to 2 per cent a year) and better fuel efficiency (growing at a similar rate).[21] In similar fashion, the average insulation levels of UK homes have been slowly improving; but this benefit has been balanced by an equal and opposite increase in average internal temperatures. We shouldn't be surprised – better insulation makes a house cheaper to heat, so rational homeowners turn up the thermostat after improving the insulation.

Successful modern economies are characterized by heavy use of energy. In sharp contrast to the complacency of European leaders, this fact is openly acknowledged by US policy-makers. European leaders often still deny their countries' economic addiction to fossil fuels. The European pretence consists of two fallacies: first, that the increasing swing to a service economy and away from manufacturing will eventually cut the need for energy; and, second, that energy-efficiency measures will dampen the amounts consumed across the economy.

Both European assumptions are highly questionable. We'll focus on the first. In fact, service industries are getting increasingly energy dependent and there's no evidence that the decline of manufacturing will do anything but slightly shave the underlying rate of growth.

Some of the reasons for this are not obvious. Why is the swing to a knowledge economy not going to cut energy demand? Importantly, service companies often operate from large buildings: glass fronted and expensive to heat and to cool. It comes as a surprise to many people that the energy needs of these buildings are enormous. Yearly carbon dioxide emissions from large buildings are often well over 2 tonnes per person, or almost 20 per cent of the average total annual output of 11 tonnes, excluding aviation. Big office blocks are prodigious users of electricity; and as they get bigger, they can sometimes use more energy per person, not less. US government data shows that offices over 50,000 square feet have electricity consumption 50 per cent above the level of smaller buildings.[22] More computers mean more heat, and more cooling in summer.

Two tonnes of carbon dioxide per office worker is a huge amount. On its own, it is not far off the total yearly emissions that the atmosphere can sustain. However, it doesn't represent an overwhelming expense to the employer. Even if all the energy is consumed in the form of electricity, it would only cost about £450 per person, or perhaps 10 per cent of the rent for a London office block. The incentives on businesses to reduce energy use are negligible. In fact, the sensible employer crams more people into the building to reduce rent costs, even if greater crowding means dramatically higher cooling costs in summer. Even a doubling of electricity costs wouldn't change this calculation.

More generally, the modern economy works best when it centralizes its business activities. Dispersed offices, placed close to customers or business partners, are replaced by a small number of larger centres. Banks close their branches and put employees in a smaller number of regional centres. Tax offices are becoming larger and fewer in number. The Post Office will close a large percentage of its outlets. Not only does this mean replacing relatively energy-efficient offices with bigger buildings, but it means that the typical journey to work or to shop becomes longer and more energy-intensive. The short commuter bus ride into the city centre is replaced by the car journey to the remote office park. The average length of journeys to work in the UK continues to rise.

So, rising employment in service industries doesn't begin to solve the problem of greenhouse gas emissions in the way that governments hope. And energy use in employment is only part of the wider pattern of increased reliance on gas and electricity. Retailing, for example, now takes place in a smaller number of much larger shops. Almost 3000 small food shops closed in the period of 2001 to 2005, a period in which the sales of large retailers grew 27 per cent, partly as the result of the continuing growth in superstores.[23] Does this add to energy consumption? Possibly not directly, though big supermarkets are major users of electricity, but certainly in terms of the much larger amount of fuel used to get to these shops by their eager customers. Of course, at the root of this switch from smaller local grocery outlets to massive out-of-town centres is the rising availability of the car and the cheapness of petrol. It's now cheaper to ship the food to a small number of huge shops and get customers to drive to the outlets. In the past, the reverse was true; customer transport was scarce and expensive, so it made sense to move the food to local shops by the lorries of retailers or, indeed, to the customer at home by a delivery bicycle.

And where does the food in these shops come from? As globalization proceeds, it comes increasingly from afar. A small number of factories, often located in a foreign country, now provide a larger and larger fraction of total groceries. All European Heinz tomato sauces are made in one factory in Holland. Proctor and Gamble's worldwide research into laundry detergents is run from Newcastle, where it also has its factory. Production efficiency is high; but it is traded off against growing needs to transport raw materials and finished products very long distances.

Against these broad trends that characterize the modern economy, the muted tendency towards energy efficiency is powerless. Incremental improvements of a couple of per cent a year are not enough to counterbalance the modern economy's need to centralize, to globalize and to transport. World trade in 2004 grew at 9 per cent per year. Air freight is growing at over 5 per cent a year in 2006. These are among the triumphs of the world economy; but their cost in greater carbon dioxide is hidden and disregarded. The advantages of global specialization – for example, the UK focuses on financial services, while China makes electronic gadgets – are so huge that they will mean increasing emissions for many years to come.

Lastly, the decline of UK (and European) manufacturing and its shift to the East may mean a fall in industrial carbon pollution in Europe; but these emissions do not disappear. They are shifted to the new centres, where energy efficiency is generally lower. We have simply exported the polluting activity to a new location. What is out of sight is now out of mind. Europe's complacent assumption that emissions will naturally fall as a consequence of the move to a service economy is unwarranted.

WIDER SOCIETY ALSO RUNS ON CHEAP FOSSIL FUEL

To a perhaps dispiriting extent, economic growth depends upon increasing consumption of fossil fuel-intensive goods and services. Continued economic prosperity, at least as conventionally defined, relies upon persuading people to buy more. As we become richer, much of what we purchase is made with prodigious quantities of energy. The Renaissance princeling might have used his wealth to commission a goldsmith or a painter; but our wealthy peers engage in frequent long-distance air travel, buy large cars and increase the size of their homes.

Of course, not all the extra money of the rich goes on activities demanding fuel. The wealthy also spend cash on private education, greater amounts of entertainment and more expensive clothing. Nevertheless, the richest 10 per cent spend over two and a half times as much as average people on foreign travel, twice as much fuelling their cars and, perhaps surprisingly, over three times as much on rail travel.[24] Rich people travel far more than the norm. Where the average person takes one return flight a year, the rich family might take five. This fact alone probably means that their emissions are twice the national average. Prime Minister Tony Blair is a terrible example, taking government jets 677 times between 1997 and 2006.[25]

Greater consumption is always a mark of the privileged of course. No society ever known has expected its rich to restrain their spending, and today's Western capitalist economy is no different. In fact, unconstrained display is a feature of many of the most successful societies. Continued growth is dependent upon it, as economists have pointed out for hundreds of years.[26]

Today, the maintenance of high status depends, as ever, on the purchase of bigger and better symbols of affluence. What prosperous person owns a ten-year-old car, a small house and takes his holiday in Skegness, or catches the bus to work? The dinner table is laden with foods flown in from Kenya or Thailand. The expensive halogen kitchen lighting is as bright as day. The children are shipped daily to a remote private school.

It's not simply that higher status requires spending on fossil fuel-intensive activities and goods, but also that failure to spend on these goods invites scorn from peers. Non-consumption can mean rejection by one's social group. Children are the worst; minor eccentricities, such as drying clothes on a line, rather than using the tumble dryer, become hugely embarrassing to them. Almost everything we do requires use of embedded fossil energy.

The close relationship of economic success and greater spending on fossil fuel-based activities is unsurprising. Perhaps less obvious is the general drift towards increasing energy use across all segments of society. Adding energy disproportionately to our expenditures as the economy grows is an embedded tendency. Look, for example, at the level of temperatures in the home. In 1970, winter temperatures in British homes averaged 13 degrees Celsius. The figure rose slowly until 1985, but then spurted ahead, and it is now about 19 degrees Celsius. As we get more prosperous, we may insulate our homes better; but then we take all the benefit in the form of more heat, not lower bills or reduced emissions.

This is an almost universal phenomenon. Car engines are getting more efficient each year; but the size of our vehicles is growing. As a result, average emissions per kilometre travelled are almost flat, and, of course, we have more cars on the road. So car transport is adding more carbon dioxide to the atmosphere each year.

Increasing prosperity brings with it a much higher propensity to travel. People in the bottom 20 per cent of the income distribution travel less than 4000 miles (6400km) a year, compared to well over 10,000 miles (16,000km) for the top quintile.[27] Equally important, wealthier people show much less inclination to use the most efficient forms of transport. The wealthiest 20 per cent typically make 29 bus journeys a year, while people in the poorest quintile make 101. The spread of car ownership – which brings with it considerably more freedom and economic independence – has tended to depress the need for bus and, to a lesser extent, rail networks.

The UK's largest bus operator, First Group, makes a related point in its 2005 *Corporate Responsibility Report*:

> *Recent work on the relationship between transport and social inclusion has shown that it is predominantly low-income groups that rely on public transport for their mobility needs. This includes accessing employment and essential services. The UK government's quality of life indicators show that those without a car are experiencing increasing difficulties in accessing health services, shops and post offices.*

The modern economy seems to require ever-greater centralization of services, increasing our need to travel. General practitioners (GPs) are being grouped into larger practices, post offices are centralized on a few high-street sites and shops are moving to the edges of towns. These broad societal trends are apparently unstoppable, but have the important consequence that people are less and less able to do without a car. Even the poor and the unwilling are obliged to have access. The acquisition of a car is likely to significantly increase the amount of personal travel taken, and the consequence for carbon emissions is obvious.

Increasing car use has the effect of decreasing the need for buses, despite their much greater efficiency in terms of carbon dioxide emissions per passenger. Bus travel in London has seen some increase since the introduction of the congestion charge; but the average distance travelled by bus outside London has fallen by 20 per cent since the mid-1980s, and the slow decline appears to be continuing. This is also the case in many European countries.

The list of the ways in which material progress drives up energy use is almost endless. We are buying larger TVs – entirely negating any benefits of energy efficiency from the switch to liquid crystal displays (LCDs) from old-fashioned cathode ray tubes. The children's bedrooms now all contain TVs and ever-more powerful games consoles, usually left on 24 hours a day. Our fridges are increasing in size, almost outweighing the very significant improvements in insulation in the last few years. We may buy some energy-efficiency light bulbs, though in much lower numbers than anybody expected; but at the same time we have added one new light fixture each year to the average home. Where our kitchens once had a couple of pale fluorescent tubes, we now have a galaxy of halogen spotlights. Our use of hot water is rising by about 1 per cent a year, increasing both the energy cost in the home and the surprising amount of power needed to pump the water to us. Our cars now have air-conditioning when we managed before with an open window.

As a general rule, we seem to take the gains we make in energy efficiency back in increased comfort, and appear to have an almost insatiable desire for an easier life, as insulated as possible from external climate or the need to engage in any form of manual work. As a result, of course, we are gaining weight. Perhaps surprisingly, we are actually not far from balance-of-food input versus energy output. I calculate that the typical middle-aged man gains about 400g (less than 1 pound) a year, and could walk this off in about 30 miles (48km) if he ate no more than before. Nevertheless, as a species we have an almost pathological laziness, and this almost universal human characteristic is reinforced by the ready availability of powered alternatives to human labour.

Power steering in cars, for example, reduces their fuel efficiency by approximately 5 per cent, although it is now absolutely standard on modern cars.[28] Few people will remember, but it used to take a real effort to turn a car at slow speed before cars were equipped with power steering. For people who drove around cities, this probably increased their own energy output by several per cent. Electric windows are another good example in cars. Reducing the amount of energy we burn off in our day-to-day activities has meant that populations of industrial societies have tended to gain weight. The response of the gradually thickening UK citizen has been to compensate by attendance at the local gym, where weight loss is attempted by using powered treadmills operating at over 1kW electric power. Compared to the typical 400W output of a middle-aged plodder trying to keep up with the running belt, this is a poor exchange. Even when trying to lose weight, we do so in energy-inefficient ways.

We all tend to use more energy as we get richer, and to substitute it for our own labour whenever we can. This is a continuing trend. The generations brought up in times when energy was much more expensive compared to manual labour are gradually disappearing. Their habits of turning off appliances or of walking rather than driving will die with them. Younger people may have never acquired these behaviours but, perhaps even more worryingly, also appear to be much less interested in environmental matters. Unlike earlier environmental movements of the 1960s and 1970s, interest in climate change appears to be lower in the young than among the old. Perhaps the footloose world travellers of today will become the environmental activists of tomorrow; but the signs are not auspicious. In a recent poll, only 31 per cent of 18 to 24 year olds said that they would voluntarily pay a £15 climate change levy on a trip to the US, compared to 40 per cent for the over 45s.[29] Eighty-two per cent of 18 to 24s agreed with the statement that 'although the problem of climate change is important, we need to deal with it in a way that will not risk the country's economic prosperity', a slightly higher figure than for the population as a whole. Similarly, the percentage of young people thinking that climate change was the most important global threat was lower among 18 to 24 year olds than older age groups. They were also less likely to have taken energy-saving measures in the home.[30] When I give talks on reducing carbon emissions to community groups, the average age of the audience will typically be over 50; the issue is much less interesting to the young.

The main forces in society all appear to point towards increasing fossil fuel use among individuals:

- Greater prosperity means more temptation to replace manual effort with fossil fuels.
- The maintenance of personal status in the modern economy demands the purchase of bigger and more ostentatious consumer goods.
- Social changes, such as the centralization of health services or places of employment, increase the need for travel and push people towards car ownership and use.
- The tradition of self-restraint and avoidance of 'waste' that characterizes the generations born before about 1960 has partly disappeared.

Will government or business change this? The next chapters look at whether the central institutions of modern society have the incentive to radically reduce carbon emissions.

2

the scope for
government action

D emocratic governments survive by following the demands of the electorate. Unpopular actions against the wishes of the voters will usually result in ejection at the next election. Unless a significant and vocal minority of the electorate lobby for action, governments seeking their own survival will never aggressively attack the problem of global warming. The inertia of governments across the world when faced with the evidence of climate change is a palpable demonstration of this truth. Governments will do what their electorates allow them: therefore, responsible individuals need to show by their individual actions that climate change measures are politically acceptable. We won't get governments to act unless the vanguard shows that it is willing to pay some price to reduce greenhouse gas emissions. At present, that willingness to accept substantial actions by our government to reduce carbon emissions is not clear to our leaders. We need to make it absolutely obvious to politicians that we expect significant measures. Without this, governments will continue to engage in token schemes of no real benefit to the atmosphere.

Not only do the leaders of the world face the indifference of the large majority of their electorate, their administrations also face huge problems coordinating international action. One of the most obvious issues is that any single government has no chance of significantly affecting the total volume of world greenhouse gas output. The UK is responsible for about 2 per cent of global carbon dioxide output and it would make little difference to the global total if it ceased burning fossil fuels tomorrow. The growth rate in emissions from other countries is sufficient to replace the UK carbon within a year. It is difficult to envisage any individual country deciding to take unilateral action over emissions if the costs – either financial or in terms of material comfort – were substantial. No democratic country has ever engaged in significant self-denial for any sustained period of time without similar behaviour from other states.

THE PROBLEMS WITH CREATING INTERNATIONAL AGREEMENTS

The UK's research group into the economics of climate change, run by Sir Nicholas Stern at the UK Treasury, has acknowledged this difficulty. Its initial discussion paper looked at ways of generating a widely based international agreement to coordinate reductions in fossil energy use in most countries at the same time.[31] Policy-makers are searching for the means to develop what is, in effect, an international cartel. Mandatory reductions in outputs of carbon to the atmosphere will be painful to all the participating countries, with little or no benefit for decades or centuries to come. This makes any proposed multilateral agreement extremely unstable. Countries will face temptations to renege on the agreement or to cheat on its obligations. Those states that do not join the contract will gain by their continued use of copious amounts of carbon-based fuels. So, any agreement can be undermined both by non-participants increasing their emissions in order to undercut the cartel members, and by participants cheating by using more fossil fuels.

The number of successful public cartels to reduce the global output of undesirable products is small. The 1987 Montreal Protocols were aimed at reducing the use of ozone-depleting chemicals, and appear to have been reasonably effective, although it will take several decades for the dangerous hole over the Antarctic to be filled. Montreal worked, so why should we be pessimistic about a future greenhouse gas deal? First and foremost, the Montreal deal involved a small number of chemicals with an important but very limited role in the economy. It was easy to define what needed to be done, and although replacement chemicals were more expensive, they could be used by the existing manufacturers of refrigeration equipment and aerosols. There was no real economic dislocation. International agreement could be easily policed and enforced. Countries that agreed to cease production were able successfully to prohibit imports of goods using ozone-depleting chemicals.

The problems in organizing a successful agreement to restrict fossil fuel use are many orders of magnitude greater. Fossil fuel use is much more difficult to measure. One tonne of steel made by a country not adhering to the agreement will be chemically identical to one made in a participating country.

The existing structure of international treaties adds to the difficulties in arranging an agreement between states to restrict emissions. The most important treaties are probably those that underpin the world trade system, monitored by the World Trade Organization (WTO). The purpose of the various international agreements over the last generation has been to reduce the barriers to international trade. All trade is good, say the policy-makers. Even though increasing international trade may well be having a deleterious effect on rates of greenhouse gas creation, the WTO pushes on with its prime objective. Attempts, for example, by one country to restrict imports of airlifted food because of the carbon cost of air travel would result in near-immediate legal action by the WTO. The agreements surrounding international aviation are even more powerful. A huge number of separate bilateral deals between sovereign states commit countries not to tax aviation fuel.[32] The UK and other states cannot increase the price of kerosene without overturning a huge number of signed protocols. And if action was taken across the whole of the European Union (EU), its effectiveness would be partly undermined by aircraft taking on more fuel in countries outside the EU that had chosen not to implement any tax. So, it's simply not going to happen, even though constraints on the growth of aviation are urgently needed.

Attempts to restrict particular activities with severe impacts on carbon dioxide emissions run into similar problems. The manufacture of aluminium is one of the most energy-intensive industrial processes; but when the German government tried to restrict the use of metal drinks cans, it faced action from the European Commission.[33] The European court eventually ruled that trying to ban the use of cans that were freely available in other member states was a restriction on trade within the EU and was therefore illegal. Any action by an individual country within the EU that tried to weight consumers' choices towards less polluting alternatives would probably suffer a similar fate.

And it is not simply the strong bias in the world economic system towards free trade that makes action by individual countries difficult. Increasingly, we see that one environmental objective can sometimes get in the way of another. For example, reducing emissions of diesel particulates from buses gives the bus operator lower fuel economy.[34] Understandably, society also wants to give consideration to the impact on human health of poor air quality in city centres, so a trade-off is made between carbon dioxide emissions and the particulates from buses that may be causing increased levels of respiratory diseases such as asthma.

THE IMPORTANCE THAT GOVERNMENTS ATTACH TO NOT REDUCING THE COMPETITIVENESS OF THEIR INDUSTRIES: THE EARLY PROBLEM WITH THE EMISSIONS TRADING SCHEME

Multi-country programmes to reduce emissions have had very limited success so far. The best known example is the EU's Emissions Trading Scheme (ETS). The ETS allocates an emissions allowance to the major users of fossil fuels in each country and then allows companies that do not use their allocation to sell the remaining allowance to other polluters. But the allowances are currently set at a sufficiently high level that they do not really bite on the major energy users. In April 2006, Germany announced that its second attempt to set limits on its major polluters would be just 0.7 per cent tighter than the first, though some industrial plants are newly included in the scheme.[35] Existing polluters are allocated at no charge nearly 99 per cent of the carbon permits that they requested.[36] The impact of this minor tightening on power stations and chemical plants will be utterly negligible, and we will see no observable effect on their behaviour.

This is no accident; a significant reduction in allowances would mean that emissions became expensive and producers' costs would rise. Imports from countries not participating in the scheme would become relatively cheaper and domestic producers would lose market share. So, individual European governments, understandably eager not to hobble some of their largest companies, have generally given their major carbon producers very generous allowances. The dramatic oversupply of permits to pollute has meant that they have very low value. At today's prices (September 2006), carbon permits for a gas-fired power station cost less than 8 per cent of the value of the electricity generated.[37] As a result, the current version of the ETS will not substantially change the behaviour of any but the egregiously inefficient users of fossil fuels. The dubious relevance of the current scheme is made clear by the willingness of the airline industry to participate in emissions trading. If the current price of permits is maintained, emissions trading would increase Easyjet's fuel costs from 2005's £7.50 a passenger by less than £1.00.

The looseness and ineffectiveness of current EU carbon limits was demonstrated in April 2006, when several major countries announced that their most energy-guzzling industries had actually emitted less carbon dioxide than they were allocated in the EU Emissions Trading Scheme. In other words, the companies in these industries would not need to buy the rights to further carbon allocations. This is exactly what pessimists had feared: most countries had exaggerated the energy needs of the companies in the energy-intensive sectors, such as steel or power generation, and had successfully been allocated pollution permits in excess of what is actually needed. If they had done otherwise, their own industries would have been disadvantaged to the benefit, usually, of a firm in another European country. No democratic government will ever wittingly allow this and the UK government is already under pressure for being slightly less generous with its allowances than some other countries. The voters don't like hearing about local job losses because carbon dioxide pollution is taxed more heavily than in competitor countries. In the language of the journalist, this is a 'race to the bottom': countries competing to protect their industries by minimizing the impact of carbon rationing on their firms.

The current failure of the emissions trading scheme to oblige carbon reductions stands in contrast to the Europe-wide increase in overall carbon dioxide generation. On 22 June 2006, the European Environment Agency announced that EU greenhouse gas emissions had risen for the second year in a row.[38] Carbon dioxide output was over 4 per cent above the level of 1990, the Kyoto baseline year. Total EU greenhouse gas emissions, including other pollutants such as methane, are only just below the 1990 level and sit well above the maximum allowed under the Kyoto Protocol for the end of the decade.

THE PROBLEMS FACING GOVERNMENT

Renewable energy

The UK government has made some efforts to reduce emissions by encouraging the generation of renewable energy. Its intelligently designed incentive system rewards renewable generation at the expense of coal and gas generators. Unfortunately, the renewable technology closest to coal and gas in terms of cost – wind – is sufficiently unpopular to restrain development. Governments facing small, determined forces of opposition and only weak and widely dispersed support will take the path of least resistance. Wind development is proceeding far less quickly than it would do with genuine political support. The UK government's energy review published in summer 2006 said that a total of 11GW of renewable energy capacity was mired in the planning system, compared to an existing 1.7GW of wind energy already installed. Most of the projects in the planning process are for wind turbines.[39] When the wind is blowing strongly, this proposed capacity might provide 15 per cent of the UK's total electricity need.

Although wind generating capacity is gradually getting through the planning process, electricity demand is increasing as well. In fact, projections made by the National Grid show UK electricity need increasing by 1.5 per cent a year, with the increased energy coming from renewables providing less than a 1 per cent increase.[40]

The dire position of UK electricity generation was made starkly clear by the formal seven-year forecasts of the operator of Britain's main power networks: the National Grid. In May 2006, it produced its annual prediction of the percentage of UK electricity that will be generated from renewable sources in 2010. This estimate was 7.4 per cent, down from a figure of 8.4 per cent the year earlier.[41] Both numbers are disappointingly low, of course, and fall well below the government's published target of 10 per cent in 2010 (I believe that this fact was completely unnoticed by UK newspapers and the electricity trade press). The small projected increase in the share of renewable energy will not even cover the loss of withdrawn nuclear capacity by 2010. As a result, our electricity at the end of the decade will actually be more dependent upon fossil fuel sources than it is now. Once again, government has simply failed to match its concerned rhetoric on climate change with – possibly unpopular – action to de-carbonize our ways of living.

Another example is the huge upgrade to the power lines in the north of Scotland to meet the increased need for the transmission of wind-generated electricity to consumers. Scotland's wind resources probably account for one quarter of the total wind energy of the EU.[42] Despite the active encouragement of wind farms by government, objectors are likely to secure the refusal of planning permission for the pylons across beautiful countryside.[43] Unless this decision is overturned, wind development in the region will be strictly curtailed. The objectors had strong points – some of Scotland's best views would be affected by the new transmission line. Caught between those vociferously protecting something they hold dear, and the weaker and less organized forces arguing for measures to protect the global atmosphere, the protesters will always tend to carry more weight.

Home insulation

The fragility of the UK government's position on climate change was demonstrated by the undemanding minimum energy insulation standards in new buildings, introduced in April 2006. Although ministers initially claimed a 40 per cent improvement over old standards, one trade body says that the underlying improvement is as little as 10 per cent, and even the government admits now that the figure is nearer 20 per cent.[44] For extensions to existing buildings, the new UK requirements are still only about half as tough as Sweden's standards. Resistance from the construction industry and a deplorable lameness from government have impeded the use of more demanding targets. The *Guardian* newspaper reported that one minister had described one of the targets as 'unnecessary gold plating', even though homes are responsible for over 20 per cent of UK greenhouse gas emissions.[45]

For the government, the problem is that most climate change initiatives are unpopular. They sound good when announced, but quickly run into the sand dunes of vested interests. Talking about inhibiting the growth of aircraft emissions, for example, makes for good headlines; but resisting the pressure for more runways in the south-east or for longer opening hours for Heathrow appears to be impossible. When significant public complaint is likely, governments in the UK and elsewhere simply back away from decisive action. Cheap air travel is one of the easiest ways in which governments can give their voters an illusion of greater prosperity, and inhibiting the growth of air miles has proved impossible across the world.

Air travel

The unrestrained growth in air travel is perhaps the most intractable climate challenge facing governments. Although air travel is only responsible for about 5.5 per cent of UK emissions at present, the amount of carbon dioxide pushed out by jet engines will probably double within 25 years.[46] And the side effects of airline emissions (dealt with in Chapter 12) make the position far worse. While we are struggling to generate the most modest of decreases in surface emissions of carbon dioxide, international air travel – untrammelled by controls imposed by Kyoto processes – races away and overwhelms any improvements we see in other fields. It is no good the government asking us to switch off our televisions when not in use (saving about 30kg of carbon dioxide a year) but waving us cheerfully away on our shopping trips to New York (over 3.5 tonnes of greenhouse gases per trip, or over 100 times as much).

So statements by the government on air travel are invariably two sided. First, the administration gives a welcome to the impact of low fares, cheap carriers and better access to a huge range of destinations. If political success is measured by the volume of travellers leaving the UK during the holiday period, aviation is the Labour government's single most successful achievement. The 2003 White Paper said that the UK needed 'a balanced and measured approach to the future of air transport which ... reflects people's desire to travel further and more often by air, and to take advantage of the affordability of air travel and the opportunities this brings'.[47] These benefits should be balanced by ensuring that 'over time, aviation pays the external costs [that] its activities impose on society at large' (note the expression 'over time' – political code for 'when we think we can get away with it')

Nothing in UK government statements indicates any intention of trying to diminish the rate of growth in emissions from air travel. There are mentions of participation in carbon trading schemes, but nothing that suggests that politicians want to reduce the number of travellers or increase the price that they pay. Cheap air travel is today's equivalent of the bread and circuses offered to Romans to bribe them out of dissatisfaction with the state. The opportunity for British holiday-makers to misbehave abroad and ruin the lives of the permanent inhabitants of Mediterranean seaside towns is too important for the administration to try to restrict access to cheap flights.

The UK prime minister does not think that it is even worthwhile trying to use the tax system to dampen air travel growth. In February 2006, he repeatedly said to a committee of senior MPs that unilateral attempts to decrease the emissions from aircraft by managing the demand for air travel were a waste of time and that we should, instead, be backing the development of more fuel-efficient jet engines and lighter airframes. He said: 'I cannot see myself that you are going to be able artificially, through mechanisms based on the consumer, to interfere with aviation travel.'[48]

The problem, of course, is that the technologies for reducing fuel consumption are improving efficiency by 1 or 2 per cent a year while air travel numbers are rising by over 5 per cent a year (and have risen by over 7 per cent in the UK over the last few years).

The government's abdication of any form of direct responsibility for managing down airline emissions is particularly important because of the central role of the UK in handling international passengers. At any one moment, 20 per cent of international passengers are travelling to or from a UK airport.[49] Aviation is a UK success story and no politician will touch it without clear electoral backing. That support is not yet there, even though a large minority of the public thinks that people would pay something towards offsetting the impact of aviation. One 2006 survey showed that 38 per cent of people thought that others would voluntarily pay a charge of £15 to counterbalance the pollution caused by a flight to New York.[50] Political support for some tax is probably rising; but the government is still concerned not to generate antagonism by even voicing a question about increasing air travel taxes. It's worth mentioning, perhaps, that if aircraft fuel were taxed at the same rate as petrol, the cost to fly a return trip across the Atlantic would be increased by £200.[51] It will probably be some time before there is widespread public support for such a charge.

What about an air travel emissions trading scheme? The EU is working on constructing a scheme that allows airlines a certain volume of emissions above which they will have to buy more permits. The idea extends the current permit system that covers major industrial users and that has, so far, proved to be virtually no constraint on carbon use. Governments around Europe – and, indeed, the airline industry – are broadly welcoming the prospect of the scheme. Our suspicions should be aroused at this point: if the airlines are in favour, can it be good for the atmosphere? Of course, it depends upon how the scheme is constructed. If airlines are given an allowance equal to half the volume of carbon dioxide that they produced last year, then emissions trading would bite. But it is very unlikely to happen like this. Airlines will be given a large quota, probably enough to cover all of the previous year's activities. They'll have to pay for growth; but at current prices, the effect will be tiny. At a permit price of 10 Euros per tonne of emissions, the effect on the cost of flying from London to New York will be about £25. At 20 Euros, the cost will be about £50. At these prices of carbon allowances, flights across Europe will rise by less than £10.

Of equal importance to the airlines is the fact that they expect to get their initial allowances free, as the electricity generators did. If ticket prices rise, they might actually be able to increase their profits as a result of the introduction of the scheme. Certainly, there's widespread suspicion that the net effect of the current European permit scheme has been to hand the power generators windfall profits of billions of Euros.

The European Commission, in charge of designing the aviation scheme, is shameless when describing its likely effect. The first page of the press release is full of quotations from European commissioners saying that the proposal would reduce emissions.[52] But read on and the story gets a little cloudy. Later in the release, the commission boasts that the impact on ticket prices is likely to be 'modest', with prices rising between 0 and 9 Euros per return flight. 'With an increase of this level', it continues, 'aviation demand would simply grow at a slightly slower rate than otherwise.' Emissions trading is going to do very little to protect the global atmosphere from the impact of rapid growth in passenger flights. The European Commission has caved in to the forces that seek to continue profiting from the ballooning growth in air travel.

Of course, this is unsurprising. Democratic societies are locked into competition with other open economies. Good, cheap aviation does not just deliver low-cost holidays in sunny Mediterranean resorts; it oils the wheels of the modern economy. Trying to restrict air travel will undoubtedly affect the ability of the UK economy to maintain its relatively fast growth and high share of investment from foreign countries. 'Britain's continuing success as a place in which to invest and do business depends crucially on the strength of our international transport links' says the UK's 2004 *Transport White Paper*.[53]

So, the government must provide more capacity for aviation. Without a revolution in politics that allows the government to abandon its plans to add runways around the UK, the only way that aircraft emissions are going to be checked is by individuals deciding voluntarily that they are not going to fly.

Private cars

Despite regularly acknowledging that transport is the most rapidly growing source of greenhouse gases, the government continues to act to encourage road travel. The 2004 *Transport White Paper* shows a graph of the cost of motoring. It depicts a projected fall of 20 per cent by 2025, during a period when real incomes are expected to rise by at least one half.[54] Unsurprisingly, the expected fall in the costs of car use is seen as feeding through to a greater mileage travelled.

The government acknowledges that the cost of private car use has fallen in recent years, while the price of bus and rail transport has risen. The pressure group Transport 2000 published a verdict on the government's policies in this field. It wrote:

> *Since Labour came to power in 1997, motoring is 6 per cent cheaper in real terms (taking into account purchase, maintenance, petrol, tax and insurance), while bus fares have risen almost 16 per cent and a rail ticket is 7 per cent more expensive than in 1997.*[55]

Understandably, UK residents have responded to this incentive by driving more and will continue to do so in future.

The government's response to the increasing demand for car travel has been to increase the road-building programme and continue to restrain rises in taxes on car use. In March 2006, Friends of the Earth noted that the duty on car fuels has not kept up with inflation since 1997. The price of petrol has risen as a result of the rise in international oil prices; but the government has damped the increase at the petrol pump by holding down fuel duties.

After initially holding back on the construction of new roads when it first came to power in 1997, the UK administration is now pushing a large number of road construction and improvement projects. As of the middle of 2006, there are about 80 major road building schemes in the UK.[56] These roads are needed, the government says, as a result of the greater congestion caused by increasing numbers of cars on the road. Unsurprisingly, this increase is largely a result of the falling cost of motoring, an outcome within the government's capacity, but not intention, to control.

As ever in government documents – in the UK and worldwide – the 2004 *Transport White Paper* devotes pages and pages to schemes for reducing road traffic. It lauds workplace and school 'travel plans', for example, that aim to reduce car travel. It quotes figures suggesting that work travel plans can cut car travel by 'between 10 per cent and 30 per cent' at negligible cost. School travel plans have a smaller impact at between 8 and 15 per cent.[57] All of these schemes are swimming against a fast-running tide if car use is forever becoming cheaper and new roads are always being under construction.

An example I know well personally illustrates how much use can be reduced if car travel to school is made more difficult, not less. Our local primary school moved three years ago to a site that was much less immediately accessible by road. Parents using a car now have to drop their children about 100m away. The result has been a sharp reduction from over 60 per cent of children being brought by car to around 20 per cent today.[58] The decline in car use appears to be one of the most impressive reductions anywhere in the country.

Similar changes around other schools might really reduce the total volume of car travel. But a policy of active discouragement of car use by making it more difficult, time consuming or expensive appears to be seen as electorally unattractive. The government praises car reduction plans in its press releases, and then discourages them, in practice, by making car travel quicker, easier and cheaper than the alternatives. And, as expected, local politicians in my neighbourhood are pressing for a new road to our school, crossing a sensitive wildlife refuge.

Government doesn't even want to gently manage downwards the emissions of its own employees. In 2002, central government announced that it would try to get its employees to drive to work less. The department with the leading responsibility for climate change issues, the Department for Environment, Food and Rural Affairs (Defra), said that it had obtained the commitment from all government ministries to reduce emissions from travel by 10 per cent by 2006.[59] Regular monitoring was promised. Two years later, the Sustainable Development Commission, a government body, commented in its annual report that 'The data provided by departments for carbon dioxide emissions over the period 2003–2004 are largely incomplete.'[60]

By 2005, independent auditors had begun to assemble the information necessary to check on whether the government was actually meeting the targets that it had set itself. Their conclusions were not favourable. The 2005 report said that 'In the same year that the government claimed to take a global lead on climate change, total CO_2 emissions from government departments have actually increased.'[61] On the question of the precise contribution of reductions in car use, the commission commented that 'over two-thirds of departments failed to report accurately on the total amount of fuel consumed in the last year, and data on CO_2 emission reduction was sometimes poor'.[62]

In similar fashion, the 2004 *Transport White Paper* committed the civil service to reducing the amount of single occupancy commuting by car to government departments by 5 per cent. Despite the exhortations directed at the commercial sector to decrease car use, and the apparently successful introduction of travel plans elsewhere, the government appears no longer to measure car use by its employees, or chooses not to publicize it. Analyses by the Department for Transport – note the 'for' – suggest that real efforts by companies to reduce car use among employees can have noticeable effects; but it cannot manage even to measure car use among its own workforce.[63]

Real reductions in car use across the economy would require uncomfortable and disruptive measures. The price and convenience of car travel would have to be made much less attractive than the use of public transport. The total amount of travel would need to be curtailed. Long-term measures would need to be put in place to reduce the distances between people's workplaces and their homes. There is little doubt that policies to achieve these objectives would be initially deeply unpopular, and no government is likely to put them in place. It is fair to mention that the government does now actively discuss charging for road use as a means of addressing congestion; but its object is the reduction of travel times, rather than cutting CO_2 emissions.

While acknowledging the importance of transport in increasing emissions, the government's hope – for which no plausible evidence is adduced – is that the UK can move rapidly to cars fuelled by biomass or hydrogen. A graph in the 2004 *Transport White Paper* showed carbon dioxide emissions from road transport peaking in 2009 and falling rapidly thereafter. There is absolutely no support in the text – not a single word – for this decline. And, remember, this is in a document that sees total road travel rising by 40 per cent by 2025. The disconnection between the pious hopes of rapid reductions in emissions and the absolute failure to actually do anything to restrain car use is a severe indictment of government. However, it is nothing less and nothing more than we can expect. Governments won't act unless a clear majority of the electorate tells them to.

In its many detailed pronouncements, the UK government always notes the deleterious effect of the rise of car travel, particularly the impact on congestion. In the case of air travel, the environmental issues are even more serious; but the discussions of climate change tend to be even more perfunctory. The reasons are clear: unconstrained growth in air travel is completely incompatible with putting a lid on overall carbon dioxide emissions.

Even the government's usual optimism about the carbon emissions going down sometime quite soon fails it in the case of aviation and it doesn't see a peak until about 2030, at around double the level of today. There is, if these forecasts come even close to accuracy, absolutely no way of getting average UK emissions per person down to an appropriate level. Therefore, the issue is avoided, and airport expansion is allowed to continue because, as the administration put it, 'Economic prosperity brings with it greater demand for travel. As people get wealthier, they can afford to travel further and more often. They can also afford to pay for goods and services brought from further afield.'[64]

Conflict with other government objectives

As importantly, government policies in areas apparently remote from climate change issues are developed with no thought to their impact on greenhouse gas emissions. Allowing parents more choice over schools for their children, or which hospitals to go to, tends to increase the volume of traffic. But the effects are dispersed, difficult to quantify and the climate cost is some distance in the future. So, increased greenhouse gas emissions are tolerated as an unfortunate consequence of some wider objective.

A good example is the digitalization of television transmission. All of the old analogue TV transmitters will be turned off and homes will either need new TV sets or will have to buy digital set-top boxes for existing TVs. There's widespread debate about the number of new boxes that will need to be bought, and the figures I've produced for a parliamentary committee have not been widely accepted.[65] But even lower estimates of 25 million new boxes humming away at 10 watts (W) will add 0.5 per cent to the UK's peak electricity demand. That's a new (possibly coal-fired and carbon-intensive) power station, just to keep set-top boxes warm when they are running in standby mode.

Faced with the problems of really addressing climate emissions – for example, by trying to hold down the growth in travel – governments back away. But they must be seen to be doing something, so they produce a steady stream of small and inoffensive initiatives to give the appearance of action. Over the past few years we've had small schemes for wind energy, tidal and wave power, and energy conservation measures. In 2006, the current fad is micro-generation – power stations on people's roofs. An impressive amount of publicity accompanied the announcement of the government's proposals in spring 2006. Nevertheless, the amount of money available to subsidize installation – £50 million – will only convert 15,000 houses, or less than 0.1 per cent of the UK housing stock. This is not enough even to catch up with Germany, which now has solar installations on well over 100,000 homes.

The UK government's wheezes are like the typical urban cycleway in the city in which I live. These end abruptly without warning, leaving the participant exposed to the threat of imminent death. Democratic governments generally do not have the patience and commitment to take new technologies from introduction to widespread use. When media interest fades, government ministers get bored very quickly. Priming the pump is easy, quite cheap and creates good headlines; but to take a new technology, such as solar photovoltaic panels, and support it until the UK has a good network of profitable and efficient installers, a wide base of satisfied users and good awareness among potential customers requires decades – not months – of consistent support. Governments never provide this unless a strong business lobby demands it; but the small renewable energy companies don't possess that authority. The government's favourite renewables company, SolarCentury, a specialist supplier of photovoltaic panels, was bitter about the failure to extend the support for domestic photovoltaic technology. Buoyed up over the years by government flattery and interest, it had promoted the administration's virtues. But in the absence of substantial action, it changed the tone of its press releases. In a comment on the massive 2006 *Energy Review*, it said: 'This is a predictably disappointing paper, which fails to deliver the "urgent action" called for by the secretary of state himself.'[66]

In addition to the small schemes and media-friendly gimmicks that exist to show governments are doing something, they provide endless advice and exhortation. There is a huge amount of information and help available to those firms and householders wanting to reduce their use of fossil fuel. Large numbers of programmes assist and advise. Unfortunately, take-up of this advice is limited; relatively few of the ideas have sufficiently short payback times for people to be interested. Energy is not a large enough proportion of most people's budgets for these schemes to work. Those people for whom energy costs are increasingly unaffordable have no money to invest in the new technologies that would save them future expenditure. New ideas, elaborate wheezes and large numbers of people providing data and analysis will not be enough to stop energy use from growing.

Government itself rarely acts in line with the suggestions it gives to other people. In both its spending and regulatory decisions, and in its own behaviour, central government has repeatedly acted to ignore the threat from climate change.

Pollution taxes and carbon rationing

Pessimism about the likely actions of government when faced with increasing emissions from transport can only be heightened by noting that since the arrival of a Labour government in 1997, the percentage of tax revenue coming from 'green' measures, such as fuel duty or air passenger tax, has fallen from 9.5 per cent to 8.3 per cent, in sharp contrast to a policy commitment made before coming to power. In early 2006, Friends of the Earth commented about this as follows:

> *The duty rate of 47.1 pence per litre following last year's budget [March 2005] is the lowest, in real terms, since June 1997 for both petrol and diesel. Since abandoning the fuel tax escalator in 1999, the chancellor has not raised fuel duties above inflation in any budget, and has frozen rates in most years. If the chancellor had even kept fuel duty at the same proportion of total taxes, rather than letting them fall, then £9 billion would have been raised between 2000 and 2004.*[67]

A rather illiterate comment from the UK Treasury in 1997 recognized the problem in increasing pollution taxes:

Environmental taxation must meet the tests of good taxation. It must be well designed to meet objectives without undesirable side effects; it must keep deadweight compliance costs to a minimum; distributional impact must be acceptable; and care must be had to implications for international competitiveness.[68]

What this statement means is that the Treasury won't increase taxes that might put the UK at a disadvantage or seriously affect the poor, even if they have environmental benefits.

The problem facing any political leader is that carbon pollution taxes that are properly effective will inevitably either impose huge burdens on the less well-off or will make the UK less competitive. As a result, the brave attempts to use market mechanisms to reduce emissions, such as through the obligations on electricity companies to subsidize renewable sources of power, are either very restricted in scale or don't really affect the operating decisions of the users of fossil fuel.

What, of course, governments should do is to demand lifestyle changes from their electorates. Less travel, better insulation and lower thermostat temperatures in the winter, fewer appliances in the home, changes in food purchase habits, and replacement of baths with short showers are all necessary. But no administration is going to demand these changes because they run wholly counter to democratic society's conventional assumption that government's role is to provide greater material prosperity, not less. So, quite reasonably in the circumstances, government will preach virtue, but actually do as little as possible.

Our governments could, of course, decide systematically to raise the price of fossil fuel energy. One sensible course of action might be to try to quadruple the cost over a period of, say, 15 years using the taxation system. The main problem would be the huge impact on the poorer members of society. The top 10 per cent of households spend less than 2 per cent of their income on gas and electricity. A major increase in prices would have little impact on these people. But the bottom decile has to spend over 5 per cent of its income on these things, and this figure will have risen considerably since the data was last collected.[69] Quadrupled gas prices would mean that a large fraction of the UK population would be obliged to go cold in winter. This is simply not going to happen in a democracy. Governments' freedom to use the price mechanism to decrease the consumption of gas for heating or petrol for cars is extremely constrained. This is one of the reasons why the plans of political parties for higher 'green' taxes are always laughably unspecific. Detailed proposals would show clearly that increasing energy prices would have a disproportionate impact on the poor.

It's fair to say that governments are continuing to search for painless ways to reduce carbon emissions. But the options open to it are depressingly few. A scheme of 'personal carbon allowances' is sometimes canvassed. Occasionally called carbon rationing, the suggestion is that each member of society is given a total allowance of carbon dioxide each year. It might currently be 5 tonnes, but would decrease year on year in order to reduce national emissions. The holder would be given a smart card containing the ration, with the balance reducing every time the holder made a purchase of fossil fuel-derived goods. Paying the electricity bill would result in a deduction from the balance, as would a top-up of fuel at the petrol station.

In some ways, this is a hugely attractive scheme. Rich people would have to buy more credits for their air travel from those who choose not to travel. Unlike using taxation, the scheme would not result in the price of home heating increasing for the poor. But carbon allowances are an administrative nightmare, impossibly complex to run, and could be circumvented in an almost infinite number of ways. Instead of driving my car, I could take a taxi. Whose allowance does that trip come from? Does the homeowner trying to keep warm in a draughty Victorian house get a larger ration? Will people off the mains gas network get larger allowances because of the greater carbon cost of heating by electricity? Tradable carbon allowances should continue to get serious investigation; but they are not a panacea within the next 15 years. In support of my scepticism, I need only point to the nearly unblemished record of total failure of most major government information technology projects in the UK over the last 20 years. Carbon rationing is an elegant and completely impractical solution.

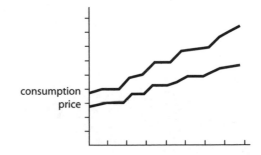

consumption
price

the inadequacy of alternative means of reducing emissions

Can we expect freely operating markets or other economic incentives to solve the problem? I don't think we can be optimistic. Conventional economic analysis has all sorts of trouble with global warming. It has helped to design the trading mechanisms that allow institutions to participate in the Emissions Trading Scheme (ETS), and it has made clear progress in helping to quantify the costs of climate change. Economists have also made robust and accurate critiques of some of the more bizarre extrapolations of energy trends contained in the scientific work on global warming.[70]

But the issues that economists can deal with are the superficial problems. So far, economics has had very little to say about how to reduce the consumption of energy without hugely increasing its price. And, it is worth pointing out, for economic forces to work, price increases would probably have to be very substantial. The price mechanism does not work well when it comes to energy. The hikes in energy prices from 2004 to 2006 have had an almost invisible effect on total consumption. Figures for Germany, for example, show that carbon dioxide emissions probably fell by about 2 per cent in 2005, though energy costs would have gone up at least 10 or 20 times this amount. Germany is one of the few large countries to see a decrease in CO_2 emissions. In most other countries emissions rose even as gas and oil prices leapt. Germany, to its credit, is making progress decoupling economic growth and energy use.

At current price levels, fossil fuel demand is what economists call very 'inelastic'. Demand does not vary much in response to large changes in price. This is unsurprising – and completely consistent with the thesis of this book that energy is so cheap that no rational individual would ever reduce consumption without enormous increases in price.

One alternative to the general increases in retail energy prices is to increase the price paid to generators of non-fossil fuel energy. Essentially, such arrangements pay more to those companies generating energy from renewable sources than those getting it from fossil fuel. One kilowatt hour from a wind farm gets a better price than the same energy from a coal-fired power station. This type of scheme – broadly approved of by economists – is pursued by the UK. It has been dramatically successful at making it financially attractive to build onshore wind farms. Onshore wind, which could easily provide 20 per cent of the UK's electricity-generating need, is now financially viable in the UK because of the virtually guaranteed subsidy of over 3 pence per kilowatt hour, paid to wind farms by fossil fuel generators. However, tidal and wave energy, which may represent larger potential sources of electricity because of their greater inherent reliability, probably need subsidies of almost 10 pence a kilowatt hour or more for many years before costs fall substantially. Solar power is even more expensive, although its costs are likely to decrease on the back of large-scale investments in sun-flooded countries in the next few years.

But raising the price paid to generators of renewable electricity has still not got the UK anywhere near the target of 10 per cent renewable energy by 2010. And even a 10 per cent renewables share does not solve the problem. Electricity accounts for only 21 per cent of the world's energy use. The typical gas-fired home in the UK takes 19,000kWh from the gas mains and 3700kWh from the electricity grid. Electricity is not as central to climate change as it sometimes seems. Even if all electricity came from non-carbon sources, we wouldn't come close to reducing UK emissions by the 75 per cent per person that we almost certainly need.

And any price rises for electricity will run into all the political problems mentioned above. The current scheme for encouraging renewables for electricity generation is intelligently designed because it forces fossil fuel plants indirectly to pay for the extra cost of producing wind energy, but only raises the retail price of electricity by a few per cent. However, the net effect is still to raise the price of electricity above what it would be in a completely free market. The impact of this on energy-intensive industries is potentially severe if they face competition from foreign companies with lower cost electricity. The backlash against the renewables subsidy has already started, and we can expect complaints to grow in intensity as the amount of subsidy rises in the next few years.

Industries facing competition from abroad need electricity costs as low as possible in order to compete. The same issue faces other countries, and without worldwide coordination of energy prices, we will always face the strong possibility of the 'race to the bottom' as countries compete to try to maintain their indigenous energy-intensive industries. Economics has no easy answer to this problem. This should not take us aback: economics generally believes that transferring production to the country with the cheapest resources, such as electricity, adds to human welfare. It takes a major leap to say that moving production to the country with the lowest energy costs is bad. Very few economists have yet to make this jump.

Of course, the profession has a far more serious problem as well. Economics holds that any growth in gross domestic product (GDP, or 'national income') is good. A large number of undergraduate textbooks would have to be rewritten if economics decided that increasing income was bad because it almost invariably involved greater depletion of the

Earth's resources and added to climate change. Similarly, economists would be rightly reluctant to suggest that people's consumption should be restricted. Very crudely speaking, conventional economics sees all consumption as something to be encouraged.

The criticism of economists for their assumption that people only pursue their economic self-interest is now almost a convention. The economics profession has begun the fight back, stressing that the subject has a more complex view of human nature than the critics suggest. Larry Summers, formerly US treasury secretary, president of Harvard and a distinguished academic economist, spoke to an undergraduate audience on reconciling economics with a more generous view of human nature:

> We all have only so much altruism in us. Economists like me think of altruism as a valuable and rare good that needs conserving. Far better to conserve it by designing a system in which people's wants will be satisfied by individuals being selfish, and saving that altruism for our families, our friends and the many social problems in this world that markets cannot solve.[71]

Global warming is by far the most important threat that 'markets cannot solve'. Economists need to recognize that the battle against climate change almost certainly requires us to give it some of what Summers sees as our limited altruism. This is the thesis of this book – nothing is going to solve the climate problem except self-restraint (or altruism by another name) by individuals. The normal price signals are simply not working properly with fossil fuel.

There are many other issues. Economics, for example, struggles with valuing biodiversity. Many people have a strong sense that maintaining the planet in a rough equilibrium and not losing huge numbers of species of plants and animals every year is a good thing. Putting a price on this is tricky, particularly when it comes to valuing the impact of maintaining a species on the welfare of unborn generations. Does it matter if our great grandchildren live in a world with no polar bears, to take the most obvious example? After all, our generation doesn't miss the dodo very much.

Weighing up the cost of climate change to the welfare of poor people in remote countries is a similar challenge. The fact that tens of millions of Bangladeshis are going to have move from the low-lying portions of their country in the next 50 years is clearly a bad thing, and economics would not deny this. However, economics has yet to devise a good mechanism for compensating these individuals by taxing today those people in the West and elsewhere who are causing the sea level to rise by their unconstrained consumption of fossil fuels (Bangladesh has carbon dioxide emissions levels of about 0.25 tonnes per head – 2 per cent of the UK figure – so it cannot itself be blamed).

The subject also struggles with what one economist I know calls the 'purple sea' problem.[72] Imagine we woke up tomorrow and the seas around Europe had all turned bright purple as a result of climate change. A very crude disparagement of economics is to say that because the sea is as useful as it ever was, economists would robustly assert that human welfare had not suffered. Despite its crudeness, there is more than a grain of truth in this criticism of the science.

Analyses by economists of the costs of global warming, such as those discussed in Bjorn Lomborg's edition of papers from the Copenhagen Consensus work, tend to completely omit any consideration of the more intangible costs of warming and focus, instead, on the highly predictable effects, such as the reduction in agricultural productivity.[73] Economists, in general, seem to place a much lower level of importance on maintaining the status quo than the populations among whom they live. I want spring to come in mid-March, not early February; but the scientific economist will only reluctantly value this apparently arbitrary preference.

There are also substantial and unresolved issues with how we choose to discount the future. Generally, we assume that £1 today is worth more than £1 in a year's time. In fact, human beings often act as if £1 in a year's time has a very low value, indeed. We give the future very little weight in our thinking. This view, carried over to climate change, implies that the benefits of cheap energy today are worth having, even if the future costs are high. We'd rather have the good things now, even if our welfare is adversely affected in ten years' time. If you agree with this line of argument, it may well not be worth trying to avert climate change. It costs a lot now to reduce greenhouse gases, and we won't value the benefit very highly in the future. As a species, we do tend to eat the entire pudding for supper, rather than making it last several days. Climate change is a sort of borrowing from the future – we get a higher standard of living today in return for lower welfare in the future. Economists generally say that this sort of free choice is to be encouraged. But those who say that future generations can look after themselves (and, after all, they will probably have much greater material prosperity) need to acknowledge that the damage we are inflicting on the global atmosphere may well be irreparable.

Reducing the carbon dioxide emissions of a household can either be done by self-denial – cutting room temperatures, for example – or by installing technologies or devices that consume less energy. Many of these things cost several hundred UK pounds per tonne of carbon dioxide saved, although this book will show that many options are far cheaper than this. They do not seem financially attractive to the average householder, and perhaps they never will. To people borrowing money on a credit card at 25 per cent, the returns from installing solar panels – at perhaps 3 or 4 per cent a year – must look very unappealing. However, without huge investments in expensive energy-saving or carbon-reducing measures, we are very unlikely even to begin to get a grasp on carbon emissions.

Conventional free-market economics cannot handle other problems. It finds it difficult to take into account the choices of the unborn. My decision to take an aircraft to

Barbados affects not just my potential standard of living in 30 years' time – if I live that long – but also that of my grandchildren and their descendants. They have had no voice in my decision to trade a nice holiday now for hotter temperatures in the future. This is what is called the problem of inter-generational equity and should be a central issue in climate change economics.

The second problem is that my choices of what to consume do not really affect my own future living standards. The individual flight to Barbados is not going to affect my future welfare to any extent. So the strictly rational individual ignores the future climate costs unless his or her conscience is unusually active.

WILL TECHNOLOGICAL PROGRESS SOLVE THE PROBLEM?

Political leaders stress the importance of technological innovation as a primary means of eventually reducing carbon emissions. This is wishful thinking on an extraordinary scale.

One good example is the much touted move to what is called the 'hydrogen economy' in which the gas replaces carbon fuels in most applications. Burning hydrogen creates no carbon dioxide, so enthusiasts say that it will naturally replace high-carbon fuels. Unfortunately, extracting hydrogen from water requires more energy than it provides when burned as a fuel, and there is no net reduction in carbon emissions.

Biofuels suffer from a similar problem. Because Western agriculture is so energy inefficient, 1 litre of biodiesel made from oilseed rape may well embed as much carbon-based energy as a similar quantity of petrol. Western countries seeking security of energy supply may well work hard to increase the availability of biofuels; but the paradox may be that more oil, or oil-derived products, are used to make the biofuels than are saved in car fuel volumes. There is acrimonious debate about this topic (see Chapter 10); but the fertilizer put on fields growing crops for biofuels possibly causes more greenhouse gas emissions than could possibly be saved by substituting for petrol. Increasing biofuel production in the UK will probably reduce, not increase, energy security and the diversity of energy sources. And most of the country's available land will have to be given over to growing oilseed rape and will therefore be unavailable for reforestation.

Nuclear and renewable sources of electricity will, eventually, come to take a larger part in the generation of power. Hydrogen, generated by renewable electricity rather than fossil fuels may come to power fuel cells in European homes. Or homes may be powered by efficient small combined heat and power (CHP) boilers. All of this is very possible using current scientific knowledge. However, moving from today's reliable, cheap, convenient sources of fossil energy is going to take decades.

Similarly, capturing the carbon emissions from power stations is theoretically feasible, and one UK generator – E.ON – has just begun to explore the possibilities for a commercial plant.[74] But it makes all too clear that it wants higher prices for electricity and a guaranteed return for its investment before it will go ahead. Even then, this first power plant would take at least five years to build, and conversion of the rest of the UK's electricity supply industry to low-carbon technologies is impossible to imagine in under 25 years, the approximate length of life of existing investments.

Capture of carbon dioxide after the combustion of a carbon-based fuel will eventually become widespread and may eventually not add significantly to the cost of energy. The UK government's 2006 *Energy Review* holds out hope, but admits that nowhere in the world is there a single working commercial power plant using this technology.

Other potential methods of carbon capture include the seeding of oceans with iron to induce faster plankton growth, which sequesters carbon, and injection of bulk CO_2 into depleted oil fields. All of these technologies are interesting and will probably eventually be useful techniques for diminishing the impact of coal and gas use – but only in several decades.

However, nothing, even in the remotest prospect, is a replacement for kerosene fuel in aircraft or will assist in capturing the gases spewed out by jet engines. The rapid rate of growth of aircraft travel and its fierce effects on warming mean that this source alone will cause us to exceed the maximum safe level of carbon dioxide emissions of 2 or at most 3 tonnes a head, however successful we are in implementing technology-based reductions to carbon emissions.

Low-carbon fuel technologies are also some way off widespread use in public transport. UK operator First Group has an extensive record of attempts to reduce emissions by using innovative and lower-carbon technologies for powering buses. In 2005 it commented: 'We ... take every opportunity to support trials in relation to alternative fuels, such as gas buses, hybrid and fuel cell technology. However, as yet the reliability of the technology itself and the supporting infrastructure is insufficient to allow the delivery of a reliable and sustainable public transport network.'[75]

These new technologies require both expensive capital investment, such as buying new buses with the appropriate kit, and an investment in training, higher levels of maintenance and greater variability in operating performance. Diesel buses are relatively reliable. Bus operators have sufficient experience to be able to plan for maintenance and for the occasional unexpected failure. They have no such knowledge of new technologies, such as hydrogen power, and buses using new equipment will tend to be unusually expensive to begin with. So, the potential operating savings to a commercial operator need to be demonstrably large if we are to get real commitment to experiment with low-carbon innovations. There's no evidence that these savings are yet present.

Despite the optimism in some quarters, and the obvious improvements in some non-carbon technologies, there is no clear way by which carbon dioxide emissions will be reduced sufficiently through the application of technology. Even were science to be working against a background of much higher energy prices, it is unclear that much carbon reduction can take place, except possibly in the generation of electricity. But easily mined and cheap coal in China and India is very likely to outweigh the effects of growth in non-carbon electricity generation in the West.

WHAT ABOUT COMPANIES, WHICH SEEM MUCH MORE INTERESTED IN THE ISSUE THAN BEFORE?

Some large and highly successful companies have made considerable play of their interest in low-carbon technologies. The best-known examples are BP and General Electric (GE) of the US, and their interest is surely genuine. No doubt they perceive the likelihood of a long-term and substantial rise in the proportion of energy generated from non-fossil fuel sources. But they cannot themselves create a market where none exists. Their interest will be dependent upon their ability to make money from new technologies.

BP is a pioneer. Unusually for the oil industry, it accepts the reality of climate change and its commitment to renewable energy seems genuine. But will it do enough? Its 2005 *Corporate Sustainability Report* indicates that it will invest $8 billion in renewable energy over ten years, or $800 million a year. $800 million is ten times the UK government's budget for micro-generation. BP's investments are probably the biggest single commitment in the world to renewable sources; but the yearly figure of $800 million compares with total 2005 investments, almost entirely in fossil fuel exploration, production and refining of $14 billion. Renewables comprise only about 6 per cent of the total. And the cost to the shareholders is hardly noticeable. In 2005, BP distributed a total of $19 billion to its investors. While BP's efforts in new technologies are hardly insignificant, they pale beside the hugely greater allocations to its conventional business. Nevertheless, it is probably doing as much as it can without upsetting its shareholders.

Another way of looking at BP's actions is to put them in the context of the company's own carbon dioxide emissions. BP's production and refining businesses were responsible for about 78 million tonnes of carbon dioxide in 2005, down slightly from the previous year. This international company is therefore responsible for 13 per cent as much carbon as the whole of UK emissions. Oil refining and production use energy – one commonly sees a figure of 15 per cent for the energy in 1 litre of crude oil that gets used in the process of turning it into functional products, such as petrol. At the current prices of $800 for a large solar panel, if BP's total yearly investment of $800 million was spend on photovoltaics, it would replace about one tenth of 1 per cent of its current CO_2 emissions. This is not a fair comparison because the solar panels will continue producing electricity for at least 20 years; but it shows the scale of BP's task if it is to maintain a drive towards a lower-carbon future.[76]

In a modern economy, in which economic competition is working actively, no company can choose to make decisions that raise its costs compared to its peers. It would only be a matter of months before its investors called for a change in strategy and began muttering about the need for a new management team. Indeed, most investors would say that companies have a duty to pursue profit, even at the expense of the wider environment, although they might not put it as crudely. Companies therefore tend to act as herd creatures, following trends as long as others are too, but never driving ahead into apparently unprofitably markets. While fossil fuel remains cheap – and it still is compared to the alternatives – we will not see much innovation from large companies.

Electricity generators – apart from the airlines, the most visible producers of greenhouse gas emissions – make persuasive claims to be committed to emissions reductions. In a recent report on its climate change programme, the UK's largest fossil fuel generator, E.ON, indicates that it plans to reduce carbon emissions per unit of electricity by 10 per cent between 2005 and 2012. But if the independent forecasts of electricity demand growth are correct, this will mean that E.ON will be emitting more carbon dioxide in 2012 than it did in 2005. It is one of the major backers of UK renewable technology; but its recent yearly investment in the field is no more than 4 per cent of its total capital expenditure. As the company says, referring to the world's indifference to the problem, 'unfortunately, climate change presents a challenge that has yet to be adequately addressed'.[77] Its own level of commitment looks somewhat limited. It sees fit to boast that its home installation arm fitted a grand total of 287 condensing boilers in 2005 in the homes of its 5 million retail customers under the Powergen brand.

Smaller companies may be more dynamic in searching for new opportunities and developments. But the history of businesses trying to make money from renewables or from improved efficiency in the use of fossil fuel is littered with truly dismal failures and slow progress even in the most successful companies. The glacial pace of developments in tidal energy, wave power, hydrogen fuels, fuel cells and small wind turbines is an indication of the profound problems experienced by smaller companies trying to commercialize new technologies against the combined weight of cheap fossil fuel and extremely well established hydrocarbon machines, such as the internal combustion engine and combined cycle gas turbine power plant. Over the past couple of years, I have tried to buy a domestic micro-combined heat and power (CHP) plant, a small wind turbine, and looked into buying a fuel cell. In each case, despite the extravagant claims on the company's website, the product was unavailable, and an apologetic email followed my enquiry. This is not to suggest that micro-renewables are not potentially extremely important as future energy sources, but simply to say that they are a long way from commercial success today.

Many lower-carbon technologies are 'stalled' – that is, they do not move from early pilots to widespread adoption in industry. Although the pioneers can often see the way of taking these technologies to much lower costs in the future, they are unable to get the customers to help them build enough units to achieve these more attractive prices.

Companies generally require paybacks on their investments in less than five years, and often much less. Virtually no carbon-reducing technologies provide this sort of return. This is not to say that business is actually opposed to cuts in the level of greenhouse gas emissions. The corporate sector simply wants to ensure that no individual company is required to manage with a small allowance when its competitors are given more. Broadly speaking, as long as emissions reductions are equitably imposed, and right across Europe, business is in favour. Though no company, singly, can do much to reduce emissions, and doesn't want to on its own, business leaders press the government to introduce schemes that universally require reductions in energy use. For example, in early June 2006, a group of the most senior UK corporate heads, including people from companies as diverse as Shell and Vodafone, visited the prime minister to push for tighter, not looser, restrictions.[78] They argued for smaller allowances under the European Emissions Trading Scheme. They spoke in favour of steps to cut emissions from transport, such as congestion charging and road pricing. They even said that building regulations should be tighter in order to improve the energy losses from new buildings.

These proposals will tend to increase business costs. Companies very rarely argue for measures that impose penalties on their activities. Why are senior executives asking national and international entities to tighten rules on emissions? I suspect that as individuals they feel uncomfortable leading companies that generate such large absolute amounts of greenhouse gases. As people – ordinary individuals with moral sensibility and a concern for the future of their race – they know that the arguments in favour of restraint are overwhelming. But as leaders paid to advance their company's wealth and size, they know that unilateral action is impossible. Shell UK is not going to stop drilling for gas just because its managers are nervous about the climate in 50 years' time. So these people want to pass the responsibility on to government, which will force them to be better behaved. We need to be clear: when business asks for lower carbon emissions, it does not intend to actually do anything unless forced by regulation. But as with many forms of regulation, equitably applied, most businesses would find greater restrictions on fossil fuel use perfectly possible to accommodate.

I can't pretend that all manufacturing and service industry leaders agree with this conclusion. Some senior executives believe that climate change initiatives will adversely affect corporate profits within a few years. Since the typical chief executive officer in a large US company can only expect to be in office for four years and the figure probably isn't much higher in the UK, it requires some selflessness to argue for measures that might start to affect profits just before the executive leaves office. As these individuals can depart with quite extraordinary sums of money – $400 million was one recent particularly egregious example paid to an oil industry executive – they are unlikely to support measures that remove part of their wealth.[79]

Nevertheless, those business leaders who think about the issue generally see the scale of the climate change problem. Many even think that initiatives to decelerate the pace of warming would have a beneficial effect on the European business sector by making it leaner and less energy-intensive. But they still won't do anything – except a few token projects for public relations purposes – that increase their costs above those of their rivals. Tesco has just started a campaign to reduce the use of plastic bags. The environmental impact of this is utterly trivial compared to the carbon emissions of the industrial food chain. However, it looks good and Tesco wants to be seen to do its bit.

OTHER BLOCKS ON THE ROAD TO A LOW-CARBON FUTURE

There's an increasing literature on the non-tangible issues we need to address if carbon emissions are to be held down.[80] Fossil fuel consumption is largely invisible and unobtrusive. Awakening people to the effect of background activity, such as keeping the house warm with an inefficient boiler, is an extremely demanding communications task.

This issue is magnified by the extraordinary pervasiveness of fossil fuel energy use. The typical consumer is unable to comprehend the multiple ways in which his or her lifestyle generates greenhouse gases. The ordinary house-owner might unconsciously take a decision to use fossil fuel several hundred times a day – boiling a kettle, flushing the toilet, buying a tin of beans, driving to the station, leaving the computer on at work – and cannot possibly be expected to weigh the carbon consequences of each action.

Many attempts to reduce carbon use are, regrettably, also the subject of potential derision from friends and colleagues. There is strong social pressure to conform to conventional behaviour. A simple decision not to use aeroplanes, the single most important statement a person can make that he or she regards climate change as an important issue, may pose problems for social relationships or prospects at work. Not going on a weekend party to Prague because of a principled refusal to fly is unlikely to endear one to friends. A willingness to drop everything and fly to the US is often a precondition of the most successful jobs. Who is going to abandon the hopes of a better paid and higher status job in order to defend a position that air travel is wrong?

Most importantly, most people have no sense whatsoever of the scale of the fossil fuel consumption attached to each activity. Here's a comment from author Deborah Moggach, interviewed about a trip to the Galapagos Islands:

> Like a lot of people, I'm a mass of contradictions. I recycle, compost and have hens that eat my leftovers and garden slugs. But I've got an old house that isn't really draft proofed and I never turn the TV off standby. I jump on planes, but I'm very good about cycling.[81]

Deborah Moggach shouldn't be criticized for not realizing that air trip to South America will have contributed 5 tonnes of carbon dioxide or more to the atmosphere, which will be

100 times more important than the impact of her recycling. No one except an expert could possibly hope to know even the approximate impacts of individual acts.

The companies that market their goods to us are aware of this, and will try to sell their products as green, even when they fail to meet the standards of even basic energy efficiency.

One good example is the Toyota Lexus hybrid, sold as an environmentally friendly car, but which has emissions somewhat greater than the average new car sold in the UK. Lexus marketing materials, which claim that the car has the same carbon dioxide output as 'a compact family car', are deeply misleading.[82] Indeed, its parent, Toyota, produces cars that it describes as 'spacious' which emit over 10 per cent less carbon. But what consumer could be expected to know all this? The purpose of marketing, particularly of strong brands, is partly to confuse. This encourages customers to throw up their hands and turn back to the trusted names. 'Confusion marketing' is an increasing feature of life, and the arena of environmental matters is no exception. As the potential impact of purchase decisions on global warming becomes clearer in our minds, we can expect to be treated to increased amounts of marketing propaganda, much of dubious accuracy. In a society in which 25 per cent (one in four) of the population do not understand the meaning of percentages, the complexities of energy economics are going to be beyond most of us.

4

. . . .

no-one else is doing much, so you'd better do something yourself

S o far, this book has commented on the difficulties of doing much about carbon emissions. Individual governments will never have the mandate, and joint action across all states is impossibly difficult to organize. Science cannot provide an answer on its own and conventional economic mechanisms will not work because fossil fuels are not in short supply.

Realizing that the ultimate responsibility rests on us, not on companies or political leaders, numerous individuals want to act on their own initiative. If the arguments in this book are correct, the only morally responsible position is to act on one's own because no institution or market mechanism has any prospect of effective reduction of fossil fuel use. It is up to individuals; we cannot rely on governments. And because our own personal actions are responsible for a larger and larger share of the total, our responsibility is increasing.

SELF-RESTRAINT: A MUCH UNDERVALUED HUMAN VIRTUE

It sometimes seems that there is an immutable law of human nature that requires us to reach out for material possessions, even when we don't really need them. Offer people the chance for a higher material standard of living and they will take it. If we can have it, we want it, even at the cost of drought in Africa or flooding in Asia. This feature of human character makes dealing with climate change especially difficult. Democratic governments and profit-driven companies are simply agents that enable us to act out the pursuit of material gain. Battling climate change requires self-restraint, a trait that modern consumer society has almost, but not quite, obliterated.

If this pessimistic conclusion is right, then the battle against global warming was lost long ago. The huge success of modern dynamic capitalism at delivering material prosperity across the world, particularly in the last 15 years, makes the battle against greenhouse gases doubly difficult. First, it has, of course, required huge amounts of fossil fuel to make the goods and services on which we are now increasingly reliant. Second, it makes jumping off the economic escalator more difficult.

This second point is a little complex to explain. I will do so with reference to a particular example. By the late 1970s, the UK was widely regarded as an economic laggard, condemned to a slow relative decline. Over-powerful trade unions, sclerotic management, an ossified class structure, an ingrained anti-capitalist culture and an absurd romantic reverence for its rural past combined to depress the rate of the UK's economic growth.[83]

Margaret Thatcher, prime minister from 1979 to 1990, did more than anybody to change this. Her mission was to rid the UK of its abiding fatalism, its sense that relative decline was inevitable. She succeeded to an extent that now seems remarkable. The most important transformation in the underlying culture may have been a growing respect for material wealth and personal economic attainment. People had previously derived a substantial portion of their status from their job title, their family history or the name of their school, and relatively little from their income or material possessions.

By the end of the Thatcher period, but certainly continuing into the 21st century, economic success – as conventionally defined by income and wealth – had become a more important indicator of social standing. The entrepreneur, City dealer or successful businessperson is a figure of far greater distinction than could have been the case during the 1970s. Of course, in many ways this has been a beneficial transition. The improvement in material economic performance – particularly in terms of the relative position against the economies of continental Europe – has given the UK a self-confidence and, unfortunately, a swagger that it lacked. Economic growth has enabled major improvements in health, life expectancy and the rate of absolute poverty. Often seen as the most sensitive indicator of physical well-being, the rate of infant mortality has fallen by over 50 per cent since 1981.[84] Between 1981 and 2002, life expectancy at age 50 increased by four and a half years for men and three years for women.[85] Of course, these important improvements may well have occurred without improvements in material prosperity; but the evidence suggests that at least some part of improved health and, indeed, life expectancy in the UK derives from the country's stronger economic performance.[86]

But the transition to a society that rewards economic success with greatly enhanced status has introduced a new compulsion to become wealthy. There is a more of a social cost to resisting fossil fuel addiction. I realize that this is a highly contentious point with powerful arguments on the other side; but the unleashing of entrepreneurial dynamism is, in my opinion, likely to inflate fossil fuel demand, particularly in the form of air travel, larger cars and bigger homes to heat. Stepping off the escalator of material prosperity is more difficult in a culture which more openly celebrates wealth and the display of material possessions. Self-restraint in consumption becomes more difficult. I think it is no accident that some Nordic countries, still partly gripped by a Lutheran self-control, are making more progress in carbon reduction than we are.[87] Personal consumption in these countries is, perhaps, less important to self-image.

A fully effective capitalism is, I suspect, a highly competitive, brutal world in which corporations are continuously under threat from new participants in their markets, from innovation and new technologies, and from cut-throat pricing from foreign suppliers. It is these conditions which keep companies on their toes. One very senior regulator once said to me that the whole aim of competition policy was to rid corporations of their autonomy. Effective competition, he said, left companies no discretion – everything they did was dictated by customers and the relentless search for better value.

The UK is a more competitive economy than it was, and in most respects this is good. But it does necessarily mean that companies have even less choice about climate change. They are left with little autonomy and they will only pursue carbon reduction if that is what their customers and their shareholders demand. Their customers are unlikely to pay significantly extra for low-carbon goods, so normal profit-maximizing companies will only reduce emissions if it makes strict financial sense. And since the average institutional shareholder owns a company's shares for a matter of months, rather than decades, it is unlikely that the owner will take a view about the price of oil in 2020 and reward a company for taking investment decisions with a view to that very long-term future.[88]

As a result, today's pattern is for companies to make marginal reductions in fossil fuel use, but only where the effort is justified by the immediate cost savings. High fossil fuel prices in 2006 are certainly increasing the incentive to reduce the use of oil-, coal- and gas-derived products; but the effects have yet to show up in aggregate national statistics.

So, the consequence of the UK's move to a more competitive, innovative and dynamic economy over the past 25 years has been to give a greater significance to consumption that uses extravagant amounts of fossil fuel, combined with a more responsive corporate sector that marches tightly in step to the drum of customer demand.

This book advances the view that voluntary self-restraint may be the most important way for responsible individuals to cut their own carbon use, combined with some personal investments in lower emissions technologies that are not necessarily financially rational.

But we live in a world that gives huge prominence to the rational pursuit of economic self-interest. The triumph of the Western capitalist model is so complete that the idea that our day-to-day consumption of fossil fuel could have a moral or even religious dimension is seen as deeply eccentric. Even those who recognize the importance of climate change rarely allow themselves to contemplate the idea that market- or taxation-based solutions might not be enough. Self-restraint over consumption is a hugely subversive idea in an economic system which has as its core proposition that greater and greater happiness will follow every increase in our personal incomes and spending.

However, deliberate self-denial is the only way in which individuals can address the global warming threat. Are there any grounds for hope that people will decide to act out moral decisions in their consumption behaviour, even if it means a higher cost or greater inconvenience? Are there analogous instances that might give us hope that individual consumers can adjust their needs so as to consume less?

The evidence demonstrates that some limited optimism is justified. Recent history shows that consumers do sometimes make purchases requiring them to pay more for goods or services which embody values that appeal to them. The most ethically conscious consumers will do this even when there is no status attached to the product. Fifteen years ago, for example, purchasers of organic vegetables were usually buying them because it seemed right, not because organic foods had a strong positive brand image. In fact, purchase of organic foods was, to use a loose expression, very 'counter-cultural'. Gradually, however, consumers may move to the next phase. This stage may be the point at which other, less ethically driven, people begin to make the purchase because of some form of cachet or enhanced status derived from using the product. Organic foods have now certainly reached this stage. Eventually, even laggards begin to switch, if only because it is seen as positively evil to continue buying the non-ethical brands. Who now, for example, would buy cosmetics that were known to be tested on animals?

The move to making low-carbon consumption patterns an endemic feature of the world economy will need to go through these three distinct phases. It does not appear to me to be enough to simply rely on the puritans who dislike consumption of all forms. For widespread personal self-restraint in carbon consumption to become successful, it needs to be developed into a high status activity and, eventually, into the conventional mode of life. The gradual move into being a standard way of living will take generations; but the high costs borne by today's innovators will diminish as low-carbon goods and services decrease in relative price as volumes increase.

It might work as in the following example. Installing ultra-efficient house insulation, for example, is now a goal aimed at by real eco-enthusiasts. It's expensive and does not produce much of a financial return above and beyond normal insulation standards. It is only the socially eccentric who have worried about the 'u' values of walls or other indicators of heat retention. But I suspect that 'eco-housing' of all types is in the process of becoming attractive to the rich and to the famous, even though, in strictly financial terms, it makes little sense. A tightly insulated house might save a few hundred UK pounds a year, but at a cost of several thousand. Nevertheless, the number of pages devoted to eco-homes in the pages of the weekend newspapers would indicate growing interest from the elite. Very well-insulated housing will become an object of desirable status, and adoption rates will rise. This will help to push down the cost of extremely good insulation, and, very gradually, ordinary folk will choose to improve their houses for financially rational reasons. It will save enough money to make investment worthwhile. Eventually, not having good insulation will be seen as slightly tacky and somewhat irresponsible.

ALTRUISTIC ACTS: FAIRTRADE PURCHASING AND RECYCLING

My optimism is perhaps a little too advanced. But in some areas of food purchasing, ethical brands are making real inroads. One example is the growth of the Fairtrade label. Starting in The Netherlands in 1988 and initially focused only on coffee, the Fairtrade brand mark provides a guarantee that the farmer obtained a relatively high and consistent price for the product. Although still tiny in terms of its share of the total grocery market, with sales of about £200 million in 2005 out of a grocery market of well over £100 billion in the UK, Fairtrade has had a disproportionate effect.

Eighteen per cent of ground and whole-bean coffee now carries the label, and the major retailer Marks & Spencer stocks nothing but Fairtrade products. In 2005, the international conglomerate Nestlé starting selling its first fairly traded instant coffee. In 2000, Fairtrade sales of coffee in the UK were only about £15 million, but rapid growth in the 2002 to 2004 period meant that large retailers and producers began to notice that Fairtrade was moving from a small niche to being a large (and potentially highly profitable) market. This has drawn in a variety of new brands and given the Fairtrade label a clearly understood position as a desirable logo.

Recycling is another activity that generally has no direct reward except a feeling of virtue. Actually, it is even less easy to explain than Fairtrade purchasing. At least with coffee or chocolate there may be a sense that the product itself is better. In the case of recycling, voluntary sorting of glass or plastics is time consuming and sometimes slightly unpleasant. It is certainly easier simply to throw the plastic milk carton in the kitchen bin, rather than washing it, crushing it and then storing it in a recycling box for a couple of weeks. Nevertheless, increasing numbers of people do make the effort to segregate their recyclable wastes and do so out of a sense of moral duty. A 2001 survey carried out in London suggested that well over half thought that recycling was a personal responsibility.[89]

Recent survey work also shows that activities such as recycling, in which the individual gains little personally from the action, become much more entrenched if organizations such as local councils make active and sustained efforts to improve recycling rates. The lesson seems to be that if people see evidence that their own selfless actions are being matched by other institutions, then their behaviour becomes more determined and committed. Perhaps 10 per cent of people are deeply resistant to recycling, and their behaviour will take a generation to change. But for almost all others, active recycling shows signs of becoming sufficiently embedded to become a social norm. In other words, those failing to recycle, in some areas of the country at least, are beginning to feel under social pressure to conform. One community group near to my home is pressuring the council to fine people for not recycling. There is no reason why, over a period of years, the same social compulsion cannot be imposed when it comes to reducing carbon emissions.

As we have come to expect, economists often despise actions that do not appear to be driven by the pursuit of what is loosely called 'rational self-interest'. The academic and polemicist John Kay, one of the most robust defenders of the power of the price mechanism, wrote this in response to a leaflet about paper recycling from his council:

> *Recycling is our penance for the material advantages of a consumer society. It is no more sensible to ask about its benefits than to enquire whether Hail Marys do the Blessed Virgin any good. The value of saving paper lies in the virtuous feelings it engenders.*[90]

John Kay's thesis in his article was that throwing waste paper away was bad for the environment and, more widely, that recycling was irrational because of the lack of personal economic return. He poured gentle scorn on those who feel a little better as they tug their paper recycling box into the street on collection day. Economists don't find it easy to empathize with those who make an effort for no return. Members of the dismal profession will always tend to bring up the rear in any campaign to get people to take personal responsibility for global warming, claiming that market mechanisms will work better (even economists acknowledge that they are among the least likely to be cooperative and altruistic in their dealings with others).[91]

Moreover, Kay's assertion that paper recycling is counter-productive is almost certainly wrong. A major review of all the available analyses of the 'life-cycle costs' of paper suggests a saving of over 1 tonne of carbon dioxide for every tonne recycled.[92]

As well as recycling and buying Fairtrade products, UK consumers seem willing to pay more for ethically sound purchases across a wide range of goods and services. The New Economics Foundation (NEF), which produces a regular tracking study of ethical consumerism, suggests that the total expenditure rose by 15 per cent in 2004.[93] One can quibble with whether some of the items included in the survey were purchases made at a higher than necessary price in order to genuinely pursue an ethical goal. Nevertheless, the pattern is very clear: ordinary people do seem to be increasingly willing to make decisions about their consumption and saving based on ethical considerations.

Probably the single most advanced ethical market is that for free-range eggs. NEF reports that 41 per cent of eggs sold in retail shops were free-range in 2004, up from 33 per cent in 2002. At the time of writing, Tesco's free-range prices were almost 60 per cent above standard eggs, so this ethical decision has some cost to the household. The NEF report also suggests that 87 per cent of people oppose the use of cages for battery hens, so buying behaviour has some way of catching up with ethical opinions. At 41 per cent of purchases, free-range eggs are sufficiently clearly the choice of ethically concerned buyers that some large supermarket chains no longer stock battery-farmed eggs. In the case of eggs, the ethical consumer has nearly won – it is now close to being socially unacceptable, at least in some demographic groups, to eat battery eggs. Stores worried about their reputations will not have them on their shelves. The average household only spends £20 a year on eggs, so the financial sacrifice from buying free-range is not huge. Nevertheless, it is a valuable model for other consumer goods.

SOCIETY'S WILLINGNESS TO PAY A PRICE FOR CARBON REDUCTIONS

Transport is a much larger target for ethical consumerism. The NEF report suggests that about 9 per cent of people use public transport 'primarily to help the environment'. This surprisingly high figure is up from 4 per cent in 2002. People seeking to diminish their climate change impact will almost inevitably need to reduce their use of cars and air travel, and the figure of 9 per cent suggests that there is a sizeable minority who have already taken steps in this direction.

Across several different markets, a reasonable percentage of people are apparently willing to act as the shock troops of environmental activism. A study for the Greater London Authority, for example, shows that about 19 per cent of the population is willing to pay an extra £5 a month or more for electricity generated from renewable sources.[94] Even at today's oppressively high prices, 4 per cent of Londoners indicated a strong interest in solar photovoltaic panels. In a completely different field, a smaller but still significant number – 10 per cent – say that they primarily buy second-hand goods for environmental reasons and 17 per cent made purchases locally in order to support nearby shops.[95] Even in financial services, there are people willing to take costly steps in order to do the right thing; the idealistic Triodos Bank has 20,000 customers in the UK even though its interest rates on deposits have historically been well below what customers could achieve elsewhere.

The evidence is that a small but growing number of people are prepared to make a personal sacrifice in order to buy goods or services that are in tune with their own ethical standpoints. The NEF study also showed a concomitant rise in the percentage of people feeling guilty about purchases that they regarded as 'unethical'. The figure doubled, to over one third of individuals, between 1999 and 2004. There were also increases in people thinking that their behaviour as consumers could affect the way in which companies behaved.

Earlier I suggested that the forces of economic competition meant that businesses were not free to act in environmentally responsible ways unless their customers changed their requirements. But when people do start wanting more ethical choices, successful companies are now likely to react more expeditiously, particularly if their reputation for stocking the eco-friendly items might be under threat. The switch of Marks & Spencer to entirely Fairtrade coffee and the supermarket chain Waitrose's move to 100 per cent free-range eggs are small but powerful illustrations of how upmarket retailers are now increasingly anxious to keep their image consistent with the aspirations of their customers.

In many different markets – whether it is renewable energy or local food – it looks as though about 5 per cent of people are serious activists, resolutely prepared to pay more and endure possible inconvenience to do what they think is right (my mention of inconvenience will be all too familiar to anybody who has had to wash carrots from a local organic box scheme or farmers' market). This 5 per cent is not composed of what marketing people usually call 'early adopters' – normal mainstream people who are quick on the uptake. Today's climate change activists are the very small group who act from moral imperatives, not because they want to get early on a bandwagon.

Getting up from this low level of acceptance to the 40 per cent share of sales at which people appear to start feeling bad about not buying the ethical choice seems to require two steps. First, the items must become fashionable: newspaper columnists must write glowingly of the celebrities who use the product and they must suggest psychic benefits that can only be obtained through extensive use. Fairtrade is clearly at this point in its development. It has an aura of goodness about it even though, to be frank, much Fairtrade coffee is of indifferent quality. The second, and more important, stage is when prosperous 'early adopters' become committed users and recommend it to their friends. At this point in the marketing of any new product the promoters can be very confident that the item stands a good chance of eventual success.

I can see several important categories of carbon saving that look as though they might cross the yawning chasm between the nutty activists and the fashionable people who populate our major urban centres. Domestic wind turbines seem a very good candidate. For a start, they are a highly visible means of displaying economic status and positively shout a concern for the climate. Our solar panels – slightly less ostentatious but still pretty easy to spot – generate regular enquiries from local people wanting to install their own. In an act that might be seen as local one-upmanship, one neighbour has recently put up photovoltaic panels with twice the power of ours. This is absolutely wonderful: solar panels might soon become a way of enhancing your local status.

Locally farmed organic food is another possible target – not only is it good for carbon emissions, it can be sold as healthier and tastier. Better central heating controls, which might save 5 per cent of the emissions from house heating, could also be candidates for entry into the shopping baskets of the rich and famous. They can be attractive electronic devices sitting visibly on the walls which the (male) owners can boast about to their friends.

But in my pessimistic moments, it sometimes seems a struggle to see how we can persuade people not to fly as regularly. The idea of avoiding winter holidays in the sun, which are such an effective badge of membership of the high-earning professional classes, is not going to be easy to sell. However, we can certainly hope that the rich will buy carbon offsets to make good part of the damage from air travel. The medieval elite were prepared to buy indulgences from the Pope's agents for their peccadilloes, and carbon offsets can fill a similar niche.

Similarly, it may not be easy to promote the value of smaller cars. But perhaps there is room for hope here. After all, Hollywood stars now climb out of their Toyota battery hybrids without embarrassment. It is perhaps conceivable that smaller, lighter, much more fuel-efficient cars could become fashion statements. But, for many people, we have to admit that the choice of a more restrained car is going to be a piece of genuine self-denial. We are years away from severing the link between high status and the capacity of the cylinders inside a large block of aluminium.

Persuasive research into people's responses to environmental messages shows the importance of establishing strong social norms that reinforce appropriate behaviour.[96] A recent series of experiments in the US looked at the influence of various different written messages in influencing whether guests reused their towels in hotels or sent them to be washed every day. Washing fewer towels saves hotels money, but also reduces the use of fuels necessary to heat water for washing.

The researchers left some messages in hotel rooms that stressed generic goals, such as 'Partner with us to help save the environment.' These texts were less influential in getting hotel guests to recycle their towels than messages that stated an expectation that the user would behave according to a social norm. The most influential message was: 'Join your fellow citizens in helping to save the environment', which got over 40 per cent of guests to reuse towels, compared to a base of 20 per cent when the card said: 'Help the hotel save energy.'

According to the academic researchers looking at the results, the message that worked best was successful because it suggested that the social norm was for the guest to request a reuse of the towels. The lesson drawn for those circumstances when the citizen is asked to be 'good' is to emphasize how many other people are already behaving that way. According to this theory, a statement that 'the vast majority of people don't drop litter' would be more effective at depressing the level of littering than a comment that emphasized that many people do, such as: 'Don't join the litter louts.'

In the case of energy use, it would be more effective to use a slogan that said 'Responsible people are reducing their thermostat settings in winter' than 'High temperatures waste energy' or 'Too many people have their house too warm.' This last statement would be particularly counter-productive because it emphasizes that the social norm may well be wasteful use of energy. It says that other people have excessively hot houses, and therefore may make it seem attractive to run the thermostat high to fit in with the neighbours.

Stressing the benefits in terms of social approval of taking the 'good' action, rather than noting the deleterious effects of 'bad' actions, is now a widely understood principle – though surprisingly often ignored in the advertising of consumer goods. Research findings separately show that instructions that tell people what not to do are more effective than those that simply describe the effects of actually doing environmentally destructive acts. For example, a statement that said 'Don't take aeroplane flights because they are one of the most important causes of global warming' would be better than saying 'Those who take aeroplane flights are helping to increase global warming.' Researchers seem to be saying that people absorb a strong injunction not to do something more effectively than they do with simple statements of fact – for example, 'Stop smoking' is better than 'Smoking kills.'

The lesson for those interested in changing human behaviour is that communications messages aimed at fostering better behaviour in response to global warming need to stress how most other people are behaving, as well as to frame the slogan with a strong statement of what not to do.

ENERGY SAVING BEGETS ENERGY SAVING

Those who have tried to make real cuts in their own carbon emissions all know a little secret. Unlike, say, dieting or giving up tobacco, conserving energy is so easy that it almost becomes addictive. A small effort can cut household electricity bills by 10 per cent and, once achieved, a little twitch on the heating thermostat can save another 10 per cent or so off the gas bill.

Why is this? If reducing energy use is so easy, why didn't we all start earlier? The reason probably lies in the insidious and unconscious growth in our personal energy demand. Energy is both cheap and largely invisible. If I leave the computer on overnight, it doesn't cost me a measurable amount of money and, in fact, it would be very difficult to see from the meter just how much energy I had used. But once I take a decision not to allow appliances to stay on unnecessarily, it is rather simple to turn everything off, and within three months the bills will be lower. If I become habituated to not wasting energy and make it a normal daily activity, it becomes easy.

The painlessness of energy saving is most noticed by people who install their own renewable energy systems, such as solar hot water. The mere act of installing the equipment seems to produce a hugely increased sensitivity to energy use. I noticed this when we put a hot water and photovoltaic system on our roof. The apparent 'savings' from the solar hot water system were about three times what could have been expected. We noticed an implausibly high figure for the reduction in electricity consumption as well. We're still quite large consumers; but we cut our bills by far more than could have been explained by the relatively small quantity of the sun's energy falling on our roof. This was not unusual; the phenomenon has been seen across the world. Before, our usage had been gently drifting upwards – like most British households; but immediately after the panels went up, the meters stopped spinning so fast and haven't increased since.

I suppose the most important change for us was a decision not to run the house at 20 degrees Celsius in winter. We moved the thermostat down to 18 degrees, and did notice the difference, but only for a matter of days. Within a few weeks, 18 degrees seemed as warm as 20 degrees had before. The gradual ratcheting upwards must have been a sort of mild addiction; we had needed a 'fix' of rising temperatures to keep feeling warm. But as with, say, strong coffee, one can take a decision to reduce one's consumption and the pain is only mild and temporary.

The upbeat tone of the last few pages has had a purpose. Many people feel a gloomy despair about climate change. Individuals can do so little directly to affect the future health of the global atmosphere. What I have tried to suggest is that there are reasons for optimism. All great social movements were started by determined and slightly eccentric individuals who refused to accept prevailing social norms. Active carbon avoidance is a principle that is worth pursuing and does have effects on friends and neighbours. It can become a communal activity. The future of the human race is dependent upon sufficient numbers of individuals eventually being persuaded to join the movement.

5

how our lives generate emissions
and what we can do about it

Divide UK greenhouse gas emissions by the number of people in the country, and you get a figure of about 12.5 tonnes of carbon dioxide, or equivalent, per person. About half of this – approximately 6.0 tonnes – is directly created by the individual in running a house, a car and taking transport. The other half – about 6.5 tonnes – is generated by other activities, such as running offices, making fertilizer, smelting iron ore and transporting goods in lorries. The total figure of 12.5 tonnes, or equivalent, certainly needs to fall to 3 tonnes or less if we are to meet any of our long-term climate change ambitions.

So, the pessimist might say, the task is impossible. Even if a person has no direct emissions from running home or car, he or she will still be responsible for the remaining 6.5 tonnes over which he has no control. This is not strictly true; for example, the food industry is a major polluter, and we can alter our buying habits to diminish indirect emissions. We can make a real dent in the indirect carbon dioxide we generate, and those emissions we genuinely cannot control, we can counterbalance by other measures. The final chapters of this book examine this point in detail.

Individuals can reduce their responsibility for greenhouse gases in an infinite variety of ways. For simplicity, I have suggested that a reasonable target is to get one's direct emissions down from 6 tonnes to 3 tonnes, and indirect responsibility down to a net figure of zero, making a total of 3 tonnes. Getting indirect greenhouse gases to zero means changing purchasing behaviour, particularly with regard to food, and, in addition, substantial cancelling-out or 'offsetting' of emissions in other ways. I have chosen to suggest, for example, that the purchasing of 'green' electricity could be thought of as a means of offsetting indirect greenhouse gases.

DIRECTLY PRODUCED EMISSIONS

The source of the 6 tonnes that we typically generate directly by our own actions is shown in Table 5.1 (more detail is contained in the Appendix, page 293).

Table 5.1 *Direct greenhouse gas emissions of the typical UK individual*

		Tonnes
House:	Heating	1.2
	Water heating	0.3
	Cooking	0.1 (assumes that cooking is done by gas)
	Lighting	0.1
	Electric appliances	0.6
	Total house	2.3
Car		1.2
Bus, rail		0.1
Air travel[97]		1.8
House and transport		5.4
Other direct emissions		0.6
Total		**6.0**

The figures in Table 5.1 are all averages. They assume a typical household composition of 2.3 people, an average-sized house and car, and standard habits for public transport and air use. For the purposes of calculating averages, we assume that the household has access to gas, either from the mains or from liquid petroleum gas (LPG), and uses mains electricity (many people without gas use electricity for heating, and their electricity consumption will be higher than the figures we use in this book).

Few people will exactly match the averages. Someone living alone in a big and energy-inefficient house, with regular trips to the US, will have emissions of several times this figure. A large family living in a small house with no car will be well under half the average (in a world where climate change is a serious issue, the poor, whether in the industrializing world or those in the less prosperous half of Western society, are the virtuous, and it is the richest people who are the worst offenders).

The carbon emissions figures in Table 5.1 are consistent with a yearly household gas usage of about 19,000kWh a year (or about 1700 cubic metres, which is how the meter generally measures household use) and electricity consumption of about 3700kWh, or 'units'.[98] You can tell whether you start above or below the average by looking at your bills for the past year, remembering that consumption, particularly for gas, is far higher between November and March. As of September 2006, these usages would equate to gas bills of about £650 (3 pence a kilowatt hour from the industry giant British Gas, plus a standing charge in the form of a higher price for the first kilowatt hours consumed) and electricity bills of about £450 (10 pence a kilowatt hour from British Gas in some regions of the country, plus standing charges).

Although any individual reader will not be typical, we can use these numbers to look at the effect of trying to cut consumption. Broadly, there are two ways of doing this: using technology or reduced consumption. Or they can be combined to produce greater savings. Can we comfortably get to 3 tonnes per person in the home? Yes, with relative ease, provided that air travel is avoided. Table 5.2 provides a summary of one way of halving fossil fuel use in the home and in personal transport.

Table 5.2 shows one possible set of actions to reduce direct personal emissions by a half. The main savings come from cutting the carbon consequences of car travel and by avoiding flights. Smaller cuts come from more efficient use of gas – for example, by installing a better boiler.

I don't intend to be prescriptive about how to get to 3 tonnes since everybody is different. But I do want to show that major reductions are possible, and, to be frank, that cutting out air travel may be the easiest way of slimming down your carbon liability. You might decide that this package is inappropriate for you – perhaps because you need to

Table 5.2 *Getting direct greenhouse gas emissions to 3 tonnes*

		Average (tonnes)	Target (tonnes)	Primary means of reduction to meet target
House	Heating	1.2	0.9	New boiler; better insulation; lower winter temperatures
	Water heating	0.3	0.2	Shorter showers; lower temperatures; 'air-mix' shower heads
	Cooking	0.1 (gas)	Less than 0.1	Use pressure cooker and microwave rather than gas oven or hob
	Lighting	0.1	Less than 0.1	Replace all bulbs with energy-efficient variety
	Electric appliances	0.6	0.4	Efficient fridge; no tumble dryer; small TV; switch off appliances at wall
Car		1.2	0.9	Small car; fewer miles
Bus, rail		0.1	0.1	No reduction
Air travel		1.8	0.0	No air travel
Allowance for other emissions		0.6	0.3	
Total		5.4	2.7	

Table 5.3 *Direct greenhouse gas emissions: Standard figures for personal calculations*

1kWh (or 'unit') of electricity	0.43kg of CO_2
1kWh of gas (approximately 11.5 kWh per cubic metre, the unit used on most home gas meters)	0.19kg of CO_2
1 litre of petrol	2.31kg of CO_2
1km of rail or coach travel	0.049kg of CO_2
1km of long-distance coach travel	0.028kg of CO_2
1km of bus travel	0.1kg of CO_2
1km of air travel	0.30kg of CO_2 (equivalent)[99]
Add 10% to reflect other emissions as detailed in the Appendix	

commute long distances to work or because you have to visit relatives in Canada every year. Other ways of getting to 3 tonnes might be easier.

Nevertheless, 3 tonnes probably represents an absolute maximum for the total emissions per person that the planet can sustain if temperatures are to come under control at about 2 to 4 degrees higher than they are today. In the UK today, I believe that the concerned citizen, willing to accept her or his share of the responsibility, ought to aim for this number.

How do you know if you have achieved this 3 tonne budget? A series of simple calculations will provide a good estimate (see Table 5.3 above). Gas and electricity estimates can be derived from yearly bills. Petrol bills can be estimated from credit card statements or other financial records. Public transport will have to be guessed at by looking at credit card statements, with an adjustment for fares paid by cash. Distances can be calculated approximately. Air travel will have to be estimated from a memory of the flights taken. Several websites give figures for the direct air distances between cities; it might be best to add 10 per cent to reflect detours imposed by air traffic control.[100]

Table 5.4 provides an illustration of a household that meets the 3 tonnes per person target.

Table 5.4 *Lowered direct emissions from a three-person household*

Electricity consumption of 3000kWh	1.35 tonnes of CO_2	About 20% below UK average
Gas consumption of 15,000kWh	2.85 tonnes of CO_2	About 20% below UK average
Petrol purchases of 1000 litres	2.50 tonnes of CO_2	Slightly below average
3000km of rail travel	1.50 tonnes of CO_2	Almost 50% above average
No air travel	0.00 tonnes	
Total	8.2 tonnes of CO_2 – or 2.7 tonnes of CO_2 per person	

INDIRECTLY PRODUCED CARBON DIOXIDE

Emissions directly under our control are only half the problem. The background workings of the economy deliver the other half. But just because these activities are in the background does not mean that we can ignore them. We cannot always control them; but we can counteract them or cancel them out.

If our own fossil fuel use in the home and when using transport still results in 3 tonnes of carbon dioxide, our indirect emissions need to go from 6.5 tonnes to a net zero to achieve the 3 tonnes overall target. Is this possible? Yes, by altering our purchasing and work patterns and by investing in technologies that counteract emissions. The individual can get his or her total carbon dioxide 'footprint' down to a total of 3 tonnes, although there may be some expense or inconvenience in getting there. For some the expense and inconvenience will mean it may be more realistic to aim for reducing both direct and indirect emissions equally (e.g. to 1½ tonnes). Each person must find their own most appropriate means of reaching the target of 3 tonnes per year. For the purposes of illustration, though, I have chosen to show how indirect emissions can be cancelled out entirely.

One way of doing this is presented in Table 5.5 (overleaf). This summary sets out a series of very simple steps. Many others are possible and details are suggested in later chapters. The most important single act is probably to change food purchase habits. The food supply chain is extraordinarily wasteful of energy and also generates large volumes of powerful greenhouse gases, such as methane, that are not directly the products of burning fossil fuel.

Buying renewable electricity is also easy. Investing in a new wind farm is a more limited opportunity. A wind turbine on your roof is more expensive, but will clearly become much easier in the next few years. Cutting consumption of new goods is also perfectly feasible, provided that the individual is willing to go against the rules of modern consumer society, which say that possessions have to be new and regularly replaced.

Office carbon emissions are a very important source of greenhouse gases: working from home is, of course, not a choice available to everybody, but is becoming more and more possible as communications and employer tolerance improves. An alternative to working from home that would have the same effect would be to persuade the employer to switch to a renewable electricity supply or even install its own large wind turbine. Many large industrial companies have begun to do this: the economics are not unfavourable, and few complain when turbines are erected on manufacturing sites. Any remaining net emissions can be cancelled by installing a solar water heater and by careful 'offsetting' emissions in other ways, such as by planting trees.

So, it is clearly feasible for the average adult to deal with his or her responsibility for arresting climate change. It requires some determination and a willingness to step away

Table 5.5 *Cancelling out indirect emissions*

Average level today	6.5 tonnes of CO_2	
Savings	*Amount saved*	*Options*
Change food-buying habits.	1.3 tonnes of CO_2	Buy local organic food, or grow on an allotment. Never buy packaged meals or processed food. Rely more on dry whole foods, rather than on manufactured food.
Invest in commercial renewable energy companies.	1.0 tonne of CO_2	Invest £600 a year in a cooperative wind farm.
Buy domestic electricity from a green supply*.	0.8 tonnes of CO_2	
Install a wind turbine on your house.	1.0 tonne of CO_2	A good wind turbine would generate about 2300kWh per year.
Buy less – for example, get a new car every 15 years, not every 10 years.	0.1 tonnes of CO_2	A new car might contain 'embedded' energy equal to 3 tonnes of CO_2.
Buy less – for example, avoid major purchases involving heavy weight of plastics or metal.	0.2 tonnes of CO_2	
Work from home.	0.8 tonnes of CO_2	
Total saving	**5.2 tonnes of CO_2**	
Remaining indirect CO_2	1.3 tonnes	
Careful purchase of carbon offset and installation of solar water heating	1.3 tonnes of CO_2	
Net indirect emissions	**0 tonnes of CO_2**	

Note: *I have chosen to regard this not as a reduction in direct emissions but rather as offsetting – see page 277.

from some of the most destructive aspects of current culture. It needs, most importantly, a willingness to reduce travel and, in particular, to all but eliminate air travel. For many people, this will seem intensely difficult and will represent significant self-denial. And this restraint will not be actively backed by government, which shows a continuing commitment to building new roads, airport terminals and runways. But government is partly encouraging air travel because it believes that the electorate really wants more cheap flights. If a reasonable number of otherwise normal individuals publicly vowed to avoid unnecessary flights, government's active support might be partly eroded.

The rest of this book gives more detail on how our day-to-day lives generate carbon dioxide and other greenhouse gases. By showing in what way emissions arise, the book enables a responsible individual to make judgements about how he or she might make changes to live a little more compatibly with the long-term health of the planet.

Some of the material in the following chapters is complex. I have tried to simplify, where possible, and I have taken the decision to round the numbers I use as much as I possibly can. I assume that people want good approximations rather than spuriously precise figures. In any event, round numbers are easier to remember and understand.

I have tried to express as much as I can in terms of kilowatt hours because I think that this is the quantity most easily understood. A kilowatt hour is an amount of energy equivalent to operating a toaster or a one-bar electric fire for an hour.

I need to make one last point. Some of the numbers and calculations that I use are somewhat at variance with official, or widely quoted, figures. For example, the regulator Ofgem uses a figure of 3300kWh for the average electricity consumption of a UK home. I cannot find a proper source for this figure and it is at variance with many other numbers, such as the electricity industry's calculations of its supply into the domestic market. In circumstances like this, I have calculated my own figures rather than rely on conventional wisdom. But this does mean that some of my figures are at odds with numbers published elsewhere. I have tried to identify the main examples of this in the endnotes.

6

home heating

Many people do not realize the importance of home heating in determining how much carbon dioxide we generate. It is, for example, far more important than emissions produced by our use of electricity in the home. Very approximately, the typical UK house uses about 280kWh of gas and electricity per year for every square metre of living space. Space heating represents over 170kWh/year of this total.[101]

The typical house (containing an average of 2.3 people) produces over 2.7 tonnes of carbon dioxide per year just to operate the central heating boiler. This means 1.2 tonnes per person. Heating the house is therefore responsible for nearly 10 per cent of a person's total responsibility for emissions, and about 20 per cent of the greenhouse gases that we can directly control.

What can be done about this? Four measures are particularly worth taking:

1   New boiler: the typical home has a boiler that is less than 75 per cent efficient at taking gas and turning it into usable heat in the home. Buying a new condensing boiler with maximum efficiency takes this up to 90 per cent or so. The savings may be as much as 0.2 tonnes. A new boiler might cost about £1500.
2   Reducing internal winter temperatures will also have a substantial effect. A 1 degree reduction may decrease fuel needs by as much as 15 per cent and takes total emissions down to not much more than 0.8 tonnes.[102] Initially it seems like a struggle; but the typical householder completely acclimatizes within days to a temperature of 19 rather than 20 degrees Celsius.
3   Better insulation, particularly of cavity walls and roofs, is important. Insulating the house's cavity wall might reduce emissions by 0.3 to 0.5 tonnes per person. Better insulation is heavily subsidized and will generally cost less than £300 for the cavity walls.
4   Intelligent central heating controls will also help. A good heating programmer will save as much as 10 per cent of the cost of gas used for heating.

Unfortunately, one cannot simply add all of these savings together to get the approximate reduction from taking all four steps. Better insulation, for example, means lower gas need, which reduces the benefit from installing a better boiler. Taking all four measures might cut 40 per cent from the heating bill and reduce personal emissions by 0.5 tonnes.

D espite improvements in insulation and far more efficient boilers, total energy use for domestic heating continues to rise. The latest statistics show that despite the rise in prices, domestic gas demand in the first quarter of 2006 was 7 per cent above the level a year earlier.[103] The impulses driving up energy use range from the understandable wish to heat our homes to higher temperatures in cold winters, to the rapid increase in the number of households as the UK population expands and household size falls. More households, of whatever size, add to heating demands because each one needs to be heated.

Until recently, another important factor increasing fuel use has been the rise in the proportion of homes using central heating. However, this percentage is now over 90 per cent and will rise only slowly from now onwards. Eventually, efficient condensing boilers and better insulation will probably reduce gas use. But we shouldn't be too confident – even with the current high prices of gas and electricity, householders have tended to increase internal temperatures rather than reduce their fuel bills as a result of efficiency improvements. Average winter house temperatures have been rising sharply in the last few years to 19 or 20 degrees Celsius. Since most people seem to have a desired comfort level of about 21 degrees Celsius, the rise in house thermostats may not have stopped yet.

For those that do want to minimize their emissions, Table 6.1 (overleaf) describes a number of measures that can be taken, with an approximate calculation of how effective each measure is.

British homes can be heated by gas, oil, solid fuel or electricity, usually from storage radiators heated by cheaper overnight power. About 80 per cent of UK households are on the mains gas supply and almost all of these use gas for heating. We'll look at the patterns of demand in these homes; but first it is worth mentioning that other countries have much more efficient means of heating their houses. The box on page 85 offers two examples of countries already heating their homes more efficiently, on average, than the UK.

THE HEAT BALANCE OF THE HOUSE

This is a complex section. Its primary purpose is to demonstrate the importance of two things:

1   Domestic boilers use more kilowatt hours of gas than they deliver as useful heat into the house. With an efficiency of 75 per cent, one quarter of the gas used is wasted because it leaves the house as hot exhaust.
2   Houses are heated by many more devices than just a domestic boiler. All of our lights, electrical appliances, hot water, the warmth of our bodies and sun coming in through the windows also heat our homes. Incidentally, this means that some advanced modern houses, such as the Passivhaus buildings mentioned in the box opposite, can do completely without central heating boilers.

Table 6.1 *Measures to reduce carbon emission from home heating*

Option	Reduction per house	Reduction per person	Comment
Install condensing boiler	0.4 tonnes of CO_2	0.2 tonnes of CO_2	Very important if the house is large or badly insulated and the existing boiler is more than ten years old.
Install cavity wall insulation	1.1 tonnes of CO_2 (theoretical maximum for average home)	0.5 tonnes of CO_2	Almost half of UK homes have uninsulated cavities.
	0.7 tonnes of CO_2 (actual probable reduction)	0.3 tonnes of CO_2	This is a clear first step and makes very good financial sense, particularly for detached homes.
Lower internal winter temperature by 1°C	0.3 tonnes of CO_2	0.1 tonnes of CO_2	It is also important not to heat unused rooms.
Better central heating controls (e.g. purchase of intelligent programmer such as a Dataterm)	0.3 tonnes of CO_2	0.1 tonnes of CO_2	Data is sparse on this, but this estimate seems reasonable.
All measures taken together	1.2 tonnes of CO_2	0.5 tonnes of CO_2	This was a difficult calculation to do and actual results may be at variance with these numbers.

HOME HEATING NEEDS: DATA FROM OTHER COUNTRIES

Sweden

A large fraction of Sweden's heating needs are met by district heating plants, usually combining electricity generation and heating distributed in the form of hot water to local housing. Each Swede typically gets 4500kWh/year of heating from such systems. This compares to a total central heating demand of about 6000kWh/year per person in the UK. These district heating plants are efficient and increasingly use low-carbon fuels, such as wood.

Germany

The average heat usage by German houses is better than in the UK even though winter temperatures are generally lower. The average German house uses 159kWh/year per square metre. In the UK, this figure is over 170kWh/year.[104] The German Passivhaus Institute is the most effective body in the world at promoting extremely energy-efficient homes, requiring less than 15kWh/year of heating per square metre. For a typical UK house size, this would mean gas consumption of 8 per cent of the current average. The Passivhaus movement has now built 6000 homes around Europe, mostly in Germany itself. These homes incorporate effective capture of the sun's energy, excellent insulation and a ventilation system that heats the incoming air with the stale air as it leaves the house. The primary importance of the Passivhaus movement is that it demonstrates what can be achieved using thoughtful design. The incremental cost of the Passivhaus elements, such as triple-glazed windows, is said to be 8200 Euros (about £5000) for a new terraced house.[105] Very approximately, this suggests that even with the new UK regulations on energy efficiency, the incremental Passivhaus costs would be recouped in little more than ten years for a typical new property.

Some readers may wish to skip these pages and just accept my assertion that the average home takes about 14,000kWh/year from the gas main to fire its boiler. This turns into about 10,500kWh/year of usable heat, to which can be added about 6000kWh/year of heat from other sources. So, the house actually gets an input of about 16,500kWh/year to keep us warm, even though the gas bill for heating is only 14,000kWh/year. The purpose of this section is to show how these figures are derived and may only be of interest to people like me, who never believe a number until they have worked it for themselves. The next few pages give us the background data to enable us to estimate roughly how much energy-saving measures might assist the householder in reducing costs and carbon emissions. After the background work, suggestions for practical measures to reduce home heating costs and carbon start on page 90.

Annual average gas use for home heating adds about 2.7 tonnes of carbon dioxide to the atmosphere. Divided by the typical number of occupants, the contribution of home heating to global warming gases is about 1.2 tonnes a year, or somewhat in excess of 10 per cent of all emissions, and not far off one quarter of all the carbon dioxide that we can directly control by our individual actions. If we are interested in reducing our personal responsibility for global warming, household heating matters. And as bills continue to climb, the financial benefit from aiming for best practice is pretty important too.

By how much do gas bills vary according to the type of the house? Accurate figures are not easily available, not least because insulation standards vary so much. But, at the highest level of approximation, typical gas consumption may vary in the way illustrated in Table 6.2. Readers may find that their own houses are larger than the typical UK property, which is only about 80 square metres, or less than 900 square feet (a total floor area of 30 feet by 30 feet).

Table 6.2 *How gas usage for heating may vary with type of house*[106]

Type of house	Estimated average gas consumption (kWh/year)
Detached	19,700
Semi-detached	14,900
Terraced	13,100
Bungalow	12,400
Flat	9800

Of course, a semi-detached may be small or large, well insulated or draughty, and run at a high or a low temperature. So, these numbers don't actually say much. Nevertheless, they are a useful reminder that house size affects heating bills, as does the number of walls shared with other households. All other things being equal, a large flat of similar size to a small detached house will have lower fuel bills because it is partly insulated by the adjoining properties, whereas all the walls of the house are exposed to the ambient air temperature.

Per household, total gas use (for water heating, cooking and heating) is about 19,000kWh/year. So, on average, heating is responsible for about three-quarters of the total volume of gas demand for homes in the UK.

Unfortunately, the calculation of the energy used to heat our homes is much more complicated than simply assessing the amount of gas that is burned in the central heating boiler. There are five important other considerations:

WHAT DOES 14,000 KILOWATT HOURS ACTUALLY MEAN IN TERMS OF METER READINGS AND COST TO THE HOUSEHOLDER?

Gas meters don't record the number of kilowatt hours a household uses. They actually measure the number of cubic metres, or cubic feet for older meters, of gas flowing into the house. The energy content of this gas can change as a result of very slightly varying pressure or gas composition. Gas supplied from the North Sea is largely methane; but gas from Russia, for example, contains a slightly higher percentage of other hydrocarbons and is a marginally better fuel in term of the heat generated by a cubic metre. Each period, gas suppliers calculate the energy value of the gas they pump through the pipes, and your bill will specify a 'calorific value' per cubic metre. They then actually charge you for the number of kilowatt hours supplied as a function of this calorific value. To get from cubic metres to kilowatt hours, you need to multiply by about 11.45. For older meters, which record in hundreds of cubic feet, not metres, you need to multiply this again by 2.83.

At the time of writing (September 2006), the price of gas to domestic consumers is almost 3 pence per kilowatt hour from the largest supplier, British Gas. In addition, some suppliers charge substantially more for the first units supplied each quarter. In effect, this is a standing charge, and all the improvements you make as a result of suggestions in this chapter will not reduce this portion of the bill. At 3 pence per kilowatt hour, plus the higher prices for the first kilowatt hours each quarter, the average home costs £500 a year to heat. Add in the costs of water heating and cooking, and the total cost rises to about £650.

1   Not all gas is turned into usable heat. Boilers work with varying levels of efficiency, and the oldest models might well only deliver 60 per cent of the energy consumed. The rest is evacuated to the outside as hot exhausts. The typical boiler in the UK stock is probably 70 to 75 per cent efficient, and I use an average of 75 per cent in my calculations. Modern 'condensing' boilers capture a much larger percentage of the heat and deliver about 90 per cent efficiency.

2   Homes typically contain other sources of heat. Electrical appliances act to heat our houses, even when they are sitting in standby mode in the middle of the day. Precisely how much energy our TVs and washing machines replace is a subject of debate; but, increasingly, our houses are full of electrical devices acting as small radiators. Those who say that their houses are entirely heated by gas central heating are, therefore, strictly speaking, wrong. All our homes are also heated by expensive and carbon-intensive electricity, even in summer.

3   The two other key sources of internal heating are, first, what is delightfully known as 'metabolic' and, second, solar. Metabolic heating is you and me, wandering about our houses giving off about 120W in heat. Solar heating from the sun varies enormously, but may be as much as 15 to 20 per cent of the total useful heat demand in some houses,

particularly those with large south-facing windows. We are, in effect, living in greenhouses and capture some heat from solar radiation, even in the winter. Passivhaus buildings capture more. (The estimates below exclude the impact of solar radiation when the house is already warm enough in summer. Similar reductions are made for all other indirect sources of heat, although these estimates are subject to considerable uncertainty.)

4   Cooking food also helps to heat the home in the heating season.
5   Hot water use also serves to heat the home – for example, taking a bath heats the bathroom.

There are various ways of calculating how much heat is used in the house. Using one set of data, the net balance looks approximately as depicted in Figure 6.1. I stress that these are only estimates from one source and, compared to other sources, they emphasize in particular the heat derived from appliances, water heating and solar gain. I will go on to give my own estimates on page 90; but I give the data in the figure below because they are derived from a very reputable source.

These statistics suggest that only about 55 per cent of the heating of a home fuelled by gas is from the useful heat delivered by the boiler. The figures are from the stupendously detailed *Domestic Heating Fact File 2003*, published by the Building Research Establishment (BRE)[107] (I have used data from this wonderful source frequently in the following pages). Other sources, including other BRE texts, suggest that the figure should be nearer two-thirds and, on balance, I think we need to use these different estimates.

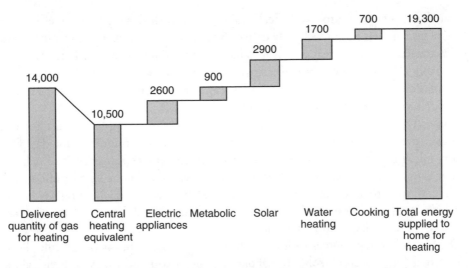

Figure 6.1 *One calculation of sources of heat for the average gas-fired home*

Note: All figures are in kilowatt hours per year (kWh/year) and were calculated in 2001.

Another way of calculating the total heating demand for a typical gas-fired house is to estimate how much energy it would take to heat the home to temperatures that we know are characteristic. In 2001, the average centrally heated home was kept at just over 19 degrees Celsius. If we assume that this figure has since risen to about 20 degrees Celsius, we can estimate the amount of energy needed to keep a house at this level.

Table 6.3 provides the average temperatures for England and Wales during the months of 2005 and the number of degrees of heating necessary to get a house to 20 degrees Celsius. It then assesses the average amount of heating, in degrees, over the period in which the gas boiler would typically be on.

The figures in Table 6.3 show that the heating system (the boiler, and all the other elements that warm the house) had to keep a house an average of 13.4 degrees Celsius above the external temperature for seven months of the year. We know from BRE data that the average UK house loses 259W (0.259kW) for every degree of difference between the internal and external temperatures. What does this mean? If the inside of the house is 1 degree hotter than the outside, 259W (the equivalent of two or three large light

Table 6.3 *Average annual heating need for England and Wales, 2005*

Month	Average 24-hour temperature (°C)	Is heating assumed to be on?	Heating need (°C)
January	5.7	Yes	14.3
February	3.9	Yes	16.1
March	6.7	Yes	13.3
April	8.6	Yes	11.4
May	11.0	Yes	9.0
June	15.0	No	–
July	16.3	No	–
August	15.8	No	–
September	14.8	No	–
October	12.6	No	–
November	6.0	Yes	14.0
December	4.2	Yes	15.8
Average	10.1		
Average during heating season	6.7		13.4

bulbs, or the metabolic energy radiated by two people) will be moving from the house to the outside. So, to keep a 10 degree difference uses 2.59kW, and a 13.4 degree gradient needs 3.47kW.

We can use this figure to estimate how much heating the house will require over the heating season. If, for example, the house needed to be heated for 4000 hours a year, then the total heating demand would be 13,900kWh/year or so (3.47 × 4000). Not all of this would be the boiler, of course, and some heat would be provided by the electric appliances and other sources. Add in the losses from leaving the windows open and opening the doors, and I think the average house probably needs total heat, including the boiler, of about 16,500kWh/year.

I therefore propose to use the following numbers in the rest of this chapter:

- Delivered energy for gas heating in the typical house: 14,000kWh/year. This is consistent with national data from the *Digest of UK Energy Statistics*.
- Usable heat produced by the boiler: 10,500kWh/year (meaning that 3500kWh/year are lost to the outside, or, by coincidence, about the same as total home electricity consumption).
- Actual heat needed by house, including the 6000kWh/year from other sources, such as electric appliances, cooking and solar gain: 16,500kWh/year.

Where the range of possible heat demands makes a difference to the calculations in the following text, I have tried to identify the issue and then provide other numbers for comparison.

My calculations assume that 14,000kWh/year is the amount of gas delivered and burned for space heating purposes in the typical home on the mains gas network. Over the course of a typical heating season, lasting perhaps seven months, this is over 65kWh a day, costing about £2. What can be done to reduce this number?

The possible steps can be divided into three main groups:

1   Improve the efficiency of the gas boiler and the controls to the central heating system.
2   Upgrade the insulation in the house or improve the capture of other sources of heat, such as solar radiation.
3   Introduce behavioural changes, such as reduced internal temperatures or ceasing to heat some rooms. Or, indeed, move to a smaller or a better-insulated home.

THE BENEFITS OF A NEW CONDENSING BOILER

Modern 'condensing' boilers convert more of the fuel they consume into useful heat for the central heating system. The exhaust gases, including water vapour, are cooled by a heat exchanger, which extracts useful heat energy. The vapour condenses into water and is drained away. By contrast, older non-condensing boilers push out large volumes of hot gas into the air outside the house, wasting the energy that it contains.

Modern condensing boilers operate at about 90 per cent efficiency. Non-condensing systems are much less efficient. Table 6.4 provides some estimates of characteristic efficiency for older boilers.[108]

Table 6.4 *Efficiency estimates for non-condensing gas-fired systems*[109]

Date when boiler installed	Typical efficiency
1974	56%
1985	67%
1993	72%
1998	74%

So, for example, a condensing boiler replacing a non-condensing version installed in 1985 will increase the efficiency of the use of gas by 23 per cent. For our typical household needing 10,500kWh of heat, the energy value of the gas delivered to the household will fall substantially.

Table 6.5 *Gas savings from replacing a typical boiler with a condensing variety*

	Typical efficiency	Gas delivered to provide 10,500kWh of usable heat
Traditional boiler installed during the late 1990s	75%	14,000kWh
New condensing boiler installed in 2007	90%	11,667kWh
Saving		2333kWh

A household switching in this way would save 2333kWh annually, or about 0.4 tonnes of carbon dioxide. The saving in gas costs for a typical house would be about £70 a year at August 2006 gas prices. The savings from reducing costs to heat water (perhaps £20) would be additional.

Recent changes in regulations mean that almost all new boilers now have to be of the condensing type. Therefore, the householder's decision is not whether to buy the slightly more expensive condensing boiler or not. It is *when* to replace an existing non-condensing boiler with a new one. Since boilers often last 20 years or more, the householder's choice may well be a voluntary one. Does it make sense, for example, to bring forward the replacement date of the home boiler by five years in order to get improved efficiency and lower carbon emissions?

The answer depends upon the age of the existing boiler and upon the level of usage in the house. A big house with an old boiler would benefit enormously from replacing the central heating furnace.

The figures in Table 6.6 show the importance of shifting to a condensing boiler if your existing furnace is more than ten years old. In a big house, with a boiler installed in 1993, carbon dioxide emissions might currently be almost 4 tonnes a year from heating alone

Table 6.6 *Savings from installing a condensing gas boiler*

	Boiler age	High gas need	Medium gas need	Low gas need
Usable heat needed (kWh/year)		15,000	10,500	7000
Savings from installing condensing boiler (kWh per year)	1974	10,119	7083	4722
	1984	5721	4005	2670
	1993	4167	2917	1944
	1998	3604	2523	1682
Annual savings in cash (3 pence per kWh)	1974	£303	£212	£142
	1984	£172	£120	£80
	1993	£125	£88	£58
	1998	£108	£76	£50
Annual saving in CO_2 (tonnes)	1974	1.92	1.35	0.90
	1984	1.09	0.76	0.51
	1993	0.79	0.55	0.37
	1998	0.68	0.48	0.32

(a need for usable heat of 15,000kWh/year, but almost 21,000kWh/year of gas burned). A condensing boiler would reduce this by about 20 per cent, or by 0.8 tonnes of CO_2. The savings in cash would not be enormous – about £125 if gas is 3 pence per kWh plus, perhaps, £35 for the reduced cost of water heating – but the benefits to the atmosphere are clear and would make a real difference to a household's overall emissions. Of course, if gas prices change, all of the savings will change proportionately.

The cost of installing a condensing boiler five years before it is strictly necessary depends upon whether you have to borrow money to pay for it. If so, then a typical installation with a full cost of £1400 might result in a five-year interest charge of £560. This cost, divided by the tonnes of carbon dioxide avoided, is shown in Table 6.7.

Table 6.7 *Cost per tonne of carbon dioxide avoided*

	Boiler age	High gas need	Medium gas need	Low gas need
Cost per tonne of CO_2 emissions avoided	1974	£58	£83	£125
	1984	£103	£147	£221
	1993	£141	£202	£303
	1998	£164	£234	£351

Note: Assumes savings are generated for five years because of the early purchase of the boiler, that the boiler costs £1400, including fitting, and that the householder pays interest of 8 per cent per annum on this expenditure.

For smaller houses, the carbon dioxide benefits of fitting a new boiler look expensive to attain. For bigger houses, the arguments are much stronger, even for houses with relatively recently installed conventional boilers.

But condensing boilers have not been popular. Until the government made it almost mandatory to use condensing technology, the rate of installation was slow. Plumbers complained that they were difficult to fit and unreliable. Others claimed that the postulated savings were difficult to achieve. Householders were wary of the plume of steam that the boiler emitted, not realizing that this steam showed that the boiler was working properly.

The issues behind these complaints appear to have been resolved. Reliability is now said to be good, and the installers are more confident that the boilers really do operate at higher levels of efficiency. The gas companies have made a better job of explaining why the plume of water vapour outside the house indicated that the boiler was more, not less, efficient (because the exhaust gases emitted from the boiler are at a much lower temperature than conventional boilers, the water vapour condenses into steam much more rapidly and closer to the house). Condensing boilers have been the norm in parts of continental Europe for up to 20 years, so it would be amazing if there are genuine problems of reliability.

Nevertheless, boilers are almost invariably bought as distress purchases, when the old stager under the stairs has finally breathed its last. Virtually nobody buys a boiler voluntarily. As a result, active selling of condensing boilers has been limited to a few organizations, such as British Gas. No doubt as a result of high sales costs, these organizations have also tended to offer very high prices. My household received a quote of over £2500 to replace our boiler with a condensing boiler from British Gas, including quotes for some ancillary pipes and valves that are over twice the price of what is readily obtainable elsewhere. Households should be able to get a reasonably powerful condensing boiler for about £1400. The reluctance to change boilers before the old one expires must change: we need to make the plume of vapour outside the house a visible badge of the household's environmental credentials.

Oil central heating

The advantages of using condensing boilers for homes using oil are somewhat lower than for gas. Oil-fired boilers have traditionally been slightly more efficient than the gas equivalent of the same year, and recently installed non-condensing units are only slightly less efficient than the condensing equivalent. The best advice is probably to wait until your oil-fired boiler really does need replacing and then go for a condensing version. Remember that the boiler itself has a reasonable amount of fossil fuel energy embedded in it.

Boiler sizing

Plumbers will generally install a boiler that is too large for the job that it has to handle. One superb eco-renovation website comments that in one case the plumber's rule of thumb would have resulted in a boiler of three times the necessary power being installed.[110] No doubt, the basis for this conventional rule is that no one ever got sued for installing a boiler that was too big, but that one that is too small would result in continuous complaints that it didn't heat the house.

Getting the right size does matter: boilers work most efficiently if they are working constantly. A boiler that it is too big will be turning on and off every few minutes, reducing its life, but also wasting heat as it fires up, cools down and then fires up again. Probably as importantly, a condensing boiler that is too big in relation to the needs of the house may not actually condense effectively because of the high temperature of the water returning to the boiler. There are good energy-efficiency reasons for not buying a boiler that is too powerful.

Unfortunately, to get the right sized boiler is not a simple matter. In theory, the calculation is easy: you need to work out the heat loss of the house on a very cold winter night and then get a boiler that can deliver this. Across the UK housing stock, this averages 259W per degree difference between the desired inside temperature and the external figure. Bigger and older houses will lose more. For the average house, and a 20 degree difference between inside and outside temperatures, the boiler should therefore be about 5kW – or 17,000 British thermal units (BTUs) per hour – to maintain the desired temperature. Increase this figure to provide the extra push to get the house to warm up after a cold night and to cover water heating needs, and the average house might need 15kW.

You will find that this is regarded as an absurdly small boiler by plumbers, who will point to the relatively small cost difference between a 15kW boiler and the 30kW variety (perhaps £120). Ignore this and remind your installer that cars with bigger engines use more fuel, even when travelling at the same speed as the smaller-engined equivalent. However, do not ignore the second line of a plumber's defence, which is that a bigger boiler will get a house up from a low temperature more rapidly than its diminutive cousin, the boiler that just meets your heating needs. You will need to make your own mind up about how important this feature is. But you should remember that the best boiler system is one that is appropriately sized, combined with good controls that mean that it fires up when it is needed and not at other times (see the following section).

Better use of central heating controls

Very little research has been done on the impact of improving central heating controls or on getting people to use their existing controls properly. As a result, this section is long on commentary and short on numbers.

Generally, a home has at least five separate control systems that affect fuel use. They are:

1 a wall thermostat;
2 a programmer for the central heating system;
3 thermostatic valves on radiators;
4 a boiler power regulator; and
5 a thermostat on the hot water tank.

The first four of these affect the efficiency of the central heating system, and the fifth influences the cost of a household's hot water.

The wall thermostat

Usually positioned at a central point in the house, the thermostat measures the air temperature.[111] It allows the householder to set a temperature level at which the boiler will turn on, provided that the central heating programmer is set to allow boiler use at that time. The boiler will turn off when the temperature rises above the level set on the thermostat.

Almost all room thermostats are turned up or down by rotating a dial. The typical product is inaccurate and imprecise. Furthermore, the conventional thermostat will tend to cause temperatures to cycle up and down. Most of them are constructed to turn on the heating when the temperature drops a degree or so below the set level, and to turn off when it reaches a degree or so higher (check this on your control: the click that tells the

heating to turn off is about 2 degrees above the temperature that tells it to turn on).
A graph of room temperature when the thermostat was set to 20 degrees Celsius
would show the actual temperature moving in a saw-tooth pattern between 21 and 19
degrees Celsius.

Typical low-quality analogue thermostats (the ones fitted in almost all UK homes)
result in inefficient use of gas, even when the owner knows what he or she is doing. They
don't, for example, instruct the boiler to start earlier in the morning when the temperature
is really low, or cut off when the temperature is rising fast and closing in on the target
warmth. These would be obvious and easily programmable features in more sophisticated
digital devices. There is no doubt in my mind that this would result in lower fuel bills, if
only because users ought to feel more confident in the effects of their thermostat. In
general, the theory goes, it would be set lower. (Despite their apparent simplicity,
thermostats are not intuitive. For example, I find it very difficult to explain to otherwise
highly rational individuals that turning the thermostat up when entering a cold house will
not increase the speed at which the house warms up.)

Furthermore, I suspect that intelligent digital thermostats would save energy by
allowing households to start heating later in the early morning, and turning it off earlier at
night. It would be particularly valuable when combined with programming controls,
allowing the users to set varying times for different days of the week.

One UK company produces a device that appears to deliver all of the electronic
functions that one would want in a room thermostat.[112] This product, called a Dataterm,
is essentially a mixture of a room thermostat and a central heating programmer. It is highly
intelligent – that is, for a thermostat – and, for example, can learn how fast an individual
house warms up. The claimed improvements are impressive, with two large local authority
installations suggesting savings of between 17 and 25 per cent on overall gas bills.
Customers quoted on the company's website say that users find it easy to operate.

Comments, reviews and independent data from domestic households are scarce for the
Dataterm or other intelligent programmers. Therefore, I hesitate to recommend it; but it
does appear to be a highly effective improvement to existing thermostats and will certainly
give an improved level of comfort. If it works as it claims, it will allow the user much closer
control over temperatures throughout the day.

The device itself is around £220 and installation would probably cost another £80 or
so. If it saved 10 per cent of domestic heating bills, which seems a reasonable possibility to
me, it would reduce the gas bill by £45 a year at current prices and cut almost 0.3 tonnes
off carbon emissions from the typical house. If it lasts 15 years before being replaced, the
cost per tonne of carbon saved would be about £70, which makes it better value than
installing a condensing boiler (of course, it could be installed in addition to a condensing
boiler, in which case the savings would be slightly lower because the percentage gas saving

would be similar, but the gas used would be lower). The device would pay for itself in about seven years.

Central heating programmer

The programmer sets the times at which the central heating can go on and off. It is, of course, over-ridden by the room thermostat if that device says that the house is already warm enough. Some research carried out for the Market Transformation Programme, one of the UK government's many climate change information bodies, suggests that many people have no idea how these programmers work and leave them on all the time, adjusting their internal temperature by yanking the room thermostat back and forward. When they want the boiler to go off, they turn the thermostat down and, conversely, turn the heating on by turning the thermostat to the right.

The readers of this book are probably not quite as crude as this. But even energy-aware folk can be confused by the difficulties of setting a complex modern programmer with its ability to set different start and finish times for different days of the week. I haven't found any estimates of how much might be saved by careful setting of when the programmer turns the heating system on and off. I suspect that saving 5 per cent of the overall fuel bill might be possible by a householder giving very close attention to setting the timings of the programmer to minimize the time that the boiler is working.

In an ideal world, houses would be fitted with intelligent room thermostats that doubled as heating programmers. The Dataterm device described above carries out both functions. But characteristically in UK homes, the programmer is sited in an obscure location, often next to the boiler itself. Unlike the thermostat, which is regarded as aesthetically acceptable, the programmer is not fit for public view. This reduces the chance of it being effectively used to moderate the household's gas consumption.

Radiator thermostats

One would be hard put to find anybody who uses these devices thoughtfully. They sit on top of the inlet pipe into a radiator and allow the homeowner to regulate the temperature in individual rooms. Properly employed, these rotation knobs could be used to maintain slightly lower temperatures in some rooms than in others. It doesn't actually seem to work that way, and they are only ever used to (at least in my experience) turn radiators either fully on or off. The useful gradations of temperature are beyond the skills of most householders.

It is, of course, a mistake to put a thermostatic control on a radiator in the same room as the main thermostat. If the radiator control is set lower than the room thermostat, and the house is well insulated internally, then the boiler will continue working furiously, heating other parts of the house to excessive levels until sufficient hot air leaks into the thermostat room to turn off the heating system.

UPGRADE THE INSULATION IN THE HOUSE OR IMPROVE THE CAPTURE OF OTHER SOURCES OF HEAT, SUCH AS SOLAR RADIATION

The previous section looked at ways of ensuring that fuel inputs to the house are efficiently converted to the right level of usable heat. Next, we need to look at how to ensure that this usable heat is retained. The scope for improvement here is considerable. The average UK home is rated E on the European Union's A to G classification of energy efficiency of domestic buildings.[113]

Homeowners can consider six main areas of improvement in home insulation:

1 cavity walls;
2 loft insulation;
3 improvement in windows;
4 improvements in doors;
5 draught proofing;
6 radiator reflectors.

It may be useful to remind ourselves of the main exit routes from the home for our increasingly expensive heat. Table 6.8 provides approximate figures for heat loss from different parts of a typical house, losing heat at 259W for every degree of temperature difference between the inside and the outside.

Table 6.8 *Loss of heat from elements of the typical house*

Source of heat loss	Watts (W) per degree temperature difference	Percentage of total loss
Walls	103	40
Windows	52	20
Ventilation	52	20
Roof	19	7
Floor	21	8
Doors	13	5
Total	259	100

These figures mean that for a typical house of about 80 square metres (800 to 900 square feet), the heat from a large light bulb is getting through the walls for every degree by which the house is raised above the outdoor temperature. For a 10 degree difference – usually called a gradient – between the internal temperature and the air outside, the walls lose the heat output from a single-bar electric radiator. Much of that is leaving the house through cracks and what are known as 'thermal bridges' – places where heat is readily conducted from the inside to the open air. Poor construction techniques make these bridges very common even in apparently well-insulated houses.

Figure 6.2 shows how heat produced in the house is dissipated through the elements of the building.

How much difference would good insulation make? For example, what happens if the heat loss through the walls were to fall to zero? First, of course, the total heat need for the house would decline by 6600kWh/year, meaning that the total input energy required will decline to 9900kWh/year. The available energy from other sources of heat, such as electric appliances, cooking and solar gain, would remain approximately the same. Therefore, the total need for heat from the central heating would fall by the full 6600kWh/year. Instead of using 10,500kWh/year of heat from the boiler, the house would only need 3900kWh/year. Miraculously, the gas delivered to the 75 per cent efficient boiler would only need to be 5200kWh/year, rather than 14,000kWh/year.

This demonstrates the magnification effect of improved insulation. If wall insulation were perfect and, as a result, reduced the house's total loss by 40 per cent, the need for gas for central heating would fall by over 60 per cent. Of course, insulation can never be completely perfect; but good construction standards – often a failing in new British housing – and sensible techniques mirrored on the European Passivhaus ideal can get close.

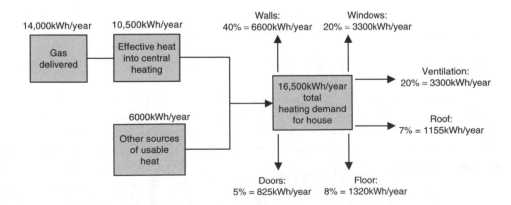

Figure 6.2 *Energy balance for home heating of the typical house*

The cost of heat losses

What would the average householder save by abolishing all heat loss from the individual elements of the home? Table 6.9 outlines some figures.

Table 6.9 *The cost of heat losses*

Element	Yearly cost* (3 pence per kWh)
Walls	£264
Windows	£132
Ventilation	£132
Roof	£46
Floor	£53
Door	£33

Note: * The gas savings arise from the reduction in heat loss, plus the heat loss in the boiler. These savings assume that the boiler is 75 per cent efficient. The savings would be lower if the house has an efficient new condensing boiler and higher if the boiler is old.

Put in this way, the cost of indifferent insulation begins to look quite minor. Stopping all heat losses through the roof would only save enough each year for one ticket to an expensive sports event. It would, however, reduce annual carbon dioxide emissions by almost one third of a tonne. Perhaps this sounds like a much more interesting target to aim for. In some ways, this illustrates one of the problems with climate change – even substantial carbon reductions can look unimpressive in cash terms.

Cavity walls and other forms of wall insulation

Since walls are typically responsible for 40 per cent of total heat losses, it makes sense to look at this target first.

Walls can be insulated by cladding the outside or the inside with a material that doesn't conduct heat. Heat loss can also be minimized by putting insulating material between the external brickwork and the internal concrete blocks. Since about 1930, British houses have generally been built with an air cavity between these two walls. This makes the house better insulated than if the walls were just brick: air is a relatively poor conductor of heat, and the gap also helps to avoid thermal bridging.

Although air isn't a bad insulator, other materials can be much better. Since the 1960s, energy-conscious homeowners have improved the insulation characteristics of their houses by injecting non-conducting plastics into the gap between the two walls. In 1974, 2.5 per cent of homes with cavities had insulation. By 2001, this had risen to about 32 per cent, or less than 6 million homes out of the 17.5 million houses with cavities. However, even today, 11 million UK homes have wall cavities that could be insulated, but leak unnecessary quantities of expensive heat to the outside world. This is about 40 per cent of all UK housing.

Effective cavity wall insulation does significantly affect energy demand for domestic heating. Nevertheless, it has only recently become mandatory for new buildings, even though the cost of adding a proper insulator during construction is vanishingly small. Until building regulations were tightened in 2002, even larger properties, which have most to gain, were usually constructed with a thin insulating membrane between the external and internal walls, rather than the full infilling of the complete gap. Perhaps this doesn't seem to matter very much – the number of new houses built each year is less than 1 per cent of the existing stock; but the cost of systematically lagging behind best practice has left UK housing as among the worst insulated in Northern Europe. (Many houses in places such as Spain are insulated to even lower standards. This is not necessarily a particular problem in winter because of the higher temperatures, at least in southern Spain; but poor insulation hugely increases the demand for air-conditioning in summer.)

The precise savings produced by cavity wall insulation are difficult to determine, depending, as they do, upon the quality of the installation and the characteristics of the un-insulated wall. The most reliable estimates I can find suggest that good insulation installed in a wide cavity (more than 60mm, or 2.5 inches) will reduce the heat losses compared to the un-insulated wall by about two-thirds[114] (these figures were provided to me by a manufacturer of insulating material, but seem to be consistent with other sources of information).

If typical losses through walls are 40 per cent of the total heat dissipation from a house, the simple calculation might suggest that total gas demand would go down by about 26 per cent. This would be an underestimate for the reason we established in looking at condensing boilers; central heating tops up the other sources of heat gain in a house, such as electric appliances. Therefore, filling the cavity in the wall will actually reduce gas demand by a larger percentage than the insulation improvement might indicate. Table 6.10 provides my estimates.

Cavity wall insulation makes most sense for big detached houses. In these cases, gas demand may fall by a huge amount. In Table 6.11, the saving for a big house will be over 2 tonnes of carbon dioxide – as well as a substantial amount of money.

These numbers are spuriously precise. They are intended to be indicative because we can't really know the characteristics of the typical house with a high gas need. Nor can they accommodate the tendency of people with well-insulated houses to run their heating at a higher level. It's a well-established fact that people take insulation improvements in what the engineers call greater 'comfort', or higher temperatures throughout the dwelling.

Table 6.10 *Very approximate gas usage savings from installing cavity wall insulation*

	House with high gas need	House with average gas need	House with low gas need
Delivered gas (kWh/year)	20,000	14,000	9333
Usable heat output from gas boiler at 75% efficiency (kWh/year)	15,000	10,500	7000
Other sources of heat gain* (kWh/year)	9000	6000	4000
Total heat (kWh/year)	24,000	16,500	11,000
Reduction from cavity wall insulation** (kWh/year)	10,667	5867	2933
Percentage saving in gas bill	53	42	31

Notes: * I assume that if a house has a high gas need, it probably also has more substantial sources of heat from electric appliances, solar gain and other non-fossil fuel sources.
** Larger houses will generally lose a larger fraction of their heat through the walls. Therefore, I have used a larger percentage than average for the loss from walls. Consider a big detached house standing in its own grounds and compare it to a mid-terraced house. The terraced house will lose relatively little through its walls because of its neighbours; but the detached house will have a high ratio of wall area to the size of the home. These calculations include an estimate of this effect.

And the cavity wall insulation won't necessarily be perfect. There will be gaps and places where the insulation doesn't reach. So, data from suppliers that estimates the impact of better wall insulation will often be lower than these figures. Good cavity wall insulation will also have the effect of reducing the amount of solar energy warming the house on a sunny winter's day. This will tend to reduce the savings in gas consumption; but the effect

Table 6.11 *Potential savings from cavity wall insulation*

	House with high gas need	House with average gas need	House with low gas need
Gas saving (kWh/year)	10,667	5867	2933
Tonnes of CO_2 averted	2.0	1.1	0.6
Financial saving at 3 pence per kWh	£320	£176	£88

will be minor for most houses. Conversely, in the summer, proper wall insulation will reduce the internal temperature increase coming from solar energy and will therefore keep the house cooler, reducing the needs for fans or other cooling devices.

Table 6.12 provides a current example of how much a cavity wall insulation supplier charges. These costs are heavily subsidized, and many people claiming state benefits will actually be able to get lower prices, or even obtain the installation free. These subsidies are a result of the government insisting that domestic gas and electricity suppliers pay a portion of the cost as part of their obligations towards improving energy efficiency.

The ratio between cost and benefit is strikingly favourable to large houses. The payback period for a big detached house is less than one year. At the other extreme, the payback for a small mid-terraced house might be two or three years.

Assume that all of these houses have another 50 years life. The cost per tonne of carbon saved is as low as £2 for a big house and £6 for a small terrace. These are strikingly low figures compared to almost any other carbon-reduction techniques. Even if the full cost, including the subsidy from the energy supplier, is included, the numbers would only approximately double.

This point is not well understood and needs to be forcibly made. The single most important contribution that the UK could make to carbon dioxide reduction is to improve the heat retention of the walls of domestic properties.

What is the scope for the UK as a country to use this lever to cut emissions? About 11 million homes have cavity walls, but no insulation. The typical house will see annual savings of 1.1 tonnes if the insulation is done well and the homeowner does not turn up the thermostat to compensate. This means that 12 million tonnes of carbon dioxide emissions could be avoided annually by a national programme of insulation of walls. This is about 2 per cent of the UK total.

If there were a national programme of insulation, handled like North Sea gas conversion, for example, the cost per household might reduce to £300, excluding subsidy. The total cost might run to about £3 billion to £3.5 billion. This would be about £5 to £6 per tonne of carbon dioxide. This is an almost absurdly good payback – and well below the European market price for carbon dioxide permits.

Table 6.12 *Costs of cavity wall insulation*

Type of house	Cost
Mid-terraced house	£250
Three-bedroom semi-detached house	£250
Four- to five-bedroom detached house	£275

Source: British Gas website (www.house.co.uk), accessed November 2006

So, why doesn't the government institute a national scheme for insulation? A large-scale scheme need not be compulsory. It could, for example, allow householders to opt out. A national programme of wall insulation could see the installers move methodically down streets so that people would see at first hand how simple and non-intrusive the process is. Even if only 90 per cent of homes allowed the insulation to take place, the savings would be huge. Indeed, there is no other single thing, excluding a large-scale transfer to nuclear power, that would have such an impact on greenhouse gases. So, why is the government prepared to allow such slow progress in reducing the number of UK homes with poor – and easily rectifiable – energy efficiency?

The first reason is probably a fear of the logistical problems handling such an endeavour. A project that sought to carry out £300 of works on 11 million homes spread across the UK would bring innumerable problems of fraud, poor performance, dissatisfied householders and unexplained delays.

CAVITY WALL INSULATION: OUR PERSONAL CASE HISTORY

We live in a house built in 2001, before recent improvements to building regulations. The walls have a cavity and a thin insulating membrane that covers the inside of the internal block wall. The gas bills for our house are not particularly low; so I investigated adding full cavity wall insulation. My calculations suggest that the house did not even meet UK building regulations in force in 2001. This is, unfortunately, typical; house builders do not seem to construct their houses with appropriate insulation standards, even by the extremely undemanding UK regulations.

Unfortunately, I was told by the cavity wall insulation firm that because we have the thin membrane – rather than simply an empty cavity – installers will not be able to put in proper insulation, except at a very high price. So we are stuck with our poor insulation standards forever, or at least until installers find a satisfactory way of blowing insulation into the cavity.

A second concern would be the political consequences of improving the insulation standards and thus lowering the heating bills of about half of UK homes, while ignoring the rest. Why should poor pensioners living in Victorian terraced housing with no wall cavities not also see their gas bills reduced?

These issues seem solvable to me. A national scheme to insulate all cavities over a three-year period would, indeed, cost more than it should. It might be beset by corruption, excess bureaucracy and inefficiency. And there would be complaints from people in energy-inefficient housing that their bills remained unaffordable. Nevertheless, compared to almost any other scheme, a determined national initiative on cavity wall insulation is a first-rate use of money. It is a pity that we don't appear to have the political will to make it happen.

About 7 million homes cannot use cavity wall insulation, either because they are part of blocks of flats or because the house walls are made from solid brick. Most houses built before the 1930s did not have a cavity wall.

The heat loss from the walls of older houses, particularly larger detached properties, is even greater than for homes with un-insulated cavities (after all, the cavity does have an important insulating effect). It therefore makes sense to contemplate covering either the outside or the inside of the wall with an insulating material. Either technique can improve the heat loss from walls sevenfold and make the wall better insulated than all but the very best-insulated cavity walls.

The installers' trade association quotes figures of between £45 and £65 per square metre for external cladding (the cost is probably ten times as much as cavity wall insulation). For a typical semi-detached house, this would mean between £3500 and £5500. My calculations suggest that the typical gas bill for such a house would be reduced by about £270 after installing external cladding, with a saving of over 1.7 tonnes of carbon dioxide per year; but figures from the trade association of external cladding firms are slightly lower. Payback periods are far longer than for cavity wall installation.

Internal cladding – achieved by fixing battens of cladding to the wall – provides equally effective insulation, but is much cheaper than external work. A do-it-yourself job can be done for about £450, and the saving should be as much as external cladding. Internal cladding therefore has a payback of about two years. Internal cladding lasting 30 years might reduce carbon dioxide emissions by 50 tonnes, meaning that the cost per tonne is £10 or less. The only reason that we do not see heavy promotion of this insulation technique is that it reduces the size of the rooms and therefore decreases the area of the house.

Grants are available for internal and external cladding, which reduces the cost by almost £500 for a detached house. In the city of Oxford, for example, these grants are supplemented by a £500 award – meaning, as far as I can understand it, that internal insulation is cost free to the householder, as well as saving almost £200 in heating bills. Unfortunately, the value of space in a town like Oxford is far greater than the worth of good insulation. A semi-detached house with a floor area of 80 square metres (about 850 square feet) might sell for £240,000. If the internal insulation caused a loss in internal area of 1 per cent, the resulting diminution of market value might be far greater than the cost of the installation itself. Very expensive living space may not make it easier to decide to add insulation.

Roof insulation

In the typical home, 7 per cent of heat losses are through the roof. In 1970, the figure was 17 per cent, and in the last 35 years the energy flowing out from the roof has fallen in absolute terms by almost three-quarters. The reason is the increase in the percentage of homes that have properly insulated lofts. From about 40 per cent in 1970, the share of homes with at least some insulation in the loft has risen to about 95 per cent (this figure excludes flats and other properties not immediately beneath a roof).

For a home left without any loft insulation today, the prospective savings are at least as great as cavity wall insulation. So, loft insulation should be part of any systematic national programme to improve insulation standards. But the number of homes left without any insulation is small, and the aggregate national saving in carbon dioxide emissions will be much less significant than the impact from wall improvements.

For most homeowners, therefore, the issue is whether to lay thicker insulation in the roof space. Early loft insulation usually only used 2.5cm (1 inch) of insulation, and owners might need to increase the thickness of coverage. Another 4.5 million or so houses have only 5 to 7.5cm (2 to 3 inches) of insulation. For these people, and owners with even less coverage, would it make sense to increase the covering to 15cm, which is the thickness usually installed today (2006 regulations for new buildings actually require a figure of 25cm)?

My calculations suggest that with typical boiler efficiencies, the savings for a medium-sized house will be about £24 a year at gas prices of 3 pence per kWh, though it would be somewhat more for a house with only 2.5cm of insulation. When done by professionals, the cost might be between £200 and £250, making the investment attractive, but not overwhelmingly good, even if gas prices increase further.[115] The carbon dioxide savings will average about 150kg a year. Over a remaining 50-year life of a house, this amounts to 7.5 tonnes, or about £30 per tonne of carbon dioxide avoided.

Buy material for loft insulation which has itself good environmental credentials. Recycled newspaper-based insulation or sheep's wool products can offer equally good insulation performance to the standard glass fibre offering and use very little energy in their manufacture.[116]

Glazing improvements

About two-thirds of homes now have at least some windows with double glazing, although the number with all windows properly insulated is no more than about 40 per cent.

Window insulation matters. A home with single glazing may well lose more heat through the windows than it does through the walls. This is particularly likely to be true if the walls are cavity filled.

But sorting out the windows is likely to be extremely expensive. A recent study of the costs of double glazing conducted by the Office of Fair Trading showed that the average price to replace eight or nine windows averaged about £500 a window.[117] To refurbish the windows of an average house might therefore cost at least £5000.

Calculation of savings is made more difficult because of two factors. Putting in double glazing will reduce the solar energy that warms the house – less will get through the windows in winter (of course, therefore, double glazing helps to reduce the internal temperature of a house in summer). Second, double glazing does seem to be installed by householders deliberately in order to be able to run the house at a higher temperature. These complications make it more complex to assess any likely savings from double glazing, either in cash or carbon terms.

Analysis shows that good double glazing reduces the heat loss through windows by about two-thirds. But note that even the best double glazing leaves the typical window still losing more heat than the same area of un-insulated wall. And so-called four season-glazed conservatories, which allow use even in winter, are absolute disasters in terms of heat loss. These glazed conservatories, often completely open to the living areas of the house, are now very difficult to build without breaching building regulations.

The maximum saving that could be hoped for from converting single glazing to good double glazing in a typical house is about £150 a year, equivalent to about 1 tonne of carbon dioxide.[118] Double-glazed windows may last, perhaps, 25 years, meaning that the cost of averting 1 tonne of carbon dioxide is about £200. Even if the full £150 yearly cash benefit is gained, this is of limited interest as a return on a £5000 investment. The saving will, anyway, be reduced by the impact of lower solar energy gain through the windows and a tendency to use increased internal temperatures. Perhaps the true saving will be less than £100, or 2 per cent of the cost. Of course, double glazing does make a house more attractive, with less window condensation and more even temperatures throughout the year, so there are other good reasons for installation. For those unable to afford full double glazing, the logical choice may be to insulate windows on the northern side of the house because south-facing single-glazed windows will capture more solar energy in winter.

Doors

Although external doors are only responsible for about 5 per cent of the heat loss from the house, it can be more economical to improve this aspect of insulation than, for example, to install double glazing. An ordinary solid wood door is a very poor insulator, leaking heat at twice the rate of an un-insulated wall.

Installing two first-rate insulated doors, front and back, may, however, cost over £500 and save no more than £15 to £20 a year. Carbon savings are likely to be about 100kg a year, with the cost per tonne of carbon being about £200 if the doors last 20 years. This is similar to double glazing; but in this case the saving may not be lost in higher internal temperatures or loss of solar energy gain.

Floors

Where possible, insulating material should be placed on stone, concrete or tiled floors. If wood floorboards are accessible, gaps between them should be filled. If cellar access is possible, it may

MEASURES TO CONSERVE HEAT

These very useful comments are from the Oxford City Council website:[119]

1   Eliminate draughts and wasted heat by fixing draught-proofing to exterior doors. Remember that some ventilation is important.
     Cost: around £5.
2   Buy an insulating jacket for the hot water cylinder. This needs to be at least 75mm thick.*
     Cost: around £10.
     Saving: £10 to £15 per year.
3   Insulate your hot water pipes to stop heat escaping from them.
     Cost: around £1 per metre.
     Saving: around £5 per year.
4   Stop draughts and heat from escaping by filling gaps under skirting boards with newspaper, beading or sealant.
     Cost: around £25.
     Saving: £5 to £10 per year.
5   Letterboxes and keyholes can let in draughts. Fit nylon brush seal or spring flap, and put a cover over the keyhole.
     Cost: around £5.

*Even if you already have some lagging, add more if needed to make it 75mm thick.

be beneficial to place insulating material, such as appropriately fire-retarded recycled newspapers, underneath the floorboards. If done on a do-it-yourself basis, better ground-floor insulation may be cost effective, although I've found it difficult to get good estimates.

Other minor measures

In addition to these measures, it may be worthwhile installing reflective panels behind radiators. These redirect some of the heat that would otherwise flow outwards through the external wall. This is particularly important if the walls of the house are solid, as heat can flow freely outwards. One website says that the carbon dioxide saving resulting from this measure can be as much as 200kg a year for a once-off cost of £45.[120] Other commentators seem much less optimistic about prospective savings.

Ventilation

For completeness, we need to mention ventilation, which is responsible for about 20 per cent of the cost of heating a home. Ventilation doesn't just mean draughts. Air needs to flow in and out of a house in order to provide the necessary oxygen for its inhabitants. Even the best-insulated house needs to sustain enough airflow to turn over the complete stock of air in the house every hour or so. This means that each hour the heating system has to heat all of the air in the house, from the external to the internal temperature (in the German Passivhaus design, this is done by passing the incoming air through a heat exchanger that uses the warm air that is being extracted from the house).

As George Marshall puts it in his inspiring and encyclopaedic website The Yellow House (www.theyellowhouse.org.uk):

> *Any house that does not have air passing through it is fundamentally unhealthy. Ventilation is vital to replace moist, stale air with fresh, clean air. The problem is that ventilation can also account for up to a third of the heat loss of the house. Just as 'weeds' are plants we don't want, 'draughts' are ventilation we don't want. The trick is to control the passage of air such that it is just enough to meet the ventilation needs and has an efficient route through the house.*[121]

The Yellow House gives useful detailed instructions for simple methods to get the right amount of ventilation in a home and to cut unwanted draughts to a minimum.

Using solar gain

To varying extents, all houses function as greenhouses, trapping heat from the sun. New houses can be built that maximize the gain in energy from this source, and simple principles can result in major savings in energy cost and carbon dioxide emissions. The very best examples of new houses can have very low needs for space heating because of their mixture of high levels of insulation and effective trapping of winter sunlight. In order to avoid overheating in summer, these 'eco-homes' also need to have a high thermal mass – that is, the ability to retain heat within the structure and slowly release it to the interior space.

What can owners of existing buildings do? The easiest and most effective method of capturing solar energy is to install a south-facing three-season conservatory. The homeowner can build what is, in effect, a greenhouse on the south side of the house, trapping heat in the spring and the autumn. Solar energy heats the air in this room, and on sunlit days, the door to the main body of the house is opened, allowing the energy to flow into the living rooms. In the dull days of winter, the door to the house is shut.

Solar conservatories work in three different ways. Godfrey Boyle's excellent book *Renewable Energy*[122] gives the following figures:

• Fifteen per cent of the value is gained because the solar conservatory effectively acts as additional insulation for the house.

- Fifty-five per cent comes from the warming of the air that circulates through the rest of the house.
- Thirty per cent comes from solar energy entering the house through conventional conduction across the external wall.

In total, Boyle says that a solar conservatory added to a badly insulated house in Milton Keynes saved about 800kWh a year (£24, or 150kg of carbon), so they are never likely to be cost effective. Moreover, the fashion for installing three-season conservatories in the 1960s and 1970s quietly developed into the building of conservatories that function as all-year-round rooms, with no barrier to the rest of the house.

REDUCING HOUSE TEMPERATURES

The simplest way to reduce bills and the carbon emissions from home heating is to reduce temperatures. This obvious fact tends not to be mentioned in textbook analyses of the impact of heating on greenhouse gas emissions. Commentators are afraid of being labelled masochists. This is unfortunate because if we are to grasp the enormity of the climate change challenge we need to understand that some sacrifices may well be necessary. The path from a 12.5 tonnes per person society to one in which carbon dioxide emissions are no more than 2 or 3 tonnes will not be easy. We can build new houses that are vastly more energy efficient than the ones we are building today, and the occupants of these homes will

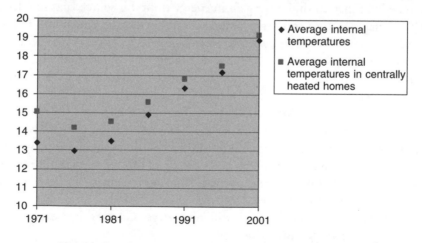

Figure 6.3 *Average internal temperatures in UK homes*

Source: L. D. Shorrock and J. I. Utley's *Domestic Energy Fact File 2003*, available at http://projects .bre.co.uk/factfile/

be able to keep their houses hot. The rest of us may need to accept that our house temperatures will have to be reduced.

As shown in Figure 6.3, internal winter house temperatures have risen steadily since the 1980s. The rise has been dramatic and shows no sign of abating. By 2001, average winter internal temperatures were about 19 degrees Celsius. It has probably gone up since to nearly 20 degrees Celsius. Better insulation standards, greater availability of central heating and rises in disposable income meant that homeowners chose to run their houses at internal winter temperatures that would have been almost unheard of a couple of generations ago. Most observers think that the rise will continue until the internal temperature reaches 21 degrees Celsius across the whole house, or at least in all of the main rooms. This figure is already reached in typical Swedish homes.

Of course, average external winter temperatures have also risen as a result of global warming and now average about 7 degrees Celsius in the heating season – although 2005/2006 was colder than this (by contrast, as recently as 1981, admittedly a cold year, the average winter temperature was as low as 5.1 degrees Celsius). The typical winter rise since the 1970s of about 1 degree or so – all other things being equal – would have allowed a 1 degree rise in internal temperatures with no extra fuel cost. But the actual rise since 1981 in internal temperatures has been about 5 degrees.

Instead of running the house at 19 degrees Celsius, what would be the impact on fuel bills of setting the thermostat for a target of 18 degrees Celsius? The numbers are surprisingly large. With a boiler efficiency of 75 per cent, turning the thermostat down by 1 degree will reduce the total amount of gas delivered to the average house by about 1750kWh/year, or about 12.5 per cent of total usage. This would save over £50 and about 330kg of carbon dioxide. A reduction of 2 degrees would double these numbers.

How difficult is it to reduce internal temperatures once a family has got used to walking about in shirtsleeves in January? The evidence is that the adoption is remarkably easy and swift. Acclimatization is aided by adding several layers of clothing, of course. What about the health impact of lower temperatures? The evidence I have seen is that as long as the interior of the house remains above 16 degrees Celsius, there is no impact on well-being. Below 16 degrees Celsius and the risk of respiratory infection does seem to rise.[123]

Heating fewer rooms

Until recently, gas prices were sufficiently low for households to consume energy profligately. Even for a family on average income, the total heating bill was not sufficiently large for economizing to have been an attractive option.

But choosing to heat only those rooms in active use does make sense for the carbon-conscious householder. Holding half of the house – the first floor, perhaps – at 3 degrees below the level of the main living rooms makes substantial sense. Turning off radiators in upstairs rooms, and closing the doors, will save some portion of the gas bill. If internal insulation is bad, as it particularly is in new houses, will mean substantial leaks of heat from the warm to the cold areas, which will reduce the saving. But careful use of radiator thermostats should enable the owner to capture savings of at least as much as can be gained by taking the whole house down by 1 degree.

Living in a smaller house

Data is sparse; but the limited evidence I have found suggests that moving from the average detached house to a terraced property might save 6600kWh of gas heating, cutting bills by about £200, and carbon dioxide by 1.25 tonnes. Although very few people would want to make this move, it would be an effective means of cutting personal emissions.

Buying a newly constructed house

New houses have much better insulation standards than the bulk of the UK housing stock. There is earnest debate among experts about exactly how good modern standards have turned out to be. Real houses tend to have much higher heat losses than predicted by the complex models used by builders and architects. They are less well constructed than predicted, with more leaks and bridges between the outside air and the interior. Householders run these houses at higher temperatures than expected.

Some 'ultra low-energy' dwellings reported on by the Association for Environment Conscious Building had total energy consumption (gas and electricity) of about 160kWh/year per square metre. This compares with 278kWh/year for the UK average and probably means that space heating costs are less than 50 per cent of the typical homes. This is a substantial improvement, but nowhere near as good as can be achieved by using international best practice. We need to continue to force UK government and construction industry to improve the lamentable insulation characteristics of British homes.[124]

What about electrically heated houses?

About 10 per cent of homes are heated using electricity, usually via storage radiators. These radiators consist of large heat stores, often made of ceramic bricks, which absorb energy during the night and release it during the day. Users subscribe to electricity tariffs that are lower during the night-time hours. Storage radiators are 100 per cent efficient: all of the heat they produce goes into raising temperatures, unlike gas boilers that have to exhaust some of their heat to the outside.

Electric heating is generally said to be more expensive and less efficient at meeting a house's needs. Our need for heating is sometimes difficult to predict because temperatures change quite rapidly. Electrically heated homes tend to be smaller than average and use less energy for heating. My rough calculations suggest that the typical electric heating system uses about 7000kWh a year, compared to 14,000kWh for a gas or oil system. Since electricity is over twice as carbon-intensive as gas, it might seem that these homes typically result in higher carbon dioxide outputs than the bigger gas-fuelled homes. However, electrically heated homes are generally taking their power during the night, when electricity demand is low, and the bulk of electricity is being generated by the nuclear power stations. Some people say, therefore, that electric heating using storage radiators is not a particularly carbon-intensive activity.

Electric under-floor heating, rather than storage radiators, is a feature of many new flats. Because it tends to provide a better sensation of warmth, it is used even in large luxury flats – and advertised as a major advantage over hot water radiators and a gas central-heating system. Sadly, these systems are likely both to be expensive to run and to produce a large carbon footprint. One source suggests that it will use about 15 per cent less energy than a conventional radiator system; but since electricity is three times the price of gas, and over twice as carbon-intensive in the UK, the cost and carbon emissions will be significantly more than hot water radiators.[126] Electric under-floor heating is attractive and fashionable, and is a good example of how economic progress tends to increase greenhouse gas emissions.

Wherever and however you live, home heating consumes huge volumes of fossil fuel energy. Reducing this is one of the major steps towards a lower-carbon life.

HOME HEATING ENERGY REQUIREMENTS: DATA FROM OTHER COUNTRIES

Home heating energy requirements obviously vary enormously between countries, depending upon the average winter temperatures. The average across the 15 European Union (EU) member states is about 14,000kWh/year, and the most recent data I can find shows the number increasing slowly since about 1995. New dwellings are much more energy efficient, with the most recently constructed homes in the EU having a heating consumption of less than half this total. Increasing sizes of new dwellings – a feature of many countries, but not the UK – added at least 5 per cent to the average heat use in new homes.[125]

Adjusted for temperature differences and for the average size of houses, the UK is the second highest consuming country in Europe, with Belgium being slightly worse. The Nordic countries and The Netherlands are the best, with temperature and size-adjusted consumption running at about 60 per cent of the UK.

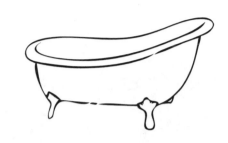

7

water heating and cooking

Hot water use is creeping upwards as more powerful showers are installed in homes. The average person now uses over 50 litres a day. The emissions from this can be relatively easily reduced by half by taking shorter showers, and not baths, and using slightly lower temperatures. The net impact could reduce the emissions impact of water heating to 0.2 tonnes per person per year. The household cost of water heating could be cut from about £120 per year to little more than £60.

Cooking should be carried out by gas, not electricity. The absolute amounts to be saved are not huge. Cooking uses less than 1000kWh/year in the average home and this number is probably falling as more prepared food is bought and larger numbers of people eat out. Best practice would be to cook as much food as possible in a pressure cooker, which saves large amounts of heat, and to use the microwave to cook pre-prepared foods.

Heating the home, examined in the previous chapter, accounts for the majority of a household's gas consumption. The other two uses are production of hot water and cooking. This chapter looks at both of these less significant activities.

WATER HEATING

Water heating uses 4000 to 4500kWh/year in the typical home with mains gas. This is about one third of the gas used for space heating. In terms of kilowatt hours, water heating is more important than the entire electricity consumption of the home. However, the cost of water heating will be lower because heat is generally provided by gas, and not by the more expensive electricity. This chapter assumes that both cooking and water heating use mains gas.

The average person uses about 55 litres of hot water a day. Total domestic water use, now about 160 litres a day – hot and cold – is growing at about 1.5 to 2 per cent a year. The limited data I have found suggests that hot water use is increasing at about the same rate as cold (for those householders using water meters, 160 litres is 0.16 of a cubic metre, the unit by which use is measured). The US uses about twice as much water per person, and France slightly less than the UK.

Households use hot water for baths and showers, for hand washing, for dish-washing and, in rare cases, for use in the washing machine (although almost all new machines are now exclusively cold fill). Of the total hot water use, I estimate that about 40 litres goes on baths and showers.[127] Other uses are relatively insignificant.

The actual amount used in a household will be substantially affected by whether the household members use baths or showers. Full-size UK baths have a capacity of between 200 and 250 litres. Researchers assume that people typically use about 80 litres of hot water for a bath, but use only 30 litres in ordinary mains pressure showers. Of course, this depends upon the length of time spent washing in the shower.

By contrast to conventional showers, the high-pressure variety using pumps to increase water flow rates can use up to 16 litres per minute, so that even a five-minute shower may be as bad as a bath using 80 litres. This is greater than the total daily UK hot water need for the average person. The welcome tendency for people to have a shower every day will continue to increase the amount of hot water used. By the way, power showers of this high flow rate are frowned upon in the more water conservation-conscious US and cannot be sold to federal government installations. In the UK, they are major contributors towards excessive water use and high water heating costs.

After taking into account boiler inefficiency and losses in the pipe work, the typical house probably uses about 4200kWh/year of gas to heat water in the home. At 3 pence a kilowatt hour, this costs about £125 (see Table 7.1).

What can be done to reduce the cost of heating water? There are three main options:

1   Improve the efficiency of the boiler. New condensing boilers will operate at 90 per cent efficiency, not the 75 per cent that I estimated is typical of the UK. This might save 700kWh/year, or nearly 140kg of carbon dioxide. The financial benefit would be about £21 a year (this is additional, of course, to the savings that would also accrue in heating the house from using a condensing boiler).
2   Water temperature can be reduced. This is either a behavioural change – learning to have cooler showers – or perhaps reducing the thermostat temperature on the hot water tank.

Table 7.1 *Gas demand for water heating in the typical household*

Number of litres of hot water used per person per day	55 litres
Energy needed to heat 1 litre by 1°C	0.0011kWh
Temperature elevation needed (10 to 60°C)	50°C
Total energy need for an individual's daily hot water	3.03kWh
Persons per house	2.3
Total water heating demand	6.96kWh per day
Days in year	365
Total per year	2539kWh
Boiler efficiency	75%
Gas need	3385kWh/year
Plus loss from hot water tank and pipes	800kWh/year
Total gas need	4185kWh/year

3   Water volumes can be reduced. The most efficient thing to do would be to move from having a bath to a shower. Assuming that this is a daily event, the reduction from one person doing this might be 20 litres a day, or up to 700kWh/year. The carbon savings will be about 140kg per year and the financial benefit about £21. The cost savings may be small; but this is a worthwhile benefit to the atmosphere.

What can be done about existing power showers? The easiest action is to change the shower head to one that constricts the flow of water. These water-saving devices create thin needle-sharp streams of water that generally do not seem to appeal much to users. Possibly a better solution is the mixing of air with the water, which can leave the apparent volume of water the same, but does significantly reduce flow rates.[128] The usual figures quoted are savings of about 7.5 litres per minute. These shower heads seem effective and the cost is relatively low at about £70. Over the course of a year, the reduction in use from having one person move from a power shower to a more miserly air-mix shower might be over 12,000 litres of hot water. For a home with a water meter, this will save at least £17 in water charges and slightly more in gas bills for each person. The reduction in carbon dioxide will be about 140kg. In a house with four people, these savings are significant and will pay back the initial cost in well under a year.

COOKING WITH GAS

Where possible, cooking should be done by gas. Although gas ovens typically use a little more energy to cook the same amount of food, the lower carbon dioxide output from a kilowatt hour of gas very much outweighs this difference in efficiency. One hundred kilowatt hours of gas costs £3, but up to £10 if delivered as electricity. The carbon dioxide produced is over twice as much.

Nevertheless, a surprising number of people use electricity for cooking, even if they have access to gas. Only 41 per cent of UK homes have gas ovens and 56 per cent have gas hobs, compared to the 80 per cent who use gas for heating.[129] Curiously, the percentage of families cooking with gas varies enormously across Europe. The market research company GfK reported that 100 per cent of cookers sold in Germany in 2005 were powered by electricity; but in Spain, 75 per cent were gas.[130]

Is it worth buying a gas oven if the house currently uses electricity for cooking? If gas cooking typically uses 800kWh/year, compared to 700kWh/year for electric cooking, the saving from switching is less than £50 a year. The carbon dioxide saving is about 150kg. The embedded energy contained in a freestanding new cooker is probably about 600kWh, or perhaps 250kg of carbon dioxide.[131] So, the carbon payback for a new freestanding gas cooker is less than two years. The cash payback would be about four years on a simple new model; but a heavier range-style model would have a less attractive return because of the greater embedded energy in the steel of the appliance. Of course, if the cooker needs replacing, then it is worth plumbing in a new gas oven rather than an electric version.

Data is sparse, but the average family seems to use the oven about 200 times a year. The gas consumption per use is probably about 2kWh over a typical 46-minute cooking period. The gas burners on the stove are used more often – perhaps 400 times a year – and the energy use each time probably averages about 1kWh. As an experiment to check this number, I've just cooked 200g of pasta in 1 litre of water, and it took about 0.5kWh of gas, although purists might say it was still a little undercooked.

Moves to improve the efficiency of gas ovens are muted, partly by the relative unimportance of cooking as a user of gas, and partly by the slow decline in the amount of home cooking. The figures given above suggest that household gas cooking uses about 800kWh/year, at a cost of about £24, and carbon dioxide output of about 150kg. Per person, therefore, gas cooking only costs about £10 a year. The typical household using gas and electricity uses about 23,000kWh/year in total – so cooking is only 3 to 4 per cent of total household energy use. Across the world, homes using gas for cooking tend to use somewhat more than the UK – the International Energy Agency offers a figure of about 1000kWh/year for the typical use of a gas cooker.[132] Another source suggests that cooking is responsible for just under 5 per cent of total energy use in homes in the 15 European Union member states, somewhat more than the UK.[133]

What information there is suggests that the most efficient gas ovens are about 25 per cent better than the average appliance in homes today. But the lack of an agreed test procedure and the absence of any energy labelling on gas ovens (but not electric) mean that consumers are unable to search for the most efficient appliance. Even if information were easily available, ditching an old gas oven for the most efficient new model would be expensive. An expenditure of about £400 for a nice new cooker might save 200kWh and almost 40kg of carbon dioxide a year. If the cooker lasted 20 years, this implies a cost of £500 per tonne of reduced carbon. This is a much higher figure than, say, the typical carbon reduction cost from an investment in a new condensing boiler.

Our estimates of energy use in British ovens may even be a little high. One source puts the total energy consumption from cooking at about 850kWh/year, including microwave use and kettles.[134] Deducting kettles (150kWh/year) and microwaves (65kWh/year) suggests a cooking usage of about 650kWh/year. Gas cookers will typically be somewhat more than this, with electricity rather less. For comparison, one survey suggested a figure of just over 500kWh/year for electric cookers in France.[135]

We know that the use of cookers is probably falling slowly in the UK. But we should not infer from this that energy consumption from all food preparation activities is necessarily falling. Paul Waide notes a strong and continuing rise in the energy use of small food-related appliances in the US. His research suggests that even automatic coffee machines are continuing to take more and more electricity, even though they have been a fixture in US homes for decades.[136] Major growth is also forecast in small appliances as diverse as waffle irons and electric grills. In the US these small appliances currently use about two-thirds as much energy as that consumed by all UK cooking activities, although, of course, the US does have a population five times as large.

Perhaps surprisingly, given the continuing importance of cooking in some family homes, cooking accounts for little more than 1 per cent of carbon emissions directly caused by our activities. And at £24 a year, the incentives to do something about the cooking bills are limited, however virtuous you are. Furthermore, much cooking is done in the heating season, when the cooker is effectively replacing energy that would otherwise be provided by central heating. Indeed, because the oven is almost always only in use when its inhabitants are in the home, it is a remarkably efficient provider of heat in the living rooms. A boiler toiling away in a remote cupboard and only working at 75 per cent efficiency may well offer less good value than the incidental impact of cooking a meal in the winter.

Nevertheless, it makes sense to carry out simple steps to improve efficiency. Using a big enough pan to cover the flames, not heating too much water, covering the pan with a lid – these are all pieces of good advice. The only significant energy-reducing appliance is the pressure cooker. This will reduce the gas expenditure to cook most foods by about 50 per cent – some sources claim an even higher figure. The energy saving comes from two principal sources: the higher boiling temperature and the entrapment of steam, rather than its loss to the open air.

The debate about whether microwave ovens save energy will run and run. Some sources suggest that they are remarkably efficient. Other reports are less sanguine. At first sight, it seems obvious that microwaves are more energy sparing; they actually directly cook the food, rather than warming up the large cavity of an oven. However, Nicola King, one of the stalwart researchers from the government's Market Transformation Programme, recently reported on cooking times for various standard UK foods (ready-prepared lasagne, porridge, baked beans and the like). Her results show that energy use was not predictably lower than hob or oven, although chilled ready meals were much more efficiently warmed up in a microwave. Photographs attached to her presentation also demonstrated that microwaved food almost always looks less appetising than meals cooked in an oven.

In Chapter 13 on the food production chain later in this book, I suggest that the growth in ready meals is inflating the energy demands of food manufacturers. I also estimate that food manufacturing may be responsible for three times as much carbon output as home cooking. It is certainly not true to assume that the swing to manufactured food and away from home-prepared meals is necessarily saving energy.

8

lighting

Seventy per cent of UK households now have at least one energy-saving light bulb. These homes typically have about four of these compact fluorescent bulbs, often in locations where they are heavily used. The typical house still has 20 or more light fittings still using old-fashioned incandescent bulbs. Switching all of the remaining lights to compact fluorescent bulbs will reduce electricity needs for lighting by almost three-quarters.

Currently, the average house uses about 750kWh/year of electricity for lighting, and this would fall to about 200kWh/year if all light bulbs were converted to the energy-saving variety. The cost would be about £80 and the yearly saving about £55, with a reduction of almost 240kg of carbon dioxide. Per person in the typical 2.3-member household, the saving would be about 100kg, or slightly less than 1 per cent of total carbon output.

There needs to be a caveat to these figures. Light bulbs act as miniature radiators. Energy-saving bulbs emit less heat, so the demands on central heating will be greater. Perhaps one third of the claimed savings in carbon would be lost because of the increased need to heat the house in winter. However, more careful use of lighting – turning them off when not in the room, for example – might restore the savings.

The last few chapters have been concerned with gas consumption in the home. The next two chapters are about electricity use, starting with lighting.

The average UK house has about 25 light bulbs. Each of these bulbs is used for an average of just over an hour a day. At a typical wattage of 75W to 80W, the home therefore uses about 750kWh/year for lighting, or about 20 per cent of total domestic electricity use. This figure is slightly higher than the average for industrial countries. The International Energy Agency reports that lighting was only responsible for about 14 per cent of domestic electricity consumption in its member countries.[137, 138]

UK usage generates about 350kg of carbon dioxide per household per year. Spread across the typical numbers of people per house, this is about 150kg a head, or well over 1 per cent of total average carbon emissions and between 2 and 3 per cent of the greenhouse gases for which we are directly responsible.

Spoken of in this way, lighting doesn't seem that important. But it is still 9 million tonnes of carbon dioxide a year, and reductions are perfectly easy although consumer resistance has, so far, been marked.

Lighting use has been far less extensively studied than domestic space or water heating. Estimates of lighting use are still far from robust, and data sources are often in conflict. I have tried to generate my own estimates in the section that follows.

Of the total of 25 bulbs, most analysis of domestic lighting has found that in a typical house about four light bulbs are in high-usage locations. These might be used an average of 2.5 hours per day taken across the year. Medium-usage bulbs number about six. These average a use of about one hour a day or somewhat more, while the remaining 15 or so might commonly be used for about half an hour a day. Across the year, this means that the each bulb averages about an hour of use per day.

Larger houses have more lights, and those lights tend to be of higher wattage. Studies in the US show that detached houses use about twice as much energy for lighting as do flats or apartments. In the UK, lighting use is also strongly associated with income. A survey of low-income households showed an average of ten light bulbs, while a similar piece of

Table 8.1 *Summary of potential savings in lighting use*

Energy-saving measure for average house	Cost	Impact on CO_2 output per person per year
Replace all remaining conventional light bulbs with energy-efficient equivalents.	£80 to buy bulbs, but save £55 a year from lower bills	0.1 tonnes
Replace all remaining conventional light bulbs with energy-efficient equivalents and estimate the heat replacement effect.	£80 to buy bulbs, but save £35 a year from lower bills	0.07 tonnes
Reduce use of lighting in secondary locations by 25 per cent.	None: this will actually mean that the bill for replacing light bulbs will fall, albeit by a minimal amount, as well as reducing electricity bills	0.08 tonnes

research showed that middle- to high-income homes had 32. A comparison of these two UK surveys shows that the higher-income households had almost twice as many bulbs per main room as the less wealthy homes. It is a small example, but again shows that increasing prosperity has a sharp effect on fossil fuel consumption.

Published data shows that the number of hours during which lights are on varies greatly during the year, from under three hours in June to about nine hours in December. Furthermore, more lights are used at any one time in the dark hours of December than in high summer, suggesting that the total amount of demand for electricity for lighting in a house may vary by far more than a factor of three across the days of the year.

Nevertheless, the main issues for those interested in minimizing their carbon emissions are transparent: how do we reduce the wattage of the lights we use and the number of light bulbs in use at any one moment? First, we need a few paragraphs on technology.

THE VARIOUS TYPES OF LIGHT BULBS

UK homes have a choice of two main types of bulb – incandescent or fluorescent. In an incandescent bulb, the passage of electricity heats a thin metal element which then emits light. This is the old technology, originating in the 19th century. It is hugely inefficient, with almost all of the energy passing through the bulb being radiated as heat. Most UK light bulbs are still of this type. Ordinary incandescent light bulbs can be dimmed and are cheap and easy to replace.

Table 8.2 *Distribution of light bulb usage in a typical house*

Type of usage	Number	Average use per day
Light bulbs in high-usage locations	4	3 hours
Medium-usage locations	6	1.25 hours
Low-usage locations	15	0.5 hours
Total	25	About 27 hours' usage in total per day

Source: various, including data produced by the Market Transformation Programme

Halogen bulbs, whether they operate at 12 volts (V) or 240V, are of incandescent type. They are more expensive, last longer and give slightly more light output per unit of electricity consumed than the conventional incandescent bulb. But they still get very hot – wasting most of the energy they use.

Fluorescent bulbs are much more efficient. In a fluorescent bulb, an electric arc is created between the two ends of the lamp. The ultraviolet output from this arc excites mercury compounds on the wall of the tube, which in turn stimulate the internal phosphor coating to fluoresce, or create light.[139] Fluorescent lamps range from tubes several metres long that illuminate factories and offices, to increasingly tiny bulbs that can be used in almost all domestic light fittings. In technical language, small domestic bulbs of this type are called compact fluorescents (CFLs); but to most consumers they are just 'energy-efficient bulbs'. These smaller bulbs consist of much longer bulbs folded over one or more times. Sometimes they are even encased in a spherical glass container to resemble more closely a conventional incandescent light bulb. Fluorescent tubes are more expensive than incandescent bulbs, last perhaps ten times longer and generate four to five times the light per unit of electricity consumed.

In ten years' time, we might be starting to replace our compact fluorescents with light-emitting diode (LED) lights in the home. These bulbs are similar, for example, to those already used to power cycle lamps. LEDs are semiconductor devices that turn electricity directly into light, with very little generation of heat. Their power consumption is measured in fractions of 1W. These bulbs are currently very expensive (up to £15), usually only illuminate a small arc, and don't deliver a very attractive light. We tried to use some in our kitchen last year and took them out again after a few days because they didn't provide enough light and the colour seemed unpleasantly white. But LEDs are improving fast and prices will decline rapidly. In our off-grid family cottage in Wales, they already provide adequate reading light powered by a battery replenished by a solar panel. Eventually, I suspect, lighting will be largely derived from devices like LEDs – but not quite yet.

CULTURAL FORCES

Forty years ago, English homes were generally lit by pendant lights hanging from a ceiling in the middle of a room. Reading light was provided by standard lamps positioned near chairs. As prosperity has increased, so has the number and wattage of lights. Where a room had two lamps in the past, it might now have four. These four lamps are often positioned around the room, and the central hanging lamp is moving out of fashion. In smaller rooms, such as kitchens and bathrooms, the tendency to disperse light fittings has moved more rapidly. Refitted kitchens are generally equipped with large numbers of 20W halogens in glass-fronted cabinets and above the work surfaces. On average, the typical house is buying about one new light fitting a year, on top of the 25 or so currently present. This increase might suggest that household use of electricity is rising by 4 per cent a year – one fitting as a percentage of the 25 existing lights. But it is unlikely that these new fittings add as much to demand: some will be replacements for old lamps, others will be put in low-use locations and some will be lower wattage halogens replacing standard incandescent bulbs.

In fact, demand for electricity for domestic lights is thought to be rising at about 1 to 1.5 per cent per year. A surprising number of different uses of domestic energy are rising by about this percentage – hot water is a good example. This rate of growth is slightly slower than gross national product (GNP) growth, allowing the government to say that the economy is using less energy per unit of economic output, but also meaning that the UK's carbon dioxide emissions will continue to rise indefinitely.

The amount of lighting used is rising for two main reasons. Smaller households tend to use more electricity per head for lighting – there are fewer people to share the light. So, the decreasing average household size in the UK, resulting from family breakdown and from increasing numbers of people living alone, tends to increase the electricity demand for lighting.

More generally, householders want the level of illumination across the house to be higher than they did in the past. Well-lit houses are seen as more welcoming, comfortable and pleasant to be in. An ageing population also needs more light to carry out its day-to-day activities. People need much more light to read with as they get older.

Unfortunately perhaps, lighting is also a form of social display. A prosperous household demonstrates its wealth partly by broadcasting its light into the street and towards adjoining houses. Few households deliberately constrain their consumption of lighting; lights are left on even when rooms are empty. This is not an entirely trivial point – the generations that saw illumination as expensive or wasteful are gradually being replaced by those who know no such inhibitions and regard lighting as essentially cost free, or at least as being so cheap as not to be worth the effort of reducing use. The average yearly cost of household lighting is about £75 at August 2006 electricity prices, so this indifference is unsurprising. An active campaign to reduce lighting use might save a householder the price of a couple of bottles of wine a year. As societies get richer, there is a strong upward tendency in the amount of light that they demand, and this is going to be extremely difficult to choke off, even by continued steep rises in the price of electricity. International Energy Agency work suggests that lighting intensity rises proportionately far more as national income increases.

THE IMPACT OF COMPACT FLUORESCENTS

Compact fluorescents have been one of the most important energy-saving innovations of the past 25 years. Their scope to reduce electricity consumption is, at least in theory, substantial, although we can see no evidence yet in the UK that the electricity used for lighting has yet begun to decline. Although the typical home now has at least one CFL, the reduction in energy use has been outweighed by the increased numbers and wattages of other lights bulbs in the house.

Currently, about 9 million CFLs are sold each year in the UK to fit in the 600 million or so UK light fittings. This compares with sales of about 180 million ordinary incandescent bulbs. The number of CFLs sold is increasing; but if 25 million new light fittings are being installed in British houses every year, the percentage of energy-efficient bulbs is barely rising. Expressed in a more optimistic fashion, 9 million new CFLs – lasting ten times as long as ordinary incandescents – are supplying about half as much future lighting as the180 million new incandescents. So, energy-efficient bulbs are gaining market share even though they are not yet reducing total energy demand.

The typical incandescent bulb lasts about 1000 hours, or three years of use at one hour a day. With 600 million in use and purchases of 180 million a year, the sceptic will note that almost all of the bulbs that burn out are still replaced by ordinary incandescent bulbs. There's very little evidence of consumers buying CFLs as replacements when conventional light bulbs fail.

Table 8.3 shows how CFLs compare with other types of light bulbs. The figures in this table show that compact fluorescents are inferior to strip fluorescents in terms of working life and light output per unit of electricity used, but are much better than incandescent lamps, whether ordinary light bulbs or halogens.

About 70 per cent of UK households have one or more CFLs. The average number of CFLs in a house is about four, usually in higher-usage locations. This means that about 60 million CFLs are in use today, or about 10 per cent of the total light bulbs in the UK. If, on average, they are used two hours a day – because they are in high-usage locations – they are supplying 20 per cent of the light in UK homes. This is a far-from-impressive figure after almost ten years of active promotion, including the huge number of free bulbs handed out as part of the energy-efficiency obligation imposed on the electricity companies.

Table 8.3 *Comparison of the main types of lighting*

	Light (lumens) per watt (W) of electricity	Typical length of working life hours	Index of light quality* (100 is optimal)
Standard incandescent	12	1000	95
Low-voltage (12V) halogen	15	3000	95
Mains-voltage halogen	20	2000	95
Strip fluorescent	80	15,000	75
Compact fluorescent	50	10,000	85
Light-emitting diode (LED) light bulbs	Eventually 150	Up to 100,000	Not yet certain, but some lamps can achieve 80 already

*Note:** Colour rendering index (CRI): a measure of how well the light enables a person to see colour accurately. Any figure over 80 is usually regarded as acceptable.

Today's sales of 9 million units a year are probably increasing the share of domestic lighting held by CFLs by about 2 per cent a year; so, in five years' time, compact fluorescents might be responsible for 30 per cent of domestic light. In the face of the growing cultural preference for high levels of light, and for increasing the number of lights on at any one time, this increase is not likely to be enough to completely halt the growth in electricity demand for lighting.

SO WHY HAVE COMPACT FLUORESCENTS NOT TAKEN OVER?

Until a couple of years ago, CFLs were only suitable for larger light fittings. We all experienced the disappointment of trying to put compact fluorescents in standard light fittings, only to find that the tubes bulged over the top of the shade. But CFLs can now be found that fit almost all sizes of fitting. They need take no more space than the equivalent incandescent, although the smaller sizes have not yet arrived in the main shopping chains.

CFLs remain more expensive than the equivalent incandescent, though the price differential has fallen markedly. An ordinary light bulb might cost 60 pence; but a CFL alternative could cost seven times as much. Of course, the bulb will last ten times as long, so the cost per hour of use is much lower. And the electricity cost is about one quarter. So, over a year, replacing a 60W bulb with a 15W CFL will save about £1 per hour of daily use. The typical bulb is on for an hour a day; therefore, only in locations of heavy use will the purchase be obviously financially advantageous to the homeowner.

The problem is actually more severe. It is a suspicion rarely voiced by those who want us to switch to fluorescents; but most householders seem not to particularly like CFLs. Today, they don't flicker and hum like the first generation; but they can still take several minutes to warm up to full light and don't seem quite to deliver the lighting power that is claimed. Their colour rendering is also slightly less appealing (see Table 8.3) and, as a result, make the room somewhat less friendly and warm. In my view, this means that CFLs will struggle to replace a large number of today's incandescent bulbs.

What is the evidence from the UK's largest retailer? When I did a swift survey, Tesco had a range of 59 bulbs for sale in its online store.[140] Only four of these bulbs were of the compact fluorescent type. As the nation's most ruthless follower of consumer tastes, Tesco is telling us something: CFLs aren't popular (but many specialist internet lighting retailers sell a full range of CFLs, large and small, bayonet and screw fitting).

The government is much more optimistic about the savings to be made from increasing use of CFLs. Its working documents show sharp inflections downwards in the previously consistent upward growth of electricity demand for domestic lighting occurring next year.

Estimates from government documents suggest that electricity use for lighting will fall by about 15 per cent from 2005 to 2010, a rate of about 3 per cent per year. My rough calculations suggest that this would require the number of CFLs sold to double immediately. Is this just pious hope? Probably. None of the various ideas that government officials present for increasing use of CFLs stand much chance of doing more than edging up sales up gradually. This phenomenon is all too common – official energy-use projections for car travel, air travel and home electric appliances, as well as lighting, all show an abrupt fall in greenhouse gas emissions a few years into the future. The evidence to back up these optimistic projections is almost invariably weak, unconvincing or completely missing.

What would be the impact of switching all of your bulbs to the CFL variety?

MAKING YOUR HOUSE 100 PER CENT COMPACT FLUORESCENT

Here are the figures for a reasonably typical house that already uses four CFLs and has a total electricity use for lighting of about 750kWh:

- Assume four CFLs in the house already. These might use about 40kWh/year
- The 21 other bulbs are of the incandescent type, providing 23 hours of daily light in total.
- These 21 bulbs average 85W each and, in total, use about 710kWh/year. Total energy demand for lighting is 750kWh/year.
- Replacing the incandescent bulbs with CFLs would save about 550kWh/year and reduce total lighting demand to little more than 200kWh/year.

- The saving would be about 15 per cent of total household electricity use.
- This equates to a saving of about 240kg of carbon dioxide, or about 100kg per person per year.

Saving 240kg of carbon dioxide will reduce your electricity bill by about £55. Some retailers are now offering significantly lower prices and it makes sense to look around. The investment will be perhaps £80 in new bulbs. These 21 extra bulbs will typically last more than ten years at the relatively low rate of use implied in this calculation. Over ten years, the carbon dioxide saving would be 2.4 tonnes. So the returns from switching to 100 per cent energy-efficient bulbs are good – about £35 per tonne of carbon reduction. The savings are therefore relatively small, but cheap to achieve.

In France, which has low electricity consumption for lighting purposes (about 450kWh/year), a 1998 survey showed that a switch to compact fluorescents reduced electricity use by almost 75 per cent.[141] An Italian study showed that replacing the six most highly used bulbs in the house captured 85 per cent of the potential savings.[142]

ELECTRICITY CONSUMPTION FOR LIGHTING: DATA FROM OTHER COUNTRIES[143]

Electricity consumption for lighting varies hugely. US houses use almost 2000kWh/year, whereas Greek homes take less than 400kWh/year for lighting purposes. The average European household uses about 560kWh/year, compared to the UK figure of 750kWh/year. The UK's relatively high total is partly accounted for by the longer hours of night in winter than in Southern Europe. But Denmark, a country on a similar latitude to the UK, only had consumption of 426kWh/year, largely because it uses much more efficient lamps. Germany's figures are very similar to the UK. According to another source, across the EU, lighting takes about 19 per cent of domestic electricity demand, excluding heating and cooking, compared to my estimate of about 20 per cent in the UK.[144]

But note that the actual carbon savings must be reduced by the 'heat replacement effect'. Having inefficient light bulbs helps to heat the house in winter. Since lighting is largely used at the same time as the house needs heating, perhaps 70 per cent of the waste heat from incandescent bulbs replaces heating fuel. If the house is heated by gas, then at least 1kWh of heating from electricity replaces 1kWh of gas in the heating season. However, gas is a much less carbon-intensive fuel than electricity, so there are still substantial carbon dioxide savings from not using incandescent bulbs to heat your home. I calculate that the net impact, even after the heat replacement effect, of switching entirely to CFLs for an ordinary house is more than 160kg of carbon dioxide a year, or about 70kg per person.

I think we should ignore the heat effect in estimating the carbon dioxide savings from switching to energy-efficient bulbs. Lighting tends to be used at times of the highest energy demand – early evening on winter nights. At these times, the carbon content of electricity generation is at its highest. Most power stations will be working, including the highly polluting coal-fired stations, and the average CO_2 emissions from 1kWh hour of generation will be higher than, say, in the middle of the night when it might be just the nuclear fleet, with zero measured emissions. And, second, a house that switches to all CFLs will almost certainly be much more conscious of lighting use – we can expect that actual hours of use will fall.

9

household appliances

The biggest users of electricity around the home are the tumble dryer, the refrigerator and the washing machine. New fridge freezers – provided that they are not American-style behemoths – can save up to 50 per cent of their energy use. If you feel you must use a tumble dryer, buy a gas-powered one or one with a heat exchanger. The extra cost will be perhaps £150 and the carbon saving is about 100kg per year.

The next greediest device is the television. The rule here is simple – buy a small liquid crystal display (LCD) screen to replace your old cathode ray tube-based TV. It will save the household 60kg per year in emissions, or about 25kg per person in the average 2.3 person family group. Big flat-screen TVs are prodigious consumers of electricity – avoid them.

Sky boxes are insidious users of power, even when not actually working. If you can get rid of digital satellite or cable, do so and replace it with Freeview. Buy a box with low standby power consumption, or make a religion of turning the box off at all times when not in use.

Other steps to improve electricity use can easily reduce consumption by another 10 per cent (simply turning everything off at the wall when not in use may save 10 per cent by itself in the average household). In an ordinary house, emissions from electricity can be reduced to below 0.6 tonnes per person with very little cost in terms of lifestyle.

A nnual electricity use by the typical household that uses mains gas for its heating is about 3700kWh, or 'units' in conventional usage. Deducting approximately 750kWh/year for lighting leaves about 2950kWh/year for other appliances, or about 1.4 tonnes of carbon dioxide. This figure is rising slowly here as well as in other countries. In The Netherlands, for example, electricity use in the home rose by 2.8 per cent a year in the period 1995 to 2002 compared to about 1.7 per cent in the UK.[145, 146]

The estimates in Table 9.1 of the cost per tonne of carbon dioxide saved assume that the house has an existing appliance of typical household efficiency, bought eight or so years ago. It compares the electrical consumption of the best new appliance with this figure. This produces a cost per tonne of carbon dioxide saved, and the numbers are all high. For people who have already decided to buy a new machine, the figures will be lower because, in these cases, it would be more appropriate to calculate the incremental cost of the best new machine over a typical model in the shops today. These figures are given in the text.

The cheapest way of reducing carbon emissions is to use appliances less frequently, to minimize standby losses by disconnecting devices and to buy smaller machines, particularly TVs. These points are discussed extensively in the following sections.

'WET' APPLIANCES

We will look, in turn, at the costs of running the major electric appliances in the home.

'Wet' appliances are those we use to wash or dry clothes, or to wash our dishes. The International Energy Agency reports that they 'typically account for 20 to 30 per cent of both the energy consumption and the water consumption in the average European home'.[147]

Table 9.1 *Electricity use by the major home appliances*[148]

	Average today (kWh/year)*	Best practice (kWh/year)	Approximate cost of new machine to achieve best practice (£)	Cost per tonne of CO_2 saved (£)**	Comment
Washing machine	270	200	300	660	More important to fill properly than to buy new machine
Tumble dryer	400	240	490	475	Spin efficiency in washing machine vital
Dishwasher	300	200	250	390	More important to fill properly than to buy new machine
Fridge	250	120	200	240	Keep in cold place
Fridge freezer	500	280	230	155	
Freezer	350	240	300	420	
Kettle	150	100	35	325	
TV (two to three per home)	500	400***	Depends on size	–	Important to buy small LCD screen
Small appliances	500	500	Various	–	
Consumer entertainment	100	100	Various	–	Most electricty used in standby
Computer	150	75	500	3,100	Laptop better than PC
Standby	400	100	Not available	–	Easiest saving to make
Wall transformers	80	40	Not available	–	

Notes: *The typical home does not have all of these appliances, so the total electricity consumption in the table is greater than the average for all households.

**Assumes 15-year life, except computer and kettle (five years).

***Based on three 26-inch screens.

Washing machines

Washing machines are to be found in about 95 per cent of UK household and are used an average of about 270 times a year, or five or so times a week. Most machines can operate at least three temperatures, and estimates have been made of the frequency of use during the year. These are shown in Table 9.2.

The typical washing machine now gurgling and splashing away in a British home uses about 1kWh per wash. So, in total, washing consumes about 270kWh/year, or just under 10 per cent of all electricity consumption, excluding lighting. The majority of this electricity is used to heat the cold water up to the wash temperature and to keep it there. In energy terms, one can think of a washing machine as a device for heating water by electricity.

Almost all washing machines now sold in the UK are filled from the cold tap and don't have a connection to the hot water system. Machines fed by hot water will tend to be more efficient because it costs less – in money and carbon dioxide – to heat water using gas rather than in the washing machine. In the US, for example, machines are generally hot water filled.

The electricity taken by the washing machine might cost £27 per year and results in over 120kg of carbon dioxide emissions. In addition, of course, washing machines use large amounts of water. A wasteful older machine, perhaps eight years from purchase, might get through 100 litres of water per wash, or 27,000 litres in a year. In a home with a water meter, this would cost up to £50 in charges from the supplier. So surprisingly perhaps, the cost in water supply may well be almost twice the figure for electricity. The careful consumer will be right to look more closely at water consumption figures when the household needs a new washing machine rather than at electricity charges.

Technical advances mean that today's machines use less energy and fewer litres of water. Less water to heat means lower electricity consumption, as well. These improvements have been encouraged by a reasonably effective energy labelling scheme mandated by the European Union (EU). Top-class washing machines with a 6kg washing capacity now use about 0.7 or 0.8kWh per 40 degree Celsius wash. Strangely, the EU energy standards measure the

Table 9.2 *Number of washes in a typical UK home*

Temperature (degrees Celsius)	Washes per year
90	5
60	83
40	186
Total	274

Source: Market Transformation Programme (2006)

electricity consumption at 60 degrees Celsius, not 40 degrees, and typically the figure for this test, legally required to be visible on all new washing machines, is now only slightly in excess of 1kWh. So, when buying a 6kg capacity washing machine, look for a figure of about 1.0 to 1.1kWh per wash on the label, and proportionately less for a 5kg machine. In a full machine, the best performing appliances will use under 0.17kWh per kilogram of washing.

Just because a machine is 'A' rated doesn't mean that it necessarily delivers efficiency of this level. The band for the 'A' category for washing machines is wide and only the best examples in the category are worth buying. As far as I can see, compared to a standard 'A' grade machine, the incremental cost of buying a really efficient washer is negligible.

Please don't be confused by the coincidence of the typical 1kW figure both for typical consumption by an older machine working away in a house today and the required figure to achieve a good 'A' rating. The typical cycle today is at 40 degrees Celsius. For a 40 degree cycle, a new machine might actually use about one third less electricity than is shown on the EU energy-efficiency label, which is assuming a 60 degree Celsius wash.

New machines are substantially more efficient than washers bought some years ago. The saving from simply switching from an eight-year-old machine to a new washer will be approximately 0.3kWh per 40 degree wash, or something like 85kWh/year. This might reduce your electricity bill by about £8 and your household carbon dioxide by about 40kg. It is therefore very difficult to encourage the householder to buy a new washing machine when the carbon savings are so small. Furthermore, a new washing machine is a fairly substantial piece of equipment and requires a lot of energy to make. It may be better to wait for your old machine to wear out.

However, water consumption is now a lot lower than for older machines. Good models can deliver their washes with less than 50 litres, or no more than half the most inefficient older models. The metered householder – now about 25 per cent of the UK total – will see savings of perhaps £25 a year. This may actually be a better financial reason to buy a machine a couple of years early than the savings in energy. (Note that there will be some indirect savings in carbon dioxide from the water company not having to push the washing water to the customer and to process it when it comes back through the sewers. Based on figures from Southern Water, the carbon dioxide savings at the water company from a householder switching to a new washing machine may be about 12kg a year.)

Are washing machines going to get much more efficient? Probably not: the savings are now largely captured and the large majority of electricity used in the machine is now used to heat the water. We're close to the limits imposed by the laws of physics. In theory, the trend towards increasing the washing capacity of the typical machine might yield some efficiency savings – fewer washes will be required. But the energy benefit of washing a larger weight of clothes in one wash rather than two will almost certainly be outweighed by an increased tendency to run the machine when it is not full. Therefore, buying a machine which can wash 9kg, rather than 6kg, may actually result in less energy-efficient operation. Be aware of this – and buy a machine whose size is best suited to your household needs.

Do the key figures for washing machine performance vary much across Europe? A recent Germany study indicates very similar results to those used in this section.[149] The researchers estimated that the average German washing machine was 14 years old when taken to a recycling centre. The typical retired washing machine was about 40 per cent less efficient in energy terms than 2004 models and consumed twice as much water.

I suspect that most people only look at the energy-efficiency rating of the *washing* cycle of a new washing machine. This is the wrong decision: they should actually pay more attention to the rating of the efficiency of the *spin* cycle if they intend to dry the clothes in a tumble dryer.

Why? Just as, in energy terms, a washing machine is little more than a device for heating water, a tumble dryer is a machine for evaporating it. Evaporating water is expensive – far more energy-intensive than washing the clothes in the first place. An 'A'-rated tumble dryer consumes about three times as much energy as a similarly classified washing machine per kilogram of dry clothes.

Buyers should therefore focus on getting a washing machine that leaves the clothes as dry as possible in order to minimize the energy consumption of the tumble dryer. The moisture level of clothes coming out of a washing machine, and how much energy they require to get completely dry, is largely dependent upon the maximum spin speeds of the machine and the number of holes in the drum through which water can escape. Generally speaking, it requires spin speeds of more than about 1400 revolutions per minute (rpm) to achieve the 'A' grade for spin efficiency. Manufacturers will need to charge more for spin speeds of 1400 rpm compared to 1000 rpm. The size and number of holes in the drum is a more complex trade-off. A drum that is more hole than metal will be good at draining water away; but it will need to be thicker and heavier in order to withstand the huge centrifugal forces experienced by something rotating 20 times or more a second. These drums are therefore more costly to produce.

How much will a good spin cycle in the washing machine reduce the energy needed to run the tumble dryer? Compare two washing machines: models rated A and C for spin efficiency:

- The A-rated washing machine will leave 3kg of dry weight of clothes with no more than 1.35kg of water.
- The C-rated washing machine will have no more than 1.89kg of water.
- The difference is 0.54kg of water. This will take approximately 0.9kWh to evaporate (this includes an estimate of the energy losses in the machine and is not just what physicists call the 'latent heat of evaporation', which is about half the total).

- Not all of the average household's 270 washes a year go into the tumble dryer. Only perhaps 150 do. So, the total saving in drying costs from getting a machine with a more efficient spin cycle may be as much as 135kWh/year. This equates to £13 of electricity cost and nearly 60kg of carbon dioxide.

The limited evidence that I can find suggests that the typical washing machine is used about twice as often as it should be. Rather than filling the typical wash with about 2kg of clothes – a figure that *Which?* apparently found in a household survey – it should be perfectly possible to aim for at least 4kg per wash. This would reduce the number of washes by 50 per cent. The reduction in energy use would not be as great as this, but could still be substantial. Savings of 100kWh/year would probably be possible, reducing emissions by 45kg.

Weigh your washing the next time you use the machine. Are you filling it close to its capacity, or are you wasting energy, heating up water for a bigger load than will actually be used?

It may also be that we could choose to wash our clothes less frequently. This might not be quite as bad as it sounds. Rather than wear lightly coloured clothes, likely to be marked on one wearing, we could switch to deeper colours, upon which the impact of day-to-day

---

HOW MUCH EXTRA DOES IT COST
TO GET GOOD SPIN EFFICIENCY?

As of March 2006, the John Lewis website was selling 45 models of washing machine, some of which are washer/dryers. Almost all of the washing-only machines were graded A for energy efficiency.

Only 11 of the 45 were rated A for spin efficiency. Four attracted a C ranking and 30 a B.

The machines graded C for spin efficiency were all among the cheapest. Three were priced at £199. To get a B machine one had to spend £219, or £20 more. But to get an A machine required a minimum expenditure of £399, or £180 more than the cheapest B.

The carbon savings achieved by moving from C to B are about equal to those achieved by moving from B to A. Getting a B-grade machine, rather than a C, clearly makes good sense: a minimum extra purchase price of £20 extra in return for savings of £6 and 30kg of carbon a year. If the machine lasts ten years, then the cost of carbon saved is £67 per tonne.

The case for going to an A-rated spin efficiency machine is not as clear. To get savings of another 30kg of carbon (a total of 60kg, as written above) is going to cost up to £180. So the cost of carbon saving is £600 a tonne.

Of course, the decision is going to be complicated by the sort of features that a family wants and various other considerations; but it is probably worth spending an extra £50 or so to get A-ranked spin efficiency above what you'd be happy to pay for a B label. Any more, and you should think about planting some trees instead and capturing the carbon that way.

activities would be less visible. But since this book is aimed at ordinary people seeking to remain part of conventional society, I won't suggest switching entirely to dressing in rarely washed polyester fleeces or hand washing of garments in the nearest river.

Tumble dryers

Tumble dryers are a good example of the developed world's continuing tendency to use more electricity without really noticing it. These machines have become standard items in

---

COOLING THE HOUSE BY DRYING CLOTHES IN IT

To get water to evaporate and change from being a liquid to a gas requires prodigious amounts of energy. We see this around us in a number of different ways:

- A kettle that is boiling isn't raising the temperature of the liquid beyond 100 degrees Celsius. Almost the entire energy from the kettle's element is being used to evaporate the water. But it still takes a long while to boil away the kettle's contents.
- Sweating is highly effective at keeping us at the right temperature. The evaporation of the water from the skin takes energy from the body, and even quite small volumes of water maintain the human body at very close to its correct temperature.
- Draping wet clothes around a fire to get them dry also uses a large amount of energy It takes about 0.8kWh of energy to evaporate 1 litre of water. This will cool the room To maintain the temperature at the desired level in the heating season, the central heating system will have to replace this loss.

Of course, when water vapour condenses back into a liquid, the heat energy is recaptured by the room. But even the best-insulated modern houses rotate the air in a house every hour or so. So, most of the energy from condensation will be lost to the house. Or perhaps the vapour will condense onto cold windows, where it will be partly lost by conduction to the outside world.

The important point is this: drying clothes inside a house will always cause a heat loss. The only way to avoid this is to dry them on a line outside the home. On wet winter days, this is impossible. The net energy effect of drying clothes in a tumble dryer in winter, above and beyond what happens by drying clothes over radiators or in an airing cupboard, may be not much more than half the gross energy cost of the operation of the dryer.

Of course, most home heating is carried out by gas; but dryers use electricity. Because the carbon cost of gas is less than half that of electricity, this still means it is much better to dry clothes in the home than it is to put them in the dryer.

In the summer, the rational householder uses washing spread about the house to help keep the building cool. A tumble dryer does not have this effect. A few wet towels placed around a hot room will have a significant cooling effect in the warmest months.

middle-class homes over the past 30 years, adding significant amounts to energy consumption. They make life easier and have replaced the often inconvenient and troublesome use of the clothes line or the airing cupboard. Two types of machine predominate: the venting type, which evacuates the hot damp air to the outside, and the condenser, which keeps the heat in the house and transfers the surplus water to a storage tank in the machine.

Most of us using tumble dryers have a strong sense that these machines – useful though they are – are prodigious consumers of electricity. The 40 per cent of homeowners who have tumble dryers will not be surprised to learn that they use about 400kWh of electricity a year, costing somewhere around £40. For an otherwise average household, the purchase of a tumble dryer would increase home electricity bills by over 10 per cent. In these homes, the tumble dryer will typically be eating considerably more electricity than the washing machine (400kWh/year versus 270kWh/year), though it will be used far less often.

But the arguments about the wickedness of tumble dryers do somewhat exaggerate the problem. It's not just the usual benefit that comes from the appliance heating the house in winter, but also that drying clothes inside a house will always use energy, even if they are draped over radiators.

Condensing dryers take about 10 per cent more electricity than venting products. Because all of the heat from the condensing dryer remains in the house, and thus reduces the need for central heating, a condensing machine probably costs less to run even though they appear to use slightly more energy.

Vented tumble dryers are actually worse for the energy balance of the house than you might think. When the machine is working, hot air is pushed out from the room containing the dryer. This means that new, cold, air will be pulled into the house. This increases the load on the central heating system.

The typical home uses the dryer about 150 times a year. The machine is generally loaded with about 3kg of clothing (and the associated moisture, of course). The cycle typically uses about 2.7kWh and costs about 25 to 30 pence. Tumble dryers operate at about 2kW, meaning that the machine is typically on for between an hour and an hour and a half each time it is used. Studies show that about 35 per cent of households with dryers use them all year round, even when it is warm, windy and sunny outside.

Rather surprisingly, the authorities seem to have put little effort into improving the energy efficiencies of these products. Perhaps the scope for reducing electricity consumption is too small, or the differences between different machines too marginal. In any event, today's dryers seem to use more electricity than ten years ago. This observation may, however, be derived from homeowners using the machines to achieve a dryer finish than they were previously accustomed to. This slight change in behaviour would, of course, be consistent with what we observe in other areas; the relatively low cost of electricity, particularly expressed in terms of household disposable income, means that normal rational people will use electricity more and their own labour less. This is still true even at today's increased prices. To a person unconcerned by global warming, a cost of 25 pence to dry clothes is nothing compared with the effort to put out the washing, peg it onto a line and then return to collect it.

Almost all washing machines sold in the UK now achieve an A rating (for energy efficiency, but not for spin effectiveness); but I could find few tumble dryers that got better than a C, though I am sure they must exist.

What should the concerned homeowner do about tumble dryers? The purists, of course, are united on this issue. We should wheel them out of our kitchens and go back to drying clothes on an outside line or in the boiler cupboard. We should use clothes that dry easily and, dare I say it, wash them less often. Some very green people whom I know take this principal a little too far.

These radical solutions will not generally appeal, perhaps even to those who recognize the severity of the climate change problem. Nevertheless, we do need to understand that tumble dryers are one of the many types of relatively new machines that provide the upwards momentum to household energy use. We can't reduce our carbon dioxide emissions if we add new appliances as fast as we increase the efficiency of others.

What can be done without too much disruption? We can use the machines less often and stop the cycle when the clothes are almost dry, rather than ready to put in the cupboard. The final drying can occur in front of a radiator, or over the hot water tank. A clothes line in summer will leave the clothes with a fresh feel, and a dry, sunny and windy day in winter will get the clothes dry faster than we might think. We can also ensure that the dryer is in a warm room because otherwise it will have to raise the temperature of the air in the machine by a larger amount, and the heat it generates will be wasted.

To get significant improvements in the carbon emissions resulting from the use of tumble dryers, we have two main options. Neither is perfect:

1   an electric tumble dryer with a condenser and a heat pump to recycle the heat;
2   gas-powered condenser dryers.

Electric condenser dryers with heat pumps

The primary reason that most tumble dryers in UK shops only achieve a 'C' energy rating is that a lot of the heat used in the machine is wasted. A heat pump system that improves the efficiency of the dryer is perhaps the easiest way of achieving significant reductions in electricity use. The heat pump recaptures some of the energy, but it adds considerably to the price.

As far as I can see, there is only one heat pump dryer available in the UK market.[150] Made by AEG Electrolux, it claims to reduce energy use by over 40 per cent over a very

Table 9.3 *Comparison of tumble dryers with and without a heat pump*

	AEG T59800	AEG T56800
Energy cost per full cycle	2.4kWh	4.2kWh
Noise	66dB	64dB
Condenser tank capacity	3.6 litres	3.6 litres

Source: AEG-Electrolux product manuals, available at www.aeg-electrolux.co.uk

long drying programme. This model – the AEG T59800 – was sold online in August 2006 for about £490. An AEG model of similar characteristics but without a heat pump, the T56800, sells for about £360, so the premium for the heat pump is about £130.

None of the websites I looked at seemed to understand the importance of the heat pump in reducing energy costs to the consumer. It is a difficult story to understand and communicate; but over a typical year the savings will be about 160kWh (£16) and the emissions reductions over 70kg. Over a fifteen-year life, the machine will save over one tonne of carbon dioxide, at a cost of about £170. This makes it an interesting way of reducing emissions, particularly in a big household that uses a clothes dryer frequently, but not an obvious priority. In terms of cash payback, at September 2006 electricity prices, the incremental cost will take over seven years to pay for itself in the average household.

Gas-powered dryers

Gas-powered dryers are more efficient than electric dryers in the same way that gas heating produces less carbon than electric heating. It uses a primary fuel source (gas), rather than a source which has itself been converted from gas and then transmitted to the home (electricity).

One manufacturer makes gas-fuelled dryers for the UK market. This company – Crosslee – makes the White Knight brand and claims savings as much as two-thirds of the cost of running an electric dryer. From the information that the company provides, the energy consumption of the gas dryers seems very slightly higher than for electric models; but because gas is very much cheaper than electricity per kilowatt hour, the cost is much lower. At current electricity and gas prices, the typical user will save about £30 and almost 100kg of carbon dioxide a year by using gas.

Crosslee's gas dryers are not widely available, but can be bought from some websites. The prices of the dryer itself are not out of line with conventional models and may actually be slightly cheaper than electric dryers with similar features. The issue, of course, is plumbing gas to the machine. Let's assume that it costs £150 to get an installer to fit the dryer. If it lasts 12 years, it will save 1.2 tonnes of carbon dioxide and the cost per tonne saved will be about £125. This makes it quite a good investment.

Combined washer dryers

Many people seek to save space by combining washing and drying in one machine. Research suggests to me that there is a slight cost in energy efficiency from buying one machine rather than two (this is the opposite finding to the comparison for fridges and freezers on page 153). The average washer dryer on the John Lewis website had combined consumption of 5.1kWh for a full cycle. If a good washing machine has usage of 1.1kWh (for a 60 degree Celsius wash) and a condenser dryer about 3kWh, the incremental cost is about 1kWh per use.

Dishwashers

Readers will not be surprised to know that academics at a German university have carefully compared the energy and water consumption patterns of hand dish-washing and machine washing.[151] Which method of washing dirty dishes used less energy?

The core conclusion of this very interesting work is that the hot water used by the average European to hand wash a full dishwasher load of dishes would take 2.5kWh to heat. Since new dishwashers today require just over 1kWh for an entire 65 degrees Celsius cycle, the researchers conclude that dishwashers are energy efficient. Unfortunately, this is probably not a robust conclusion:

- A dishwasher uses electricity to heat water to wash the dishes. 1kWh of electricity equates to 0.43kg of carbon dioxide emissions.
- In a household using gas for water heating, 2.5kWh of heat requires about 3.3kWh of gas to be burned in a boiler that is 75 per cent efficient (this is about the average figure for the UK). This produces about 0.63kg of carbon dioxide.
- Dishwashers look better. But they have to be full for the benefit to be realized. If half empty, or as badly loaded as they typically are in our household, then the energy cost is the same. In this case, hand washing would be more effective in energy terms.
- The situation is made even less clear by the findings of the German researchers on British habits when it comes to washing dishes. The Germans observed that the British subjects used far less water than average to clean the dishes (they also left them dirtier than any other nationality). So, the balance is even further in favour of hand washing.
- In our household, doubts about the efficacy of our dishwasher mean that we actually pre-wash some of the dirtier plates in running hot water. This makes it even clearer that

we would do better by washing by hand, as long as we did so in a bowl of hot water and not under a constantly running tap.

- As a final thought, the standby power used by dishwashers when not in use also adds to the advantage of hand washing (but, to be really picky, a dishwasher also helps to keep the kitchen warm, and so replaces some gas heating).

Energy-efficiency buffs always say that it makes sense to use a dishwasher. But actually the evidence doesn't really bear this out as clearly as it seems. Although a typical dishwasher uses quite small amounts of water – as little as 14 litres in new models, or less than one quarter of that used by a good washing machine – the fact that this water is heated by electricity means that carbon dioxide and energy costs may be higher when compared to hand washing water heated by gas. This would be particularly true in a household with a high-efficiency condensing boiler for water heating, or if the householder has a surplus of solar-heated water in the summer.

George Marshall's eco-renovation website, www.theyellowhouse.org.uk, has a good go at dishwasher manufacturers for not having hot water feed models that would allow the householder to power the dishwasher with water heated by gas. Of course, he is right; but we are all now too used to being able to turn on the dishwasher whenever we want, and not just when the boiler has heated hot water.

About 27 per cent of UK households have automatic dishwashers, a much lower number than in most European countries. On average, the household uses these appliances about 250 times a year, or about five times a week (this number appears to be falling as households eat less at home). The installed population of dishwashers typically uses about 1.2kWh per cycle, implying a yearly electricity consumption of about 300kWh. Buying one of the newest models might reduce the consumption by one third, saving 100kWh/year, or 45kg of carbon dioxide, and with a financial benefit of £10. Provided that the householder's old dishwasher is working reasonably well, there is little financial reason to switch to a new model as the cost per tonne of CO_2 saved is about £390.[152]

Dishwashers clean plates more effectively than all but the best hand washer. But, as we have seen, they aren't necessarily more energy efficient. The implications for committed dishwasher users are clear: the machines should only be used when absolutely full. When the cycle is finished, the machine should be turned off in order to minimize standby power consumption.

Some research data suggests that the typical user only manages to fill the dishwasher to half its capacity before turning it on. In our case, this is certainly true. The shape of our plates makes it difficult to fit in a full load, and we would certainly benefit from buying new tableware. But the saving in cash terms from being able to run the dishwasher less frequently might only be £10 a year, not enough to pay for the cost of new plates and cups.

If the householder has surplus hot water from solar panels, then it makes a lot of sense to break the habit of using a machine and to wash the dishes with the free hot water in the months of high summer. The water is certainly abundant enough in June and July in our house.

As with many electrical appliances, most of the potential energy-efficiency savings were captured at least five years ago. Improvements are now marginal. So, once again, the crucial change may not be to buy a new and more energy-efficient machine. Rather, it is probably to use the existing machine in a way that maximizes its effectiveness, using it less frequently and in an intelligent way that reduces its total energy use.

'COLD' APPLIANCES

Major improvements have taken place in the energy efficiency of fridges and freezers over the last ten years. The EU Energy Labelling Scheme has been very effective at improving the typical energy consumption of new machines. In 1995, the average fridge freezer in the shops would consume over 600kWh of electricity a year, or about 20 per cent of total electricity consumption, including lighting. The ten cheapest fridge freezers in John Lewis in March 2006 are projected to use an average of 318kWh, a reduction of over 45 per cent. The best ones are now well below 300kWh, but cost no more than other machines.

Industry studies suggest that the total electricity consumption of cold appliances, including all types of fridge and freezer, has fallen by about 25 per cent in the last ten years. This is a rare success story; efforts to improve efficiency have worked, and have not been entirely compensated for by increased size of appliance or by a greater number of fridges or freezers in the home. If there is an energy-efficiency success story, this is it.

The dramatic improvements in energy use have come largely by improving the insulation of the doors and walls of cold appliances. Very approximately, 80 per cent of the running costs of an appliance are due to heat coming in through the external covering. Only about 10 per cent comes from the energy cost of opening doors, and the remaining 10 per cent from the impact of cooling the food that is placed in the fridge or freezer. Still greater efficiency is possible in the insulation of walls and doors, so we should see a slow decline in the energy consumption of new machines.

Household ownership of cold appliances

The average UK household owns about 1.5 cold appliances. Almost all households have either a fridge or a fridge freezer. Slightly less than half of all homes also have a separate freezer.

The total electricity consumption from these devices averages about 500kWh/year. A house with just a new fridge, and no freezer, may have a lower usage of perhaps

160kWh/year, while a home with ten-year-old fridge freezer and a separate freezer might be using over 1000 kWh/year, or over one quarter of total average electricity consumption.

As with UK school exams, merely getting an A grade for energy efficiency is not necessarily good enough. The range of A performance is so wide. It is worth looking for A+ and A++ machines, although they are generally few and far between in the UK retail market.

The electricity consumption figures above are calculated by running the machines in a laboratory at a consistent temperature. They do not pretend to be an accurate assessment of actual electricity consumption when the machine is in ordinary domestic use. For example, the tests do not involve any opening or closing of the fridge door. However, independent studies have shown that the laboratory tests are reasonably accurate predictors of the actual electricity use. Although the tests do not simulate real household conditions, the laboratory is kept at a high temperature compared to the typical home. This has the effect of increasing electricity consumption because of the larger heat difference that the appliance has to maintain between the cold inside and the warm outside.

Testers in other countries do attempt to model the real use of cold appliances more accurately. Japanese tests, for example, include measurement of the effect of opening and closing the fridge door 50 times a day. Not surprisingly, other testers regard this as excessive and have tended to use 25 door openings as their standard. However, the time between opening and closing is set at 10 seconds, which anybody observing a small child trying to decide between four flavours of yoghurt will know is hopelessly insufficient.

The main tips for reducing energy use

Whether or not the household fridge is a new, shiny, curved stainless steel appliance or a grubby enamelled veteran, good practice can reduce energy use. The most important advice is probably to try to put fridges and freezers in the coldest room in the house. Placing the appliances in an unheated storeroom may save over 30 per cent of electricity costs according to one European study. Putting the machines in a cold room minimizes the work they have to do to maintain a low temperature (this advice is the opposite from that for washing machines and dryers, which benefit from being in a hotter room). It may be an obvious point, but all fridges and freezers also need to be kept out of the sun. Some machines will not work properly when kept in a place that gets particularly cold, such as an un-insulated garage. Very low winter temperatures may mean that the machines' thermostats will not operate correctly.

The second important step is to run the appliances at the highest possible temperature consistent with food safety. According to a French study, the typical freezer is set 3 degrees below the recommended −18 degrees Celsius. It may be worth buying a thermometer to check that your appliances are achieving the right temperature.

The external coils that dissipate the heat extracted from inside the fridge or freezer should also be kept free of dust and dirt and need to be properly ventilated to allow the hot air easily to escape. If the seals on a fridge door are beginning to perish, it is almost certainly time to trade it in. Of course, there is an extra worry now; the coolant in fridges is often itself a powerful greenhouse gas – usually known as hydrofluorocarbon (HFC) – and this gas needs to be carefully removed to avoid it entering the atmosphere. When buying a new fridge, it is now thought to be preferable to look for a hydrocarbon-based coolant, usually going by the designation R600 or HC600a.

Fridge freezers

Table 9.4 shows that the scope for reducing electricity consumption by replacing an old fridge freezer is more substantial than for almost any other home appliance. The most energy-efficient fridge freezers I can find that are easily available in UK shops in August 2006 are made by Indesit. The BAAN10 and BAAN12 machines use 284kWh/year, at least according to the John Lewis website (the manufacturer is silent on this topic). These machines are not obviously more expensive than their less efficient equivalents with comparable internal space and electronic features. The cheaper machine in this range (the BAAN10) is on sale at John Lewis for £229, and though less expensive fridge freezers can be found at other shops, this A+ model does not look expensive by comparison to less energy-efficient brands.

Anyone buying the ultra-efficient Indesit machines will save over 300kWh/year compared to the average ten-year-old device. At today's electricity prices, this is worth £30 and the carbon dioxide saving is 130kg a year. So, all other things being equal, the average home electricity bill will fall by over 8 per cent simply by replacing an old fridge freezer with the best new one. In other words, you may even notice the difference in your electricity costs by buying one of the Indesit models. There are no other types of appliance of which this could generally be said when comparing with a ten-year-old equivalent.

The main disadvantage is that the range is not 'frost free' and ice will occasionally need to be scraped from the interior of the freezer compartment. Most other appliances currently on the market are advertised as frost free – this means that they have a cycle that will periodically defrost the freezer coils. Machines of this type are inherently less efficient

Table 9.4 *Approximate figures for electricity consumption of typical cold appliances*

	Percentage of household ownership	Average machines in shops ten years ago (kWh/year)	Reasonably efficient machines today (kWh/year)
Fridges (short and tall)	42	300	160
Fridge freezers	63	600	320
Freezers (upright and chest)	40	420	250

than the small number of models on the market today that are not frost free. Buying a frost-free fridge saves some effort and inconvenience, but may add 50 to 60kWh to the annual consumption, or 25kg of carbon dioxide or so. This is another instance of convenience being traded for energy efficiency.

Fridges

Small stand-alone fridges can now be strikingly efficient. Whereas the Indesit BAAN range of fridge freezers has yearly electricity consumption of 284kWh, the very best A+ fridges can now achieve figures as low as 120kWh or below (for comparison, this is less than the power consumption of today's generation of Sky boxes and no more than about 3 per cent of the typical household's electricity bill). The internal capacity of the most efficient fridges is small; but even full-size fridges now use as little as 160kWh/year or so.

Buy an efficient small fridge and the benefit of switching from a ten-year-old model may be as much 200kWh/year or £20. These models cost around £200, so the payback is ten years at August 2006 electricity prices. Over a fifteen-year life, the saving will be about 0.9 tonnes of carbon dioxide, implying a cost per tonne of carbon of over £220.

Freezers

Stand-alone freezers are in about 45 per cent of homes. There is a small swing towards upright freezers. A decade ago, the way to run an energy-efficient household would have been to have a chest freezer kept in a cold room, such as the garage, surrounded by sheets of extra insulation. A small fridge would be kept in a cool place in the kitchen, well away from sources of heat such as the cooker. Advances in insulation, particularly in fridge freezers, have made this a much less common arrangement.

A good energy-efficient large freezer, with a capacity of more than 150 litres, should use no more than about 240kWh/year. Smaller worktop height freezers should be obtainable with consumption of no more than about 200kWh/year. So, where possible, buy a smaller freezer, or fridge, rather than a larger version.

Which is more efficient – a fridge and a freezer, or a fridge freezer?

A full-height fridge freezer, standing about 1.80m tall, might typically have 180 litres of refrigerated capacity and 80 litres of freezer. A good model might use less than 320kWh/year.

A very good freestanding freezer that gives 80 to 100 litres useful space would use 180kWh/year and a 180 litre refrigerator might consume 160kWh/year. Added together, the consumption of even very good individual machines will almost certainly be greater than a fridge freezer.

Table 9.5 gives the details of the very best models that I could find as of August 2006 on the John Lewis website, and compares the cost and energy consumption. This table indicates that it is currently unlikely that separate machines could meet the efficiency of the combined fridge freezer and still be cost competitive in the shops. In the example, the two machines would cost £200 more than the single and would not save any energy. The usable capacity would be less. All in all, running two separate machines is bound to use more electricity. Of course, the numbers will change as retailers and manufacturers rotate their models; but this conclusion seems fairly robust.

Table 9.5 *Getting the best possible energy efficiency from fridge freezers, refrigerators and freezers*

	Model name	Height (m)	Price	Capacity (litres)		Energy consumption (kWh/year)
				Fridge	Freezer	
Fridge freezer	Indesit BAAN12S	1.75	£279	180	110	284
Fridge	Bosch KTR 18P20	0.85	£219	154		117
Freezer	Siemens GS12DA 70GB	0.85	£299		97	179
Fridge plus freezer			£518	154	97	296

The marketing of energy efficiency

Searching for the 'most efficient' machines is difficult. I could find no UK retailer with an internet site that allowed me to search for these appliances by their energy-use characteristics. As importantly, the quality of the descriptions of energy use and of energy efficiency, more generally, are absolutely dismal. Since good retailers do what their customers want, this must reflect a lack of interest. Whether we like it or not, the market seems to be telling us that consumers don't regard energy efficiency as particularly important. They have to be told about electricity costs, and don't want actively want to know about it. While the EU energy labels have undeniably pulled down average energy consumption (alongside the very clear threat to ban inefficient machines), pressure from consumers is apparently non-existent.

Is this consumer indifference rational? Are consumers right not to actively search for the best machines? Let's look at the variety of energy consumption figures at the main price points for fridge freezers. Instead of going to the John Lewis website, this time I looked at Comet in mid-March 2006.

At the time of the research, Comet had slightly more than 100 fridge freezers on sale. They ranged in prices from £150 to a jaw-dropping £2000. The mid-point is about £450. The expected energy consumption ranged from just under 200kWh/year to almost 500kWh/year.

The more expensive machines were generally slightly bigger than the cheapest appliances, but the difference is not great. The least expensive fridge freezers were typically at least 70 per cent of the size of the biggest. The prices per litre of internal capacity in the fridge or the freezer rise sharply. But does spending a few more pounds mean that energy consumption is better? The answer was clearly and unambiguously 'no'. There is absolutely no relationship between the price per litre of capacity and the machine's energy consumption. Whatever people are paying for when they spend – say, £800 on a fridge freezer – it is certainly not better energy efficiency.

Anyone looking for energy efficiency should concentrate the search on the smaller fridge freezers. Going from a 300 litre capacity machine to a 400 litre will typically add about 60kWh/year to electricity consumption, so it makes sense to try to buy a moderately sized appliance. A 300 litre fridge freezer (over 10 cubic feet) is a reasonably big machine. The buyer should probably follow a simple rule – look to buy a 300 litre machine that uses less than 300kWh/year and costs less than £300. No appliance quite met this specification on the Comet website; but several come close and careful shopping around will get you a machine that fits these targets.

THE EXAMPLE OF AMERICAN-STYLE FRIDGE FREEZERS

When researching this case study, I found that Comet sell a range of huge American-style fridge freezers. These monsters started at £300 and went up to a scarcely believable £7500. With one exception, they were graded 'A'; but almost all of them used over 500kWh/year, or nearly twice the best-performing conventional fridge freezer. The biggest and most expensive machines consumed the most electricity, with the champion using almost 700kWh/year, but still capturing the 'A' rating because it is so huge. American-style fridges are gaining market share in UK homes, partly because of their conveniences and partly because they represent a mark of affluence. We can be sure that the downward trend in emissions from home refrigeration would be rapidly reversed if more UK homes had the space and the money to install these energy-hungry appliances.

But does it actually make sense to do this search? How much better efficiency do you get by a careful search compared to walking into the store and buying the first 300 litre machine you come across? In the case of Comet, a randomly chosen machine of approximately the right size would have an energy consumption of 338kWh/year.[153] Therefore, random choice might cost a buyer 40kWh/year or so (338kWh/year minus the target I suggested of around 300kWh/year). The saving in yearly energy bills is potentially only £4. This means £40 over a ten-year life and a carbon dioxide benefit less than 200kg.

When what economists call 'search costs' are high – and it took me five hours to enter all the Comet data into a spreadsheet and do the calculations – no economically rational individual will focus his or her attention on energy use. It is simply too costly to look through the 100 or so models on the Comet website merely to save £4 on the yearly electricity bill.

Intuitively, most human beings recognize this. They will not spend much time over small savings. Because energy is still very cheap in relation to the cost of time, it is not worth seeking out the most efficient machine. Energy labels might help; but all bar a few fridge freezer models on the Comet website were rated 'A'. It doesn't help much to have such indiscriminating targets. But imposing stricter requirements to attain the A grade is opposed by manufacturers, particularly if it is accompanied by any move to penalize larger appliances. At the moment, the biggest fridge freezers can still be classed 'A' even though they have much higher electricity consumption than smaller machines. The grades are allocated on the basis of energy use per unit of refrigeration capacity. But from the perspective of the national consumption of electricity, we need to discourage electricity use, even if it means reducing the size of appliances. We ought to base our labels on the absolute value of energy consumed.

The introduction of EU labels on electrical appliances has clearly had some success. It pushed the pace of technical innovation and removed the most egregiously poorly insulated 'cold' appliances from the market. Now that all appliances are of a reasonable standard, technical improvement will be quite slow (this is also true for washing machines and dryers).

LARGE APPLIANCES: DATA FROM OTHER COUNTRIES[154]

Large appliances ('wet' and 'cold' machines) consume about 1100kWh/year in the average UK home. Other European countries are generally a little higher than this, in part because of higher ownership levels of appliances, such as dishwashers. Germany's levels of consumption are lower than the UK after adjusting for ownership levels; but Sweden and France are higher, at between 1400 and 1500kWh/year. Large appliances typically represent about 45 per cent of household electricity consumption for all appliances and lighting. In the UK, the comparable figure is less than 40 per cent. As in the UK, improvements in refrigerator efficiency are pushing down electricity use; but European dishwasher use is rising and dryers now absorb two or three times the energy that they did in 1985.

Therefore, the fight has got to move from labelling to reducing the size of appliances and the number that we have in each home. This is an enormously challenging political issue.

KETTLES

Kettles are responsible for a surprising amount of energy use. Almost all households own one, and they typically use them over 1500 times a year, with an average content of about 1 litre of water. The energy used per home is probably about 150kWh/year, or approximately 5 per cent of the total electricity consumed excluding lighting. To put this in perspective, the cost to boil 1 litre of water is no more than 1 pence, even after the price rises of 2006.

Kettles are efficient devices for converting electrical energy into heat. Therefore, improvements in technology are unlikely to significantly cut energy use. In fact, the evidence suggests that kettles are demanding more electricity, not less. Three forces are at work:

1   In recent years, kettles have moved from 2kW to 3kW heating elements. Although kettles operating at 2kW are still on sale, the bulk of the market is now composed of more powerful 3kW devices. Why does this matter? After all, it will simply mean that it is quicker to boil 1 litre, but the total amount of energy will remain the same. The issue is a behavioural one. A 2kW kettle boils 1 litre of water in about three minutes, compared to two minutes for a 3kW model. Waiting three minutes for a kettle to boil is, of course, almost equivalent to an eternity, so the tea drinker is relatively careful about boiling approximately the right amount of water. A 3kW kettle boils 33 per cent faster, and the incentive on the user not to overfill the kettle is proportionately reduced. So, the kettle is filled less accurately and hot water is wasted. And at less than 1 pence per litre of boiled water, you have to be very worried about global warming to carefully measure how much water you need.

2   Having once been simply a functional and utilitarian device that sat on a gas stove, the kettle is now regarded as something of a fashion item. They come in brushed metal, with pastel panels. A recent trend sees them coordinated with kitchen toasters for maximum visual effect. In addition, they have lights to flicker or glow and 'keep warm' buttons that ensure that the contents are always hot – thus further reducing the time to deliver boiling hot water. These add to energy consumption. One estimate says that a kettle being 'kept warm' uses a constant 66W to maintain the temperature.

3   A further fashion trend is for kettles to spread further in the base, much like the British population itself. Ten years ago, jug kettles were cylindrical. Now they are often far wider at the bottom than at the spout. Why is this important? It means that for many kettles the minimum fill is much greater than in the older machines. Where it was possible to run a kettle just with one cup of water, it now often requires two.

HOW TO BOIL WATER

Even simple tasks can demand some detailed calculations. The maximum efficiencies of the main methods of boiling water are as follows:

- The electric kettle converts about 80 per cent of electricity used into energy that heats the water.
- The similar figure for a light pan on a gas hob is about 40 per cent.
- The figure for a microwave is about 55 per cent.

If users filled the electric kettle with just enough water to make their tea, the kettle would clearly be better than the microwave for boiling water (the kettle's efficiency is higher than the microwave's). But is this a realistic conclusion? Probably not. Studies of consumer behaviour suggest that people usually use about twice as much water as they need when filling a kettle. Water gets boiled, doesn't get used and then gradually falls back in temperature.

Therefore, a mug of water placed in the microwave should be compared against the equivalent two mugs boiled in an electric kettle. The greater efficiency of a kettle isn't enough to compensate for the wastefulness of most users in overfilling the kettle. But many new kettles don't indicate how much water they contain. So people guess and will tend to err on the conservative side, putting too much water in the kettle.

What about the gas hob? More heat is wasted using gas: the efficiency is less than electricity. But does this mean that it would be wrong to use the stove? No: on the grounds of expense and carbon emissions, water should be boiled using gas (see Table 9.6, overleaf).

So, for the very careful person, boiling a kettle on a gas stove is better than using an electric kettle. But the differences aren't great and could be outweighed by many things. Electric kettles turn themselves off, for example, while kettles on a hob will be left while boiling. Sometimes gas kettles aren't placed efficiently on the stove, with some of the heat being wasted. On the other hand, electric kettles may be more susceptible to efficiency-reducing lime scale. Electric kettles may also be 're-boiled' more often if the user has gone away and wants to reheat the water.

Assume for one second that the raw calculations are correct: the cost per litre is, indeed, nearly twice as much for electricity as for gas. What will be the yearly savings of moving to a gas kettle? If the average household use is 1500 litres, the saving might be around £8 – and the carbon dioxide abatement less than 10kg. What person in her right mind would switch to gas merely to save this small amount of pollution? The extra time taken to boil a kettle on a gas stove is perhaps two minutes a time, or over 20 hours a year. No British person values time at as little as 40 pence an hour, which might be what it would take to rationally justify using gas instead of electricity for boiling water.

It is far more important to fill the kettle accurately with what the user needs, de-scale the element with vinegar regularly and only boil once. Some of the sources I have consulted suggest that herbal teas and fresh coffee taste better with water just below boiling temperature, not with water at 100 degrees Celsius or above.

These three things make it more and more difficult, in physical and behavioural terms, for the user to make the effort to reduce the amount of water boiled to the minimum. Where before we might carefully fill the kettle to suit our immediate need, we are now almost encouraged to be wasteful.

There's one advance that has been leaped upon by the energy-efficiency specialists. The Eco Kettle is divided into two compartments. When the user wants to boil one cup of water, he or she presses a button and precisely the right amount of liquid drops from one compartment to the other, and is then boiled. Because the amount of water boiled is more accurately tied to the user's needs, much less is wasted. Initial studies on this machine suggest that it saves about 30 per cent on energy use.

Does it make sense to buy this machine? It retails for about £35 and has a 3kW element and a 1.5 litre capacity, which is a bit low compared with the 1.7 litre machines that clog the market. The nearest equivalent conventional machines are between £15 and £20. So, a careful shopper might be spending an extra £20 on the Eco Kettle. If it does, indeed, save 30 per cent of electricity use, it reduces the typical electricity bill by about £5 a year. The payback is therefore about four years. Since many kettles don't last this long, it is not necessarily a good financial investment. If it lasts five years, then the carbon dioxide savings in the average house will be about 100kg, and therefore the price to save 1 tonne of greenhouse gas is about £200. This makes it quite expensive in carbon terms, although it is an appealing device for those offended by obvious waste. However, it will not appeal to those who like the energy-guzzling 'keep warm' feature in other kettles.

Does it make sense not to use conventional electric kettles at all and, instead, rely on an old-fashioned semi-spherical whistling kettle on a gas hob?

Table 9.6 *The costs of boiling water*

Fuel	Amount used to boil 1 litre	Price per kWh	Cost per litre of boiled water	CO₂ emitted per boiled litre
Gas	0.25kWh	3 pence	0.75 pence	0.05kg
Electricity	0.125kWh	10 pence	1.25 pence	0.06kg

TELEVISIONS

TVs in the home are major users of electricity. The typical household uses about 500kWh/year powering the multiple televisions around the home. This is over one sixth of all electricity consumption, excluding that for lighting. It exceeds the figure for tumble dryers, normally thought of as the worst energy guzzlers in the home.

The average number of TVs in the home is rising. Now over 2.4, it will probably rise to about three TVs by 2020. In other words, the home typically has more TVs than inhabitants and this imbalance is likely to become marked as the number of people per house continues to fall.

Each television uses about 200kWh/year. When working, old-fashioned cathode ray tube (CRT) televisions use about 80W, though this varies somewhat according to the size of the screen. TVs are typically being used more than six hours a day, although they may not be watched all of this time. They are, of course, increasingly used as background entertainment and as radios in many homes with digital set-top boxes.

Government projections show typical household electricity demand to power televisions rising from about 500kWh/year now to well over 600kWh/year at the end of this decade.[155] To put this in context, this increase alone will add well over 1 million tonnes of carbon dioxide to UK emissions (this assumes no change in the energy efficiency of TV sets). The rise in household demand is driven both by increasing numbers of television sets and a rise in their power consumption. New sets bought today absorb a lot more power than those bought five years ago. The increase in liquid crystal display (LCD) screen sizes now in the shops suggests an even faster increase in total electricity demand from televisions.

Technology changes

In a relatively small number of months, TVs sold in shops moved from CRT to plasma or, increasingly, to LCD technology. Although these new display technologies remain more expensive than CRT televisions, they have the huge advantage of being very slim and occupying a much smaller area of a room. As a result of their success, it is now almost impossible to obtain an old-fashioned CRT set.

An LCD screen of 17 or 20 inches consumes little, if any, more power than a similarly sized CRT model. A 20 inch LCD screen might need 60W to 70W to power. Most of this energy is going to illuminate the bulbs that light the screen from the back. But as LCD TVs get bigger, their power consumption goes up as the square of the screen size. Thus, a 30 inch LCD screen will consume well over twice as much as a 20 inch display. This is also true for typical flat-panel computer screens.

And TV screens are getting bigger all the time. Massive screens of over 40 inches are now, if not common, at least beginning to appear in the shops. Prices are awesomely high, but are falling rapidly as LCD manufacturing technology improves. At the moment, 40 inch screens consume over 200W, and this power usage will probably not fall markedly over the next few years. The degree of the problem posed by the growth of the size of domestic LCD screens is illustrated by an Australian survey which showed that the typical new LCD TV consumed 50W in 2003, but 92W in 2005. This increase in the average size of TV screens will continue for several years.

Plasma screens, which are losing market share to LCDs, have even worse power consumption patterns. The largest devices can take over 300W.

There is some relief in sight. Within a few years we will (probably) see the replacement of LCD as the dominant technology by new display techniques that use very little power. The most likely candidate is something known as an organic light-emitting diode (OLED). Light-emitting diodes (LEDs) are already used for lights such as those on bicycles and may eventually spread into the home (see Chapter 8). LEDs use very little energy and TV displays employing this technology are already in trial. Within five years, perhaps, new TVs will use significantly less electricity than at present. But by that time, most UK homes will have one or two (long-lasting) large-screen LCDs.

Typical usage patterns

The average person watches TV for about three and a half hours per day; but surveys seem to suggest that TVs are left on for about six hours. In the remainder of the time, the TVs are almost invariably left on standby, when the electronics in the machine are still on, but merely ticking over. In this state, the TV might take 3W to 5W, though it can be lower than 1W.

For a typical CRT TV, still dominant in UK homes, the position is approximately as outlined in Table 9.7.

Table 9.7 *Power consumption for a full-size conventional TV*

	Time	Watts (W) used	Total (kWh/year)
Hours of use per day	6 hours	80	175
Hours of standby per day	18 hours	4.5	30
Total	24 hours		205

How does this change if you add a monster LCD TV to your home entertainment options?

Table 9.8 *Power consumption for a typical 32 inch LCD TV*

	Time	Watts (W) used	Total (kWh/year)
Hours of use per day	6 hours	150	328
Hours of standby per day	18 hours	1	7
Total	24 hours		335

If the new LCD TV replaces the old CRT, the increment to household energy consumption is 130kWh/year (about 60kg of carbon dioxide, or £13). On the other hand, if, as is more likely, the old screen ends up in another room, still being left on some of the time, the total increase in energy consumption might perhaps go up to double this level.

Is it reasonable to assume that the typical new LCD TV is as large as 32 inches? Perhaps not; but over one quarter of the models on sale at Comet in August 2006 were this size or larger. Of course, sales patterns are likely to be biased towards the cheaper machines; but as prices fall, 32 inches is going to be a pretty conventional purchase. As in many other ways, technology and rising prosperity are tending to increase our need for electricity in the home. Although it might now cost almost £35 a year to run a large LCD TV, those who paid out more than £700 to buy it are unlikely to be very sensitive to the price of electricity.

The impact of the growth of LCD TVs

About 6 million TVs are sold in the UK each year.[156] By the end of 2006, almost all will be LCD or plasma. When householders buy a new television, some old TVs are retired; but the total number in UK homes is probably rising by over 3 million a year. If the average increment to household consumption is 200kWh/year from the purchase of a new LCD TV, the 6 million TVs sold will add over 0.5 million tonnes of carbon dioxide to the atmosphere every year.

Why has this been allowed to happen unchecked?

There are no labelling schemes of any importance covering TVs. In fact, you have to look hard to get information on energy use from retailers' websites. The sites provide enormous and unfathomable detail on the various aspects of picture quality and often include 30 or more separate pieces of information, such as brightness or audio output power. But electricity use is often completely omitted. The website of the major UK retailer Comet is even worse: in August 2006, it said that its 32 inch LCD TVs have 'low energy consumption', even though this is completely untrue in any generally understood sense. To get accurate data, I had to use manufacturers' brochures for my research. Even these are sometimes completely coy about energy use. Toshiba, for example, often misses out mentioning energy utilization when the machine is in use, though it does give a figure for consumption in standby mode.

The well-developed labelling schemes for washing machines and other appliances have had some effect and are highly visible reminders of the energy implications of a poor purchase. But consumers have no such assistance when buying a television. This is remarkable; sales of consumer electronics have introduced a new buoyancy in home electricity use that is outweighing the energy savings in other areas, such as refrigerators. It's TVs, satellite decoders and Freeview boxes that are responsible for pushing up domestic electricity use; but nothing is done to alert or restrain the public. Other countries have introduced voluntary labelling schemes; but in the UK the problem is ignored. I suspect that policy-makers have simply not yet realized how fast LCD TV power consumption is rising. After all, few of them will yet own one of these ghastly massive TV sets with their enormous price tags.

Nevertheless, we need some action. Consumers eager to avoid higher electricity bills need to buy small-screen LCD TVs, turn them off when not being watched and throw out any old CRT appliances. And we can all read books rather than watch the TV.

DOES IT MATTER WHEN YOU WATCH TV?

Domestic electricity consumption varies by a factor of two or three during a typical day. The peak is reached at about 6.00 or 6.30 in the evening, when people are home, cooking is taking place and the TV is on. After this time, electricity use fades away slowly. A disruption to this pattern is caused by breaks in extremely popular television programmes. At this time, demand shoots upward. Important events on TV in the later evening sometimes produce a spike in electricity demand that exceeds the highest level of demand at 6.00 pm. These jumps are usually predictable events, and the TV companies give the National Grid notice of expected peaks. Nevertheless, at these times the grid has to bring into production power stations that are relatively costly producers of electricity. Today, these stations tend to be coal fired, although this depends crucially upon the relative prices of gas and coal. Coal generation produces two to three times as much carbon dioxide as gas for every unit of electricity generated. So the (perhaps excessively) concerned householder needs to bear in mind that watching TV at moments of great national interest, such as the death of a much reviled character in a soap opera, will tend to cause higher levels of carbon pollution than watching it when electricity demand is low and the least polluting fuels are being used. Moreover, coal power stations have to be warmed up – literally – in order to be ready for the moment the kettles are turned on at the end of a particularly gruesome episode of *Coronation Street*. This also wastes carbon dioxide. The really carbon-phobic household would always seek to watch TV at times when the base-load electricity generators – nuclear, hydro and wind – are the only power stations working. Or, since VCRs typically use much less electricity than TVs, record *Coronation Street* and watch when other people aren't using their TVs. 'Shaving the peak', as it is known, is a good way of cutting the carbon output from electricity generation. Other countries pursue much more active policies to even out electricity demand than the UK, and the effects can be substantial.

SMALL APPLIANCES

Modern living demands a range of little devices that burn huge quantities of electricity, but only for a few minutes a day. Anything with a big motor or a large heating element will be taking 1kW or 2kW to do its work. Table 9.9 focuses on four appliances.

How much are these appliances used every week? I've not found good estimates, so I'll make up my own. I think irons might be used for 90 minutes in a typical house, vacuums for 60 minutes, toasters for 40 and microwaves for 20. With this pattern of use, these appliances together take somewhat over 300kWh/year. Of course, this will vary hugely with the size and type of household. But if my estimates of usage times are right, the iron is a particularly intense user of electricity. On its own, it might be using over 150kWh/year.

The new type of iron, in which steam is generated in a separate container, uses somewhat more energy than the conventional steam iron. However, retailers claim that the time needed for pressing is up to 50 per cent less. Perhaps this is so; but it would be one of the rare appliances where power increases actually reduce total energy consumption.

Table 9.9 *Power consumptions of four small appliances*

	Typical consumption when in use
Irons	2000W
Vacuum cleaners	1800W
Toasters	1000W
Microwave ovens	1500W*

Note: * The typical microwave seems to take about twice as much power as it delivers in useful energy to warm food.

Microwave ovens deliver about half their energy use in useful heating to food. So a machine advertised as 800W may actually be typically taking over 1.6kW from the mains. Nevertheless, for some types of food they are effective and energy efficient. The following summary is from a US website:[157]

Take the simple matter of baking a potato. You start out with a very hot heat source: a gas burner or a set of electric coils. You heat up the inside walls of the oven, the grill, the pan and all of the air trapped inside. Just to bring the oven up to the required 400 degrees [Fahrenheit] takes four to five minutes. You then overwhelm the potato with a massive onslaught of heat from all sides. The potato, heating from [the] surface inward through conduction, requires an hour to bake. Cooling down time for the oven is an additional three to four hours.

On the other hand, the microwave oven starts instantly – like a radio – from a cold condition. The minute you turn it on, the potato begins to absorb heat throughout its entire bulk. It's baked ready to serve in four or five minutes – the same time it required to bring the conventional oven up to working temperature. And when you turn off the microwave oven, it's cool. There's no wasted-heat hangover.

This seems to make good sense, though I very much doubt that a decently sized potato will be cooked in four or five minutes – 15 minutes is more like it.

You'll see estimates of microwave efficiency that suggest they save up to 90 per cent of the energy that might be used by a conventional oven. Of course, it is not always this simple. Cooking a large quantity of potatoes in a gas oven won't be quite as inefficient as a couple of small specimens. Nevertheless, the point is broadly that if we are solely interested in energy efficiency, microwave cooking is used far too little.

Table 9.10 shows that a toaster is quite efficient as well, at least by comparison to a gas grill.

Table 9.10 *Toasting a piece of bread using electricity or gas: A comparison*

	Electric toaster	Gas oven
Time taken	3 minutes	5 minutes
Energy used	0.05kWh	0.24kWh
CO_2 produced	22.5g	45.6g*
Energy cost	0.5 pence	0.7 pence

Notes: * The piece of toast only weighed about 80g.
This experiment may overestimate the relative disadvantage of cooking with gas since the large grill was cold at the start of the experiment. Further pieces of bread would take much less time to cook.
Source: personal experience of cooking two pieces of toast for lunch, 22 March 2006.

Other small appliances may take about 100 to 200kWh/year in total. They will vary enormously by household. For example, we use our bread-maker almost once a day and it probably consumes the best part of 1kW in each cycle. Other homes will use high-consumption appliances such as hair dryers or wine chillers. The hair dryer is a good example of an appliance that is using more and more electricity. New models often use 2kW, up from half this level a few years ago. Six minutes a day of active use means 30kg of carbon dioxide a year.

The person interested in energy efficiency will seek to minimize the use of these products and be boringly diligent at taking the plugs out of the wall. Even the bread-maker consumes standby energy!

CONSUMER ELECTRONICS

Entertainment

The TV is usually the most important consumer of electric power of the electronic entertainment devices in the home. But in an increasingly large number of households, other electronic appliances now take more electricity than the home TVs. There's every reason to suppose that within ten years the power consumption of the ever-growing number of electronic entertainment products in the household will significantly augment total electricity use.

As is becoming increasingly well understood, much electricity use in these devices occurs when they are apparently not in use. 'Standby' power, usually utilized to keep the product ready for use at a moment's notice, means that the appliance may be using up to 20W when not in use. This sounds an insignificant amount of energy; but, over the year, this will amount to over 175kWh, or over 80kg of carbon dioxide. More and more homes have large numbers of these products, and growth will almost certainly continue at an unchecked rate.

Table 9.11 shows how much electricity typical home electronics products consume when in use and when on standby. These estimates should be treated with caution: the standby function, in particular, varies enormously in power use from model to model and manufacturer to manufacturer.

Table 9.11 *Power consumption in use and in standby mode*

	Homes (million)	Power use when on (W)	Power use in standby mode (W)
Sky	8	17	16
Sky+[a]	1	24	16
Cable	3	17	16
Freeview	10	10	7
VCR (video cassette recorder)	20	22	8
DVD player	15	10	1
DVD recorder	3	20	2
Radio (digital or analogue)	25	8	0
Home theatre	1	200	1
Games console	8	60	5

Note: * The Sky+ box includes integrated digital recording capacity using a hard disc.

Table 9.12 *Energy consumption of consumer electronics*

	Hours of use	Hours of standby	Energy use when on (kWh/year)	Energy use in standby (kWh/year)	Total energy use (kWh/year)
Sky	6	18	37	105	142
Sky (two rooms)	5	19	62	222	284
Sky+	6	18	53	105	158
Cable	6	18	37	105	142
Freeview	5	19	18	49	67
VCR	1	23	8	67	75
DVD player	1	23	4	8	12
DVD recorder	6	18	44	13	57
Radio	2	22	6	0	6
Home theatre	6	18	438	7	445
Games console	4	20	88	37	124

Some homes will possess all of these appliances, while others will only have one or two. Therefore, generalization is difficult. From published data on hours of use, it is possible to estimate with reasonable accuracy how much each type of appliance adds to electricity usage.

What do these figures suggest for total power consumption from consumer electronics in people's homes? I've set up four stereotypes: the addict, the heavy consumer, the moderate user and the home that hasn't quite caught up with the 1990s yet (see Table 9.13).

It is easy to see the consequence of the household's choice of home entertainment appliances. There's a tenfold variation between the addicts and the homes stuck in the 1980s with a VCR and a few radios. The aficionados use a megawatt hour (1000kWh) just to power their gizmos and I haven't included the little devices, such as MP3 players and clock radios plugged in around the home. And much of this is invisible in the sense that it occurs when the machines are not in use, but are sitting quietly humming in standby mode. VCRs are relatively rarely used; typical estimates suggest that eight times as much power is consumed by a VCR in standby than when it is in use.

Will standby power losses increase in the future? The pattern is not as clear cut as we might expect. VCRs are major users of standby electricity; but their replacement in sophisticated homes is the recordable DVD player. These machines use much less energy when in standby. So though standby power for electronics is a major source of electricity consumption in almost all homes; it isn't likely to rise as a proportion of total power use.

Table 9.13 *Energy usage by the four stereotypical households for consumer electronics*

	Energy used actively (kWh/year)	Energy used in standby mode (kWh/year)	Total energy used (kWh/year)	Home contents
Stuck in the 1980s (light)	23	76	99	VCR, DVD, two radios
Moderate	99	296	395	Sky, Freeview, two VCRs, four radios, DVD
Heavy	207	256	463	Sky+, two Freeview, two DVDs, games console, four radios
Addict	739	377	1116	Sky+ (multi-room), two Freeview, two DVD-R, home theatre, games console

The UK government is actively pushing the introduction and adoption of digital appliances in the home. Perhaps its most celebrated policy in this area is the switching off of the analogue television signal and its replacement by an all-digital system. This means that every household in the UK will need to buy equipment to receive TV after the transition. This may require new TV sets or multiple Freeview boxes attached to the TV sets (and some of the VCRs, too). A typical home with about 2.5 TV sets and 1.5 VCRs may decide to buy three new Freeview boxes. Unless power consumption is improved – which is technically extremely feasible – the total extra electricity is going to be 200kWh/year, or nearly 6 per cent of total home electricity consumption, adding about 50 per cent to domestic standby power consumption.

Some homes have converted all of their sets to digital already, and some have yet to start; but the total impact of going digital across 25 million UK homes is going to be about 5000 million kilowatt hours a year, or about 2.3 million tonnes of carbon dioxide. This is over 3 per cent of the UK's total greenhouse gas emissions. As in so many other areas, in the headlong rush for progress, the government flings energy efficiency aside. A few more years of gentle movement towards digitalization of TV, and most consumers would have been ready to buy digital-ready TVs and recording DVD players. Instead, the pace towards digital TV has been forced and pressured – as a result, this switch alone may mean that the UK's Kyoto Protocol target may be missed.

The move towards the full digitalization of television broadcasting is one force at work increasing power consumption among the electronic devices in the home. It may not be the most significant because of the rapid trend towards increasing power consumption among existing types of devices. Take one example: the games console. Microsoft's latest model, the fearsomely cool Xbox 360, is said to take 160W when in use. It replaces the older version of the console, which only needed 70W to 80W. The older Sony Play Station requires 50W. Progress in games technology means, at least for the moment, very substantial increases in power to drive the realistic graphics on screen. A player using the Xbox 360 for four hours a day – and leaving it plugged in when not in use – will use 330kWh/year, compared to about 150kWh when using the earlier model.

So Xbox 360 is an important additional consumer of electricity. But the electricity bill will be perhaps £30 to £35, or less than the cost of one new game. The trade-off is clear – there is virtually no incentive for manufacturers independently to reduce energy use. Computer gamers buy machines based on the quality of the graphics in the games and on the speed and realism of the gory action. At today's energy prices, neither Microsoft nor its customers will seek to reduce power consumption if this entails any diminution whatsoever in the quality of the gaming experience. Energy is still too cheap.

Of course, the new home theatre devices are just as much of a problem. These packages, combining powerful speakers and DVD/audio players, can use huge amounts of energy to power. But they are clearly a product whose time is coming: in March 2006, Comet stocked 13 different packages, all of which were major users of electricity when in use. By August, it had 21 different home theatre bundles on its website. The lesson is all too obvious: advances in consumer electronics are very likely to mean continuing increases in power sucked from the mains. But because TV is such an important part of everyday life, no government finds it easy to meddle with power consumption.

Computers

Similar forces are at work in home desktop computers. Increasing processor speeds tend to increase electricity consumption. More electricity use increases the heat given off by the chip, which means a bigger fan. This also takes more power. Top of the range PCs now use 200W – equivalent to two large incandescent light bulbs – when in full activity. Even when droning along, not doing very much, these machines use over 100W. A machine advertised as 'green' uses over 100W when running a programme and CD drive.[158] By the way, these are figures for offices; but the person working at home will, of course, see similar figures.

Computers have various different states of alertness. A PC whose processor is working hard, probably processing graphics, will use more electricity. But even when the machine is just turned on and a screensaver is hopping around the screen, it is probably using 30W. It surprises most people, but the computer is still consuming electricity even when it is turned off. Unless the plug is pulled out of the socket or turned off at the wall, the machine is typically burning about 8.5W – or 55kWh/year if it is 'turned off' for

16 hours a day. As a senior engineer at Google once said, the power companies might soon start providing people with a free computer in return for signing up to a long-term electricity contract.

Modern PCs are bad news for carbon emissions; but there's little economic incentive on people to do much about the power drain. For the typical user, it is hardly likely to be worth unplugging the machine rather than leaving it with the screensaver overnight. The saving might be as much as £15 to £20; but even a new and uncluttered machine might take five minutes to move from turning on to the point where the key programmes are all working. So, leaving the machine on probably saves 1000 minutes a year of valuable working time. The electricity cost of this time is less than 2 pence a minute. In the economist's language, the 'rational' individual therefore doesn't turn the computer off. Even at today's high prices of electricity, the exchange rate between money and carbon dioxide is so unfavourable that no one has sufficient incentive to reduce their carbon dioxide emissions in return for more cash.

This is not just a problem in Western economies; the price of fossil fuel is so low that even newly industrializing nations will use coal and oil rather than human labour. And for many people, this is the end of the matter. The price mechanism has spoken and most people simply follow its signals. Human beings who behave differently and try to conserve energy even if it is not worth the effort are eccentrics and cranks. I hope that some of the readers of this book might see a moral quality in saving energy; but most people simply respond passively to the price of energy compared to the value of their own time. No one can blame them – but the consequences for emissions are increasingly severe.

The problem of power-hungry PCs is likely to get worse before it gets better. Not only are desktop machines getting bigger and more powerful all the time, we are buying more of them. The two- or three-PC household is now commonplace, and this often means more expenditure on electricity to power the little grey boxes that link the network together, whether wirelessly or via cables.

The laptop is the only computer product in which power use is very carefully managed. Laptops are probably twice as energy efficient as desktop computers, even those with efficient flat screens. Because users value the length of time before the computer needs to be plugged in for refreshment, the laptop has been engineered to use as little power as possible (this is the case even when the computer is powered by the mains and not just when it is working off the battery). Research and development is focusing on further reducing the power use of the laptop screen, which is the major cause of power drain.

Should you work with the laptop plugged or run it off its battery? This partly depends upon whether you set your computer to dim its screen when working off battery; but, in general, it makes sense to run it from mains electricity because there are electrical losses in charging and discharging the battery. One study saw 20 per cent efficiency losses from running off the battery rather than the mains, although it commented that this was much better than observed with other battery charged devices.[159]

The rest of computing is not following the good example set by laptop manufacturers – power use is going up. About 60 per cent of homes now have a PC, and the energy consumption in these households will be tending to rise as a result of computing. The increasingly ubiquitous broadband modem, present in over 10 million homes, is another small cause of rising emissions.

The rules for computers are reasonably simple. Use a laptop rather than a desktop. Turn off machines when you can, and ensure that the plug is removed from the wall (or the wall switch turned off). If possible, don't use processor-intensive activities. And don't be in a hurry to upgrade to the latest machine with a faster processor. It will probably use more energy. Networking of computers is relatively cheap in energy terms; but excess peripherals should be turned off completely when not in use. If you continue to use a desktop, rather than a laptop, ensure you have an LCD ('flat') screen rather than a CRT (one that looks like an old TV). As we discussed when talking about TVs, these are more energy efficient for the same size screen.

STANDBY LOSSES

It is not just consumer electronics that waste power when in standby. Most of today's appliances are using electricity even when they are apparently turned off. Sitting waiting to be used, these devices are burning a few watts in standby state. Many people's reaction to this is of understandable outrage. The typical homeowner is not aware of the leakage of electricity through the increasing number of appliances that sit in the average home. Simple proposals to reduce the electricity trickling around the house are listed at the end of this chapter. The important point I want to make is that halting progress in getting manufacturers to reduce unnecessary power losses is dwarfed by the increase in the number of appliances using standby power.

Some household gadgets, such as mobile phones, also use little black transformers that plug into a socket. These chargers, or 'wall warts', as they sometimes used to be called in the US, also use electricity even when they are not working. And when they are being used, they often don't efficiently convert mains power into the lower voltages that the appliance is designed to handle. Some of these transformers lose over 50 per cent of the power in the form of heat. This problem is described in following section.

The average UK home probably has at least 20 devices that consume electricity when on standby. They range from telephone answering machines to smoke alarms, microwave ovens and digital set-top boxes. Even that recent addition, the domestic bread-maker, is chewing up current. One obvious symbol of their continuous drain of electricity is the little light that stares at you at all times, day and night. However, it isn't just the red light, or even the clock on the oven, that is consuming electricity, but also the slow trickle that is needed to keep the electronics ready to switch on without a second's delay.

In the office where I have written this book, I can see ten small green lights without turning my head. They indicate appliances that are using electricity even when they are not doing any useful work. There's a laser printer that might actually run off 20 pages a day, but which I am sometimes too lazy to turn off when I have finished using it. A cordless telephone sits erect in a small cradle. A fax machine, now rarely used, has two lights. A new and unreliable system for linking the three computers in the house via a network has a total of a further five unblinking bulbs. When my own computer is turned off, the screen tells me it is still ready by showing a weak yellow signal. Some of these lights I can turn off; others stay on all the time. But even though I nag others in the household about turning appliances off at the mains, I myself sometimes cannot be bothered to spend the 30 seconds or so shutting everything down at night and then powering it up again in the morning.

Typically, these gadgets consume 3W to 4W of power while not working (the light itself is a small fraction of this electricity consumption, but usually signifies that background electronics are working, too). So, a house with, say, 15 devices is burning 50W every hour of the day for no obvious purpose. That's over 400kWh/year, or 180 kilos of carbon dioxide per household. The cost is almost £40 a year. Between 10 and 15 per cent of all the domestic electricity that we use is wasted in this way.

The newest types of devices are sometimes the most expensive to operate. Sky satellite boxes use up to 17W even when the TV is off. Home security systems such as mains-powered burglar alarms can be over 20W in standby.

Unless action is taken, the percentage of domestic electricity used for standby is likely to rise substantially. Even the simplest device is now equipped with electronics that need power dribbling through. And we have more and more such devices in the home. Almost every person over ten has a mobile phone and the charger is usually permanently in the socket. The number of set-top boxes will continue to increase, perhaps rapidly. Battery-powered devices such as electric toothbrushes, cordless power tools and hand vacuum cleaners are all rapidly penetrating UK homes. Our five-person household could never be called a home of gadget fans; but we have over 30 appliances that will use standby power when plugged into the mains. Most of these have been acquired over the last five years. Unsurprisingly, the International Energy Agency says that standby power is already responsible for roughly 1 per cent of global carbon dioxide emissions.

The standby mode, whether used by the device itself humming quietly in the corner or, in addition, by the wall block that delivers its electricity, will always require a small amount of power. But most of today's devices use far more than is necessary. The high power usage levels are partly a function of laziness in design and partly because lowered standby power levels require slightly more expensive components. Good data is not available for the UK; but, for example, the US government estimates that three-quarters of the electricity consumption of home electronics is used when the products aren't actually working. I think that this figure is probably somewhat lower in the UK.

Today's most efficient devices use substantially less than 1W when on standby. For example, a good mobile phone charger uses between 0.25W and 0.5W when not charging the phone. Televisions can also be less than 1W. However, the typical appliance still runs at several times this level. If the appliance uses a wall wart, you can tell whether it has a significant power loss by touching it with your hand. If the transformer is warm, the appliance attached to it is using a measurable quantity of electricity.

Governments have latched onto the importance of the standby power issue. Around the world, energy-efficiency bodies are pushing manufacturers to introduce maximum standby power limits of 1W. European compliance is, however, entirely voluntary and progress here is probably even slower than in the US. Cheap set-top boxes bought to receive the Freeview digital television service, for example, have a high power consumption – possibly averaging as much as 15W – and do not have a proper standby state. In other words, they burn 15W whether they are working or not (see the box below). Contrast this tolerance of high wastage of electricity with the position in the US, where President Bush signed an executive order in 2001 obliging the US federal government to buy only appliances with standby losses of 1W or less. Australia and South Korea have also formally adopted a target of 1W standby power.

The US also has a much better energy labelling system than in Europe. Here we rely on a complex categorization that gives each appliance a letter from A to E. The US Energy Star programme, by contrast, simply sets a single target. If the appliance meets the criterion, it can use the Energy Star logo. If not, it can't. To get an Energy Star designation for a wall transformer, the device must lose less than 0.75W for a major appliance. The limit is even tighter for a transformer for a small appliance. The requirements were

---

STANDBY LOSSES: DATA FROM OTHER COUNTRIES

The average German home has continuous standby losses of 45W (the figure means that an average of 45W is being used at all times simply to keep appliances ready for use).[160] This equates to just under 400kWh/year. Add in standby losses in the non-residential sector and the figure rises to about 4 per cent of German electricity consumption, at a cost of about 14 million tonnes of carbon dioxide.

Danish homes lose 10 per cent of their electricity to standby consumption and Japan has a similar figure. Estimates from other European countries are 5 to 10 per cent of total domestic electricity use. The UK is a relatively poor performer, probably because of the greater penetration of inefficient digital set-top boxes.

introduced in early 2005. These limits are perfectly manageable, and manufacturers will probably fall into line. No such pressure exists for companies selling into the UK market.

TRANSFORMER LOSSES

As I mentioned earlier, all wall transformers lose electricity when in standby mode. It is usually not much, but it is measurable. The transformers generally also aren't particularly efficient at converting mains electricity into lower voltages. Many older transformers, recognized by their large regular shape, operate at no more than 50 per cent efficiency. Newer, less wasteful, transformers can achieve efficiencies of 90 per cent or so (laptop transformers are generally very good). These power supplies are also much smaller and are often irregularly shaped, rather than cuboid. Older transformers are about the size of six or eight matchboxes put together, and often are so large that they block the adjacent wall socket. The more efficient types occupy perhaps one quarter of the space so that you can easily recognize which type you are using.

The losses from the older type of transformer are enormous. The appliance itself might use 10W or 20W, and the transformer effectively doubles this. For some appliances, the transformer almost has to be on all the time, but is used for ten minutes a day. A cordless telephone would be a good example. The Energy Saving Trust in the UK recently reported evidence that the average UK home has five wall transformers, which jointly consume 18 per cent of the energy used by domestic electronic appliances.[161]

WHAT DO WE DO?

Recommendations are reasonably clear and easy to implement:

• **Turn off all appliances at the mains – or pull out the plug – when not in use.** For the average appliance, this will save roughly 3W to 4W. This is a simple recommendation for things such as mobile phone chargers. For other devices, such as clock radios, for example, it is clearly nonsensical. Larger and larger numbers of appliances come equipped with digital clocks that flash crossly and require resetting every time the device is turned on. Try to buy versions of these products that don't have lights, displays or clocks. They do exist.

    Some people will also protest that turning off appliances is not always advisable. Users of the early personal computers were told that turning the machine off would shorten the life of the hard disc. This was probably true; but modern computers are now typically engineered to withstand 40,000 start-ups and shutdowns. Talking of computers, don't be confused into thinking that the screensaver conserves electricity.

It doesn't. It is there for entertainment, not energy saving, and the screen generally continues to use the same amount of power as when the display is actually in working mode.

Look round the house. You'll probably find many appliances that constantly use electricity without telling you. That nice new bread-maker that you leave plugged in? Two to three watts. The inkjet printer? Five watts or so. And so it goes on – you can probably reduce your background electricity consumption by 25W without any problem at all simply by walking room to room (perhaps saving £20 a year). The simple rule is that if the machine doesn't need to be plugged in, it shouldn't be.

- **Where possible, avoid buying products that use external power transformers ('chargers').** Where the product isn't available without these transformers, such as mobile phones, make sure that you buy one that uses a small non-cuboid transformer (any irregularly shaped charger is probably better than the big cube transformers that are still used on some appliances). In general, mobile phone manufacturers have come into line and their transformers are efficient. But other manufacturers are still using power supplies that lose a lot of energy when they are powering a device and considerable amounts when they are inactive. The Energy Saving Trust identified cordless phones and digital radios among the categories of electronic devices that used poorly designed transformers.[162]
- **Own fewer devices.** Buy less electronics. This is the real winner. More electronics in the home means more power consumption. A hard-headed assessment of whether it really is necessary to run a third TV, another DVD player or a new cordless power tool will sometimes force the concerned buyer simply to reject the new purchase.
- **Consider buying a device that tells you exactly how much electricity the house is using every second.** These simple displays demonstrate the amount of power appliances are using in standby and the huge impact of turning on tumble dryers and other electricity guzzlers. The device from Electrisave costs about £65, though the price is likely to fall significantly in the next year. The makers claim that householders can use these devices to cut electricity use by up to 25 per cent, although competing manufacturers suggest that the real figure may be as low as 6 per cent.

10

car travel

The average car in the UK emits 180g of carbon dioxide every kilometre. Typical new cars are only very slightly better than this average. Change your car for a small (or medium-sized) diesel with manual transmission and you can get this number down to below 130g per kilometre. Such a car doing typical mileage will cut the emissions per person down to 0.9 tonnes from 1.2 tonnes.

Reducing the car's mileage down to, say, 7000 miles (11,300km) a year, rather than the UK average of 9000 miles (14,500km) and the figure goes to 0.7 tonnes. Hire a car or belong to a car club, and the number falls ever further. Other choices, such as buying a hybrid electric car, can help to reduce emissions, but at a high financial cost.

D omestic cars, typically weighing well over a tonne, will always use large amounts of energy to move around the country. This is a simple outcome of the laws of physics, and we should distrust those who claim that any new type of car will somehow avoid being bound by the usual rules. Hydrogen or electric cars don't escape this generalization. In fact, though fuel efficiency continues to rise, the increase in the typical size of cars means that total petrol consumption is not declining in the UK. Even taking into account innovations in alternative fuels, the impact of car transport on global warming is not going to decrease. Nevertheless, the typical car user can reduce his or her carbon dioxide emissions by 50 per cent by making some simple choices.

Despite the widespread impression to the contrary, car use is only increasing very slowly in the UK. The number of cars on the road continues to rise; but the average mileage per car is flat, or even slowly reducing. Nevertheless, private car transport is already responsible for over 10 per cent of total carbon dioxide emissions. Per UK citizen, cars contribute about 1.2 tonnes of emissions per year, and for each car, the figure is around 2.6 tonnes. Car driving represents over one fifth of the emissions that we can directly control by our individual actions. Car journeys represent a higher percentage of all land travel in the UK than any other European Union (EU) country and show no sign of falling.[163]

Individuals and families face an array of alternative choices for reducing the emissions for which they are responsible. Broadly speaking, these options divide into three groups:

1   driving fewer miles or using a lower-emission car;
2   using lower-emission fuels;
3   harnessing technology to get better fuel consumption.

Halving the miles driven will, of course, approximately halve emissions. Combining this with driving a small, efficient diesel car, preferably with manual transmission, might reduce consumption by a further third. This would cut the impact of using a car from 2.6 tonnes down to about 0.9 tonnes. This effect is much greater than can be accomplished just by using lower-emission fuels, such as liquid petroleum gas (LPG) or diesel. We're also going to hear a great deal more about biofuels, such as ethanol or biodiesel; but the emissions impact of these fuels is controversial. Because of the enormous amounts of fossil fuel used in the growing of crops for biofuel, the emissions savings may be non-existent. Getting better fuel consumption by using a hybrid car, such as the Toyota Prius, is extremely helpful; but once again the effect is not as great as simply driving less in a smaller car.

Table 10.1 looks at the main alternative ways of reducing emissions from personal car travel. It tries to show that there isn't an easy technological solution to carbon emissions from cars. The two best routes forward are either to drive a small car fewer miles or to use the only genuinely near-zero emission vehicle – a car powered by used oil from a fish and chip shop.

This chapter looks at how responsible people can cut the carbon dioxide that comes from driving cars. Some people can simply give up their car; but others do not easily have

Table 10.1 *The main options for reducing emissions from car travel*

Option	Main impact on typical CO_2 emissions*
Hybrid car, such as Prius	Reduce emissions by 1.1 tonnes
Liquid petroleum gas (LPG) car	Reduce emissions by 0.35 tonnes
New efficient car	Would only reduce emissions if old car is at the end of its life
Drive less	Just cutting out short journeys isn't enough to make much difference
Smaller car	A small diesel with manual transmission can halve emissions compared to a 2.0 litre petrol car
Auto versus manual	Switching from automatic to manual transmission saves 0.3 tonnes
Diesel versus petrol	A small manual diesel car offers savings of up to 0.9 tonnes
Electric car	Reduces emissions to about half the level of a small manual diesel
Car clubs	Joining a car club typically reduces car use by two-thirds, saving perhaps 1.8 tonnes
Biofuels	Complex calculations, but no convincing evidence that agricultural biofuels reduce fossil fuel use; cars using old frying oils are, however, very close to zero emission

Note: *Compared with an average car doing 9000 miles (14,500km) and adding 2.6 tonnes of CO_2 to the atmosphere each year.

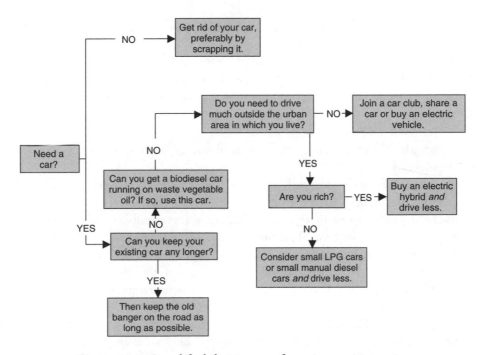

Figure 10.1 *Simplified decision tree for assistance in assessing whether to buy a new car and, if so, what type*

this option. Therefore, the analysis tries to provide guidance as to what people can do to reduce emissions without giving up the car altogether. It quantifies some of the main options by their effectiveness in challenging global warming and in terms of their cost per tonne of carbon dioxide saved.

We all know the usual instructions about how to drive a car for maximum fuel efficiency:

- Don't accelerate hard.
- Try to drive so you never have to brake (because you waste energy getting the car up to the speed from which you were required to brake).
- Keep the tyres inflated and replace filters frequently.
- Try to drive at the speed that is optimal for fuel efficiency (generally around 55 to 60mph).
- Air-conditioning use increases fuel consumption, perhaps by about 5 to 8 per cent, on average.[164] Try not to use it.

Taken together, these behavioural adjustments might save 10 to 15 per cent of all fuel consumption, or perhaps reduce emissions by 150kg per person per year. This is valuable; but more radical options need to be explored, as well.

CAR TRAVEL: THE MAJOR TRENDS

Influenced, perhaps, by the increasing levels of congestion, our perception is that car travel is growing rapidly. Actually, the underlying picture is more complex. Although private car travel is an important source of greenhouse gases, it has not been rising at a particularly speedy rate:

- The number of private cars in the UK is about 27 million, or just under 1.1 cars per household.[165]
- The number of households without a car is still falling – 26 per cent now, it was 33 per cent in 1990.
- Households with two or more cars have increased in number significantly in recent years to about 29 per cent. The bulk of the rise occurred in the 1990s, and the number of two-car households has not risen much in recent years (social changes have seen a rapid rise in one-person households – if this trend continues, we will eventually see a fall in two-car households since few individuals choose to own more than one car).
- Although the number of cars is increasing, the amount of car travel per person appears to be gently declining, although commuting distances are rising. Typical personal car mileage seems to be a couple of percentage points lower than in 1999.
- The distance travelled in typical individual car trips is also flat or falling slightly.
- Therefore, the simple picture that we should have in our minds is of an increasing number of cars, but a very gradually diminishing amount of use of these vehicles, resulting in almost flat total amounts of car travel.[166]

These trends will probably continue. More and more people will own cars, particularly as the average life of vehicles seems likely to increase; but they won't necessarily use them for a much greater number of miles. The number of roads won't increase much – they already occupy an area the size of Leicestershire – and so congestion from private cars will increase slowly. Lorries and vans make the problem worse.

What is the impact of these trends on greenhouse gases? New vehicles are getting more fuel efficient; but consumers are tending to buy bigger cars with heavier equipment, which pushes up their fuel use. Sports utility vehicles (SUVs) are simply the most visible example. Unsurprisingly, therefore, the government's fuel efficiency targets are unlikely to be met. The EU agreed a voluntary figure with the motor industry of 140g of carbon dioxide emissions per kilometre to be achieved by 2008; but the current UK level is 169g and is only falling slowly. Moreover, these figures are from official tests. Actual performance is somewhat worse as a result of poor maintenance and hopelessly inefficient driving from a large percentage of the population.

Taken together, all of these forces – more cars but slightly fewer miles per car, better fuel efficiency but bigger vehicles – will probably mean that private car transport gradually increases in importance as an emitter of greenhouse gases, although the situation is not as apocalyptic as some commentators claim. The prognosis for goods vehicle traffic is far less favourable.

Most organizations working in the field think that the average car travels about 10,000 miles a year, or about 16,000 kilometres. This number looks slightly high to me. Table 10.2 provides another estimate, based on calculations from UK government emissions figures.

Table 10.2 *Estimate of average distance travelled per year by UK private cars*

Data	Source
67.8 million tonnes of CO_2 from private cars	Office for National Statistics, 2005
27 million private cars = 2.51 tonnes CO_2 per car	National Travel Survey, 2004
Average CO_2 output = 180g per kilometre	Estimate based on average figures for new cars over the last 15 years
Total kilometres driven = circa 14,000km	

As a compromise between the industry wisdom and my guesswork, the rest of this chapter uses an average figure of 14,500km per year, or about 9000 miles. It doesn't matter much if this number is slightly inaccurate since I am only using it as a number upon which to base estimates of improvements in carbon dioxide emissions levels. I also use an assumption that the average car on UK roads emits 180g of carbon dioxide per kilometre driven (the typical new car is slightly more efficient than this). Put another way, this means that a car generates 1kg of extra carbon dioxide for every 4 miles (6.5km) on the road. For the purpose of calculations of lifetime savings, this chapter will assume that new cars last 16 years before retiring to the scrap heap.

CAR TRAVEL: DATA FROM OTHER COUNTRIES

In the UK, there are just over two people per car. Per person, therefore, car travel amounts to about 6000km to 7000km per year (around 4000 miles). This figure is about the same as most European countries – Finland and Italy are a little higher, and Norway and The Netherlands somewhat lower. France and Sweden are about the same. The US is about 13,000km (8000 miles); but in Japan, car travel amounts to less than 4000km (2500 miles).[167]

This chapter will always use estimates of the direct carbon dioxide emissions arising from car use. In fact, a full analysis would include many other consequences of operating a car. Probably the most important of these is the carbon cost of producing the petrol that goes into the car. All of the figures for fuel consumption need to be inflated by about 15 per cent just to account for the energy cost of turning oil into refined products. And what about the costs of running the forecourts, the repair shops and the car dealerships? Some analysts have even allocated carbon costs arising from the insurance and licensing activities necessary to keep private cars on the road. To keep it simple, I do none of this and refer only to fuel burned in the engine of the motor vehicle.

Hybrid cars

I'll try to demonstrate later in this chapter that trading in your old car and replacing it with a new, more efficient vehicle makes no sense if the old vehicle still remains on the road. In replacing your old motor, you have added one car to the stock of cars on the road, and although it can be argued that the incremental car adds little to the total number of miles driven by UK residents, it will certainly have some effect.

So let's assume, instead, that your old car sits smoking in the drive, having driven its last mile. Its only function now is to be broken down and recycled back into the steel and plastics from which it came. Does it make sense to buy a Toyota Prius – by far the best-selling hybrid electric car – to replace it, or not?

ALTERNATIVES IN BUYING CARS: SOME COMPLICATIONS

When weighing up alternatives for buying cars, some complexities need to be borne in mind:

- Different fuels have different energy contents. So, 1 litre of liquid petroleum gas (LPG) is not the same as 1 litre of petrol: it contains a lot less energy. Saying that LPG is half the price of petrol does not mean that the LPG owner's fuel bills will be halved. LPG will deliver fewer miles per litre than petrol. LPG advertisements tend not to talk about this.
- Advertised fuel economy figures are lower than are actually achieved in practice. Perhaps paradoxically, this means that the advantages of new technologies such as hybrid petrol/electric car tend to be understated when compared to alternative vehicles. If both hybrid and petrol cars use 10 per cent more fuel than the advertisements say, the savings from the hybrid will actually be greater than they appear (to be conservative, I've always used the published figure for low-emissions cars).

First of all, we need to ask why hybrid cars save any carbon emissions. After all, they are still fuelled by petrol and contain internal combustion engines like any other vehicle. In the case of the Prius, the energy saving comes from capturing the kinetic energy lost by braking and turning it into electric power in an internal battery. As a car brakes from 70mph on a motorway to 30mph on the slip road, it loses energy. In fact, the energy of the vehicle has declined by a factor of five as it makes this transition. Where does it all go? As we all know from the laws of thermodynamics, energy does not disappear. Most of the car's energy of motion becomes heat as the brakes capture kinetic energy and turn it into increased temperature. The Prius works by turning the energy transformation during deceleration into potential energy in an electric battery. This electricity is then used to power the car at low speeds, replacing the requirement for the engine to be working. Importantly, this means that the car no longer needs to idle when it is stationary in traffic – instant battery power is always available to move the car.

The question we need to ask is whether the Prius's innovative technology offers a significant improvement over conventional petrol or diesel cars. The standard fuel economy tests show that the Prius generates 104g of carbon dioxide per kilometre compared to the UK average of 169g for the average new car, or 168g for the nearest equivalent Toyota model, a conventional Corolla. What is the likely saving in emissions from choosing the Prius?

For the driver of the average number of miles, the Prius will save about 1 tonne of carbon dioxide a year compared to the typical UK new car. Compared to the nearest Toyota equivalent in terms of size and power, the saving is slightly less.

Does this make it a good purchase? In one sense, the answer is yes. The Prius delivers significant savings over petrol cars that the owner might buy. Even if the expected savings aren't realized, perhaps because of unusual driving patterns, the Prius is probably the lowest emissions petrol-powered car on the road. The Prius owners whom I have spoken to are happy with the car's fuel economy, although they sometimes express reservation as to whether the car achieves all of the savings that it claims.

In another sense, the Prius is bad value for money. Comparing the prices of cars is always difficult; they come with very different accessories and equipment. But on the basis of the list prices, the Prius is about £5000 more expensive than the nearest Toyota equivalent. Perhaps the Prius is significantly more luxurious or commodious than the typical Toyota Corolla; but at £18,000 or so, it is a very pricey alternative. On the basis of lifetime savings of about 15 tonnes of carbon dioxide (about 0.9 tonnes a year over 16 years), the incremental cost is £350 per tonne not emitted. If you have £18,000 to spare and want to reduce carbon emissions, there are many more effective alternatives, both when considering motoring and other activities. The world is doomed to a very impoverished future if reducing carbon emissions by 1 tonne always costs £350: if the developed countries need to reduce emissions by 10 tonnes a head per year, then the total bill will be £3500, or almost one fifth of gross national product (GNP) per capita. This would be good justification for those who claim that significant reductions on emissions are 'too expensive'. As we have seen, emissions reduction generally costs a small fraction of the figure implied by the Prius. Indeed, the price of 1 tonne of carbon dioxide reduction, when traded on the international carbon exchanges, is currently (September 2006) about £11, or about one thirtieth of the extra price that the buyer pays for the Prius's low fuel consumption.

Later in this chapter, we will look at the impact of increased car weight on emissions. The Prius is a slightly heavier vehicle than its near equivalents – by about 100kg. Most of this extra weight is metal and metal contains what is usually called 'embodied energy'. In other words, it took fossil fuels to manufacture the components of the car, whether it is the engine or the Prius's battery. This would tend to reduce the lifetime carbon savings gained by the Prius's owner; but the effect is not large enough to outweigh more than a few per cent of the savings from the Prius's capture of braking energy.

Don't assume that all hybrids necessarily save on carbon dioxide emissions. The Lexus hybrid SUV's CO_2 emissions are over 10 per cent above the average of new cars entering the UK fleet. Buying a small hybrid car may be a good idea – but buying an SUV that just happens to also have a battery makes no sense whatsoever from the environmental point of view. Nevertheless, we can expect heavy advertising of the emissions reductions impact of buying such cars. It can be ignored. Focus on the published carbon dioxide estimates and always look for cars that are much better than the current UK average new car figure of about 170g per kilometre.

Toyota hybrid cars are expensive compared to their conventional alternatives. After all, the Prius's hybrid technology is relatively new, and the manufacturer may rightly claim that the extra costs compared to other cars will tend to fall over time. So, buying a Prius does help Toyota to move down the manufacturing learning curve. Another complaint about the simple numbers contained in Table 10.3 is that high-mileage drivers, doing two or three times the UK average hacking up and down motorways, may be able to achieve much better carbon savings. This may be true, although the Prius's best performance is probably generated on a mixture of local driving, when it uses the battery, and long-distance travel, when the battery is quietly recharging. If the driver is only using the car for long journeys on higher speed roads, the average petrol consumption of a hybrid car will be worse than expected.

But in the minds of a customer, the Prius also has significant advantages over conventional cars. For example, it is exempt from the London congestion charge. It is, in fact, probably the most 'normal' of all cars that don't have to pay the charge. Some other vehicles, like the all-electric G-Wiz that I talk about later in this chapter, involve real trade-offs for the customer, such as having to plug in the battery every 40 miles (64km) in exchange for lower fuel consumption. The Prius is just like a normal car; but the regular central London motorist saves up to £2000 a year. Such a buyer will find the extra £5000 cost a small price for freedom from the congestion charge.

Table 10.3 *How much carbon dioxide does the Toyota Prius save?*

Car model	Kilometres per year	Emissions in standard test	Yearly CO$_2$ emissions (tonnes)	Extra CO$_2$ emissions compared to the Prius (tonnes per year)
Toyota Prius	14,500	104g CO$_2$ per kilometre	1.508	
Toyota Corolla 1.6 litre manual	14,500	168g CO$_2$ per kilometre	2.436	circa 0.9
Average UK new car, 2004	14,500	169g CO$_2$ per kilometre	2.480	circa 1.0

The exemption from congestion charging is, in effect, government incentives to use low-emission cars. Central government also encourages the purchase of a Prius by reducing the annual road tax fees. A Prius costs £65 compared to the £150 of a Corolla of similar power and size. Over the course of its life, this saving will be over £1300, and the tax discount for very high-efficiency cars is probably likely to increase over the next decades.

More important, perhaps, are the lower petrol bills. At a price of 90 pence a litre, the typical owner of a competing Corolla will spend about £950 on fuel every year. The Prius costs about £360 less, thus saving somewhat more – over £6000 – over the lifetime of a car than the incremental cost compared to buying a similar Corolla. Of course, it might be thought that the cheaper cost of motoring might cause the Prius owner to drive more miles. With a petrol cost of about 6 pence a mile, compared to 10 pence for a conventional car of similar size, the hybrid owner may slip into a habit of greater use.

Similar behaviour is noted in Chapter 6 on central heating – better-insulated homes with lower energy bills tend to be run at a higher temperature than draughty period properties. The owners take the saving partly in increased comfort. The point? Protection from climate change isn't necessarily provided by high efficiency.

In fact, I'll try to argue later – in the section on 'Car clubs' – that the best way to get vehicle emissions down may be to encourage vehicle rental. Commercial car clubs offer short-term rental at high hourly rates; but users never buy the car or pay the annual fixed charges, such as insurance and duty. This addresses the problem that conventional car owners – you and me – tend to only notice the petrol costs of running a car. The purchase price, possibly paid ten years ago, is a distant memory, and our decision about how much we can afford to drive is only affected by what economists term the 'marginal' costs of driving: the extra costs of driving another mile. In most cases, this is just the petrol used; but car clubs load the full cost of driving onto the hourly rates. There's abundant evidence later in this chapter that this really does affect total car use.

Liquid petroleum gas (LPG)

Liquid petroleum gas (LPG) is an alternative fuel for motor vehicles. Many LPG vehicles – and there are 120,000 or so on the road in the UK – are conversions of existing petrol (not diesel) cars to run both on LPG and on petrol. The presence of the 'dual-fuel' label on the back of some conversions and the two fuel caps on the side of the car help to identify these vehicles. These cars have both a petrol and a gas tank. The typical LPG driver will actually only ever use LPG, because it is cheaper, but will keep petrol in the petrol tank just in case the gas runs out.[168] Around the UK, 1300 LPG filling stations make it reasonably easy to avoid ever running out of gas.

The typical cost of converting a petrol car to LPG is about £2000, and a large number of approved installers are able to do the job, typically in the course of a working week. Generally speaking, insurance costs are no greater than a similar petrol car. The only significant disadvantages are said to be the loss of car storage capacity as a result of the installation of the gas tank, usually at the expense of the spare tyre, and some complaints about the car's performance after conversion. Neither of these concerns seems to worry many LPG users. The ones whom I have spoken to are very happy with their cars and their fuel bills.

As well as producing less carbon dioxide, LPG produces less of the main other pollutants from vehicle use. Compared to diesel engines, for example, LPG reduces particulate emissions by 90 per cent. There is also a potentially significant impact on nitrogen oxide and carbon monoxide emissions.

In other countries, a large fraction of all high-mileage cars and light vehicles have been converted to LPG, and users such as taxi drivers would benefit most from using gas in the UK. The tax regime has, however, not always been sufficiently advantageous to justify conversion, rather than, say, saving on fuel bills by buying a diesel car instead.

LPG is a mixture of two chemically simple gases – propane and butane. In the UK, LPG is largely propane, but is nearer a 50:50 mixture in other European countries. The fuel is rich in energy and is slightly more powerful than petrol per kilogram. But even in liquid form, it is much lighter than petrol and so the energy content per litre is not as high. One litre of LPG is not equivalent to 1 litre of petrol. Nevertheless, advertisements for conversion often simply advertise the headline price of LPG without mentioning the shorter distance that 1 litre of the fuel will take the car.

Figure 10.2 gives a simple example of what this means in practice.

These figures suggest that the carbon dioxide savings from converting a car to LPG are about 15 per cent. Proponents of LPG sometimes claim higher figures of 20 per cent or more; but these estimates do not seem to be consistent with the energy content of the fuel and its carbon dioxide production when burned in an engine. To me, 15 per cent or so

LPG cars use more litres of fuel...	But emit far less CO_2 per litre...	Meaning that emissions per kilometre are lower
Kilometres per litre	CO_2 per litre (kg)	CO_2 per kilometre (kg)
LPG – 10.4	LPG – 1.51	LPG – 0.145
Petrol – 13.6	Petrol – 2.31	Petrol – 0.169

Figure 10.2 *What are the carbon dioxide savings from using a liquid petroleum gas-powered car? An example of a manual 2005 Vauxhall Vectra 1.8i*

Source: various, including the LPG Association (data from the LPGA website, www.boostlpg.co.uk). Some of these numbers are slightly different from the ones on the www.vauxhall.co.uk site. For example, Vauxhall says that the carbon dioxide emissions for the petrol car are 0.175kg per mile (0.109kg per kilometre).

seems the right percentage saving, and in the Vectra example given in Figure 10.2, the CO_2 saved would be about 350kg per year for a typical driver.

The savings in the cost of motoring are more significant.

For the average car driver, the savings will be about 35 per cent of the cost of a petrol equivalent. This assumes that the current relationship between the price of petrol and the price of LPG remains the same; lower taxation of LPG means that the forecourt price of gas is about half the price of petrol at the moment. This difference is partly an artefact of taxation because the government is using the lower tax on LPG as a means of increasing its appeal. It would therefore be an entirely reasonable view that LPG's price advantage could fall as a result of government losing enthusiasm for LPG at some stage in the future.

Currently, for the average car driver doing 14,500 kilometres (approximately 9000 miles) a year, the savings will be, perhaps, £300 to £400, depending upon the size of the car. The incremental cost of purchasing the car will be somewhere about £2000, meaning that the payback will be about six years. For a heavy driver, the return could be much quicker, which is why many taxis and other high-usage vehicles have moved to gas.

Most LPG cars – but not all – get beneath the carbon dioxide emissions levels set for exemption from the London congestion charge. Vehicle licence taxes are also lower than for the equivalent petrol-only car. The Vauxhall Vectra owner would save £65 a year at current rates, paying £95 and not £150.

What about the carbon dioxide benefits? In the Vectra example (see Figure 10.2), we estimated the savings at about 350kg a year, or about 5.6 tonnes over the 16-year life of a car. If the cost of an LPG, conversion is £2000, and the price per tonne saved is about £360. This is very slightly higher than the equivalent figure for the Toyota Prius.

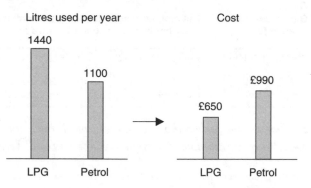

Figure 10.3 *The savings from switching to liquid petroleum gas (LPG)*

Buying a new car

Does it make sense in environmental terms to sell your old vehicle and replace it with a new and more fuel-efficient car? Of course, the answer to this depends upon a number of different questions:

- Does the old car get scrapped or does it remain on the road?
- How fuel inefficient was the old car in relation to the new?
- How much energy was consumed building the new vehicle?

If a very old car that consumes a huge amount of petrol is scrapped and replaced by a light and low-emission vehicle, it may be that the net impact of the change is beneficial to the progress of global warming. But in most circumstances, the purchase of a new car results in a net addition to the atmospheric stock of carbon, largely because the old car also remains on the road.

What is the correct way to show this? We need to do a sum in three parts:

1   First, we need to calculate the remaining emissions of the older car.
2   Second, we must calculate the savings from the lower level of emissions of a new car.
3   And, finally, we should estimate the energy cost of building a car and allocate it pro rata to the remaining life of the *old* car, or the number of years of useful life that we could have used it for.

As an example, let's examine the trading-in of an eight-year-old car during 2005. When new, this car was typical of its year of manufacture and generated, as can be seen in Table 10.4, just under 190g of carbon dioxide per kilometre.

Table 10.4 *Average new car emissions by year of manufacture*

Year	Average emissions (grams of CO_2 per kilometre)	Year-on-year change	Percentage change since 1997
1997	189.8	–	–
1998	188.4	–0.7	–0.7
1999	185.0	–1.8	–2.5
2000	181.0	–2.2	–4.6
2001	177.6	–1.9	–6.4
2002	174.2	–1.9	–8.2
2003	172.1	–1.2	–9.3
2004	171.4	–0.4	–9.7
2005	169.4	–1.2	–10.7

Source: 'UK motor industry failing to tackle climate change', Friends of the Earth press release, April 2006

As an aside, we should note that the figures in Table 10.4 are taken from a Friends of the Earth press release, but are published by the government as a result of an EU directive aiming to reduce typical new car emissions to 140g per kilometre by 2008. It can be easily inferred from these figures that at current rates of progress, this represents an unattainable target. The rate of improvement in underlying fuel efficiency is not insignificant; but the pesky customers keep on buying bigger cars, so average carbon emissions are now falling far less fast than is necessary to reduce total emissions.

Go back to the eight-year-old car. When sold, it will stay on the road for probably another eight years. It will typically become the second or third car of a nearby household (it always used to be said that cars in the UK typically move northward at about 4 miles, or 6.5km, a year as prosperous Southerners sell their cars to buyers typically from slightly further north).

The discarded car will typically travel relatively few miles a year for the remainder of its life. Four thousand miles (6500km) seems an appropriate average figure, although this estimate is no more than a guess.

In the eight remaining years of its life, the car will therefore produce a total of 9.8 tonnes of carbon dioxide. How does this compare to the savings generated in this time by the use of the lower-emissions new car bought to replace it? A typical new car in 2005 will generate emissions of about 170g per kilometre. The better fuel efficiency of the average new car will mean a saving of about 2.2 tonnes of carbon dioxide in its first eight years.

Therefore, the replacement of an old car with a new car will typically result in a net increase in emissions of about 7.6 tonnes of carbon dioxide, or almost 1 tonne a year in the period before the old car is retired from the fleet. This figure is before calculating the effect of actually making the new car.

Studies of the energy taken to manufacture or process new goods are often controversial. For example, the two sides of the acrimonious British debate on the merits of wind farms are locked in an intricate argument about whether the energy used to make the turbines, their masts, the concrete approach roads and the electricity transmission plant are greater than the electricity generated during the useful life of the farm. At one extreme, the proponents of wind suggest that the energy balance swings positive over about 18 months, while, at the other, some suggest that onshore wind farms never reach energy neutrality. With such huge divergence in opinion, we need to approach the energy cost of any manufactured item with extreme caution.

I'm going to calculate the energy cost of a car in an extremely imprecise way. First, I say that the average car contains about 1 tonne of steel (experts will know that cars increasingly use aluminium; but steel still provides the majority of metal in the world's existing cars). Steel is generally made by creating iron in a blast furnace or an electric arc and then adding alloy metals. The energy taken to make 1 tonne of steel is about 19 gigajoules (GJ), or, in equivalent terms, about 5500kWh (more than a typical UK household uses as its annual electricity consumption). Most steel-making is fuelled by coal, and coal releases about 88kg of carbon dioxide per GJ of energy released. So, the CO_2 released to make 1 tonne of steel is 88kg multiplied by 19, or about 1.6 tonnes, if the process is 100 per cent thermally efficient. A more reasonable assumption might be that the steel-making process is only 50 per cent efficient. This would double the energy needed – and the amount of carbon dioxide produced – to 3.2 tonnes. Add in all of the other energy costs of making a car and the total is very unlikely to be less than 5 tonnes, or about two years' worth of emissions on the road. If the steel is made in an electric arc furnace, the figure is probably higher.

That was the third step in the chain; the total environmental cost of swapping an eight-year-old car for a more efficient model is over 12.5 tonnes, or more than the total yearly emissions of the average person. The lesson? Don't replace your car – drive the old jalopy until it retires from the road. Take pride in the age of your car and boast your credentials even as you fill up the tank for the third time in a week.

Perhaps it is obvious, but switching your car also makes no financial sense. The maximum saving in fuel efficiency is probably worth £200 for the mainstream driver. Buying a low-emissions car can also cut £100 a year from your vehicle taxation bill, although this number is certain to rise. Perhaps the lower maintenance charges will save £500 a year. Bluntly put, the total savings will little more than pay the interest charges on the purchase of a new motor.

Drive less

Most people need a car. Some families need two. But many of us can adjust our behaviour so as to use the automobile less. I will ignore the appalling possibility that, by reducing congestion, using your car less will encourage others to use theirs more, thus wiping out any benefit from your actions. This kind of economist's logic creates inertia and despair.

In a more optimistic frame of mind, what happens to carbon dioxide when one decides never to take the car on journeys of less than 2 miles (3km) and replaces these trips with a walk?

Table 10.5 shows that replacing all car trips of less than 2 miles does not result in a substantial reduction in car travel. Although these trips account for a total of about one quarter of all journeys, they represent only about 3.5 per cent of the 5000 or so miles that each person typically drives every year. (But note, however, that the National Travel Survey data seems to underestimate the actual amount of car travel by as much as half. The actual mileage of car travel per person should certainly be over 8000 miles. Perhaps the survey results contain a phenomenon well known to market researchers – 'virtuous' rather than accurate answers.)

Table 10.5 *Impact of always walking rather than taking the car on trips of up to 2 miles*

Distance	Driver or passenger?	Estimated average distance (miles)	Number of trips per year	Distance travelled (miles per year)
0 to 1 mile	Driver	0.5	27	13.5
	Passenger	0.5	17	8.5
1 to 2 miles	Driver	1.5	67	100.5
	Passenger	1.5	42	63
Total				185.5

Source: 'National travel survey', Department for Transport, London, 25 July 2005

If we were to assume that the survey respondents did accurately report the number of car trips of less than 2 miles, how much carbon dioxide would be saved by shifting to walking?

Short trips will typically be fuel-inefficient trips; but, at average fuel economy, the saving might be no more about 55kg of carbon dioxide a year. And even if the respondents had underestimated their journeys by 50 per cent, the benefit is unlikely to average more than 80kg.

This demonstrates an uncomfortable fact – it may be the short, needless car trips that most enrage environmentalists; but cutting out the guilty dash to the corner shop will not substantially reduce emissions. To reduce carbon dioxide, we would need to attack commuting journeys and visits to friends. Commuting journeys are responsible for 18 per cent of all personal trips and visiting friends, 19 per cent. Neither of these activities is increasing much; but the typical distance travelled on these trips is drifting slowly upwards. Ten years ago, the typical commuting car trip was 6 miles (just under 10km); it is now about 8 miles (13km).

We need to further explore the question of whether reducing the number of short car trips and replacing them by walking actually saves carbon dioxide. Walking is not zero emission because we need food energy to move ourselves from place to place. Food production creates carbon emissions. Does the energy used when walking a mile, rather than driving, result in a net rise in carbon dioxide because this energy needs to be replaced by extra food?

This is an unconventional question, of course. Most people see walking as a means of using up food calories that would otherwise become extra body weight. To put it another way, most people consume very slightly more calories than they use, so, little by little, body weight increases. Figure 10.4 demonstrates this for a cohort of English men, showing that the typical weight of a person in this group rose from 81.5 kilos in 1993 to 86.5 kilos in 2004. During this 11-year period, the average weight rose by 5 kilos (about 11 pounds), or about 0.4 kilos a year (1 pound).

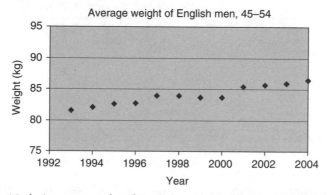

Figure 10.4 *Average weight of English men aged 45 to 54 (1992–2004)*

Source: Health Survey for England, UK Department of Health, London, 2005

However, the striking fact is that a tiny amount of extra walking would work off this extra 0.4kg (see Table 10.6).

Table 10.6 *How many miles of walking does it take to reduce weight by 0.4kg a year?*

Typical energy intake	1,050,000 kilocalories per year
Approximate surplus required to add 0.4kg a year*	2734 kilocalories
Rate of energy expenditure walking at 3 miles per hour	264 kilocalories per hour
Number of hours of extra walking required to balance energy input and output	10 hours, 20 minutes
Number of miles of extra walking	31 miles

Sources: Various. *I have used a crucial figure from lecture notes provided online by Dr J. A. Illingworth of the University of Leeds, UK. Dr Illingworth says that a person typically consuming 1.3 per cent more energy than he or she requires will put on 2kg a year.

Table 10.6 shows that weight gain occurring in the UK population could be completely avoided if the typical person walked an extra 31 miles (50km) a year, or about 150m a day – provided that he or she didn't compensate for the extra exercise by eating a jam sandwich or two. The National Travel Survey (disparaged for its possible inaccuracy above in Table 10.5) says that the typical individual walks about 200 miles (320km) a year, and so the exercise necessary to restrain any weight gain would only add about 16 per cent to the distance walked.

Why is this digression relevant to the calculation of the environmental impact of switching from car to foot? My argument is this: avoiding weight gain in the UK population requires 31 miles (50km) extra walking a year; but switching to foot for all car journeys under 2 miles would require 185 pedestrian miles. So, the typical person would lose weight if he or she stopped using a car for short journeys. In fact, they would lose more than 2kg a year (4.5 pounds). This is assuming that they didn't eat more as the result of the extra exercise. Instead, if they chose to hold their weight constant each year (31 miles' walking), they would have to eat enough to replace the energy burned by walking 154 miles (185 miles less 31 miles).

Producing food takes energy. In fact, most assessments show that Western industrial food manufacture – I include the processes on the farm – absorbs more than nine times as much energy as in the food itself contains (see Chapter 13). So 1 calorie of lettuce or bread or beef takes at least 9 calories of fossil fuel to make. The question is this: does the high 'embedded' energy content of Western food mean that walking rather than driving is necessarily good for the global climate?

At one extreme, the answer is almost certainly no. The calculations in Table 10.7 show that drinking a glass of milk to replace the energy lost during a walk probably produces more greenhouse gases than the car would have done. Home-grown food, cultivated without fertilizers, would have different consequences, of course.

Table 10.7 *Energy balance from walking rather than driving*
if the energy replacement is from dairy products

Distance walked		1.5 miles
Kilocalories used		132 kilocalories
Milk needed to replace this energy* (165 kilocalories)		154ml (about 1 cup)
Methane	Typical methane production from intensively farmed cows per 154ml**	3.79g
	Methane to CO_2 multiplier***	21
	CO_2 equivalence	80g
Carbon dioxide	Energy (kWh) equivalence to kilocalories	0.00116kWh per kilocalorie
	Energy multiplier to convert fossil fuel energy into food energy	9
	Kilowatt hours of fossil fuel energy to produce 165 kilocalories	1.73kWh
	CO_2 output per kWh (e.g. from natural gas)	0.20kg
	Total CO_2 produced in the food chain to deliver 154ml of milk	345g
Total CO_2 equivalent		80g + 345g = 0.425kg
Equivalent CO_2 cost for a typical car for a 1.5 mile (2.5km) journey		0.45kg
Saving		0.025kg
But CO_2 cost of walking if *two* people travel by car instead of walking		0.40kg

Notes: *Assumes that food energy is converted by the body at 80 per cent efficiency.
**This figure would be even higher if the milk was organic because organic cows produce more methane per litre of milk produced.
***Methane's impact on global warming is generally calculated as about 21 times that of carbon dioxide.

Even though I have tried to simplify it, where possible, Table 10.7 is complex and confusing. It has four stages:

1   First, it establishes the energy needed to replace the calories in a short walk. Then it looks at how milk is needed to provide that energy.
2   It goes on to calculate the methane output from the cow that provides that milk and multiplies this by 21 to reflect the disproportionate impact of methane on global warming.
3   It then works out the carbon dioxide cost of the fossil fuels needed to get the milk to the home.
4   And, finally, it compares the carbon dioxide equivalent cost of drinking milk compared to travelling by car.

Table 10.7 shows that if one person walks rather than drives, she saves some emissions – but the difference is marginal. But if the car carried two people, the short journey would be better done by car.

Most books written about the climate change problem use the assumption that human-powered motion is carbon free. Table 10.7 is intended to show that this is not necessarily the case, but is not meant to demonstrate that car travel is inherently better than walking or cycling. The primary point of the calculation is to show the impact of modern intensive farming on carbon emissions. What are the implications of these conclusions? Reducing personal carbon dioxide emissions may require cutting the amount of travel both in private cars and in the food supply system. Merely shifting a small number of miles from car to foot will have virtually no impact, and may even harm the cause you are trying to promote. On the other hand, cutting your personal mileage by 20 per cent by taking the bus to work might save 0.5 tonnes of carbon dioxide.

Switching to a smaller car

When the time comes to retire your old car, you will save money and carbon by switching to a smaller, less powerful vehicle. Smaller car engines produce less carbon dioxide than big ones. This is not quite as trivial a statement as it sounds; some of the most efficient engines in the world, such as those that move huge ships, are highly efficient at turning fossil fuels into kinetic energy. What makes large car engines relatively fuel inefficient is that they are engineered to produce high power and to move larger, heavier vehicles with faster acceleration.

A statistical examination of the current Toyota portfolio is shown in Table 10.8. Very approximately, the move from a 1.0 litre car to a 2.0 litre model adds about 60–70g of carbon dioxide per kilometre driven.

Table 10.8 *Carbon dioxide emissions of Toyota petrol cars, early 2006*

Model	Engine size (litre)*	CO_2 (g/km)
Prius	not applicable	104
Yaris	1.0	129
	1.3	133
Corolla	1.4	159
	1.6	168
Avensis	1.8	171
	2.0	193
Previa	2.4	226

Note: *Petrol fuel and manual transmission.

Source: www.toyota.co.uk, accessed January 2006

For the household using the car for an average distance a year, the saving in carbon dioxide arising from using a 1.0 litre engine rather than a 2.0 litre monster is about 1 tonne of carbon dioxide. This is about 40 per cent of the average car's emissions, so is a more than worthwhile contribution.

Change to diesel or manual transmission

The car industry has done a good job of ensuring that few people recognize the fuel-efficiency deterioration from moving to automatic transmission. On the Toyota range, the equivalent automatics have emissions that are typically 12 per cent higher than the manual model. In the case of automatics, the process of transmitting engine power to the wheels through the transmission system turns a larger percentage of engine power into heat, rather than kinetic energy.

With a typical car and an average mileage, a manual transmission saves about 0.3 tonnes of carbon dioxide.

Diesel versus petrol

Diesel is much heavier than petrol and although its energy content per kilogram is lower, the greater density more than makes up for this deficiency. So, although diesel is more expensive at the pumps than petrol, it delivers more energy per litre. Better fuel economy in the diesel engine also improves carbon dioxide emissions.

I have seen a wide range of estimates for the characteristic improvement in comparably powered engines from switching from petrol to diesel. Some are as high as 40 per cent; but comparisons of similar petrol and diesel Toyota models suggest an average figure of about 17 per cent. To quote an example: the 2.0 Avensis engine produces 155g of carbon dioxide per kilometre in the diesel variant, compared to 193g in the petrol form.

If the average carbon dioxide output is 2.6 tonnes per year, then switching to a diesel car of similar size will save over 400kg per year (note that the average figure for all UK cars mixes petrol and diesel vehicles and would be higher if it only included the petrol cars on the road). Over a 16-year life, the savings will be over 6 tonnes of CO_2.

Diesel cars are, however, more expensive. The typical vehicle seems to be about £1000 more expensive than a similar petrol motor car. So, the cost per tonne of carbon dioxide saved is about £150 – much better than for an LPG or a hybrid electric car. Each year, the fuel savings might average £160, giving a seven-year payback. There will be a small saving in excise duty as well.

Strict environmentalists frown on diesels because of the higher levels of emission of particulates and some other pollutants. Cleaner diesel engines will reduce these problems over time. Or you could use an LPG car instead, which reduces particulate emissions to very low levels.

And, as usual, there's the possibility of the cheaper costs of running a diesel, which act as an incentive to the driver to travel more. One study in France showed that drivers who moved from petrol to diesel cars increased their travel by an average of 17 per cent.[169] We need to absorb this lesson – make something cheaper and people will consume more.

Small diesel manuals compared to average petrol automatics

A small diesel car with a manual transmission offers the best carbon dioxide performance of conventional cars. The Toyota Yaris, in its 1.4 litre diesel form, manages emissions of 117g per kilometre, and the Nissan Micra almost matches this with 119g. These cars would save about 0.9 tonnes of carbon dioxide a year compared to the characteristic UK petrol car. These cars are, of course, far cheaper than the Toyota Prius, the only car that beats them for emissions.

Electric cars

Decent electric cars have been promised for years; but true equivalents to internal combustion cars are still not here. Batteries are too large, performance is poor and none of the factors that enthuses car buyers – speed, acceleration, comfort and looks – are possessed by the current range of products. Attempts in the US to build vehicles to help meet stricter emissions control standards have generally flopped.

The only possible exception to the gloom is the success of some very small short-range 'city' cars, which barely improve on the speed and acceleration of electric postal delivery vehicles. The most obvious current example in the UK is the Bangalore-made, but California-designed, G-Wiz car. It seats two people in reasonable comfort; but you wouldn't want to drive it on a motorway. It claims to have the space to put a couple of children in the back, as well. They would have to be quite small children.

The car needs about 9kWh of electricity to charge the battery. This – the retailer claims – will take the car about 40 miles (64km). How does this compare in terms of carbon emissions? Using an estimate of the average UK carbon emissions from electricity generation, this car puts out about 63g per kilometre. This figure is slightly more than half the figure of ultra-low emission diesels. What about the cost of running it? If a charge of 9kWh (at about 7.5 pence per kWh) takes the car 40 miles (64km), the cost is about 1.7 pence per mile (1 pence per kilometre). The lowest figure for a small diesel driving in the city is likely to be about 8 pence per mile, or more than four times as much.

Of course, such a car would never drive 14,500km (9000 miles) a year; but if it did it would (indirectly) emit about 0.9 tonnes of carbon dioxide, compared to the 2.6 tonnes UK average. For the typical urban-only user doing perhaps 8000km (5000 miles) a year, the saving over the smallest conventional cars would be about 0.5 tonnes. The benefit over a Prius would be as little as 0.3 tonnes, although at about £7000, the G-Wiz is a fraction of the price of the hybrid. In addition, the low weight of the G-Wiz means that far less energy is used in its manufacture.

The vehicle escapes congestion charge and vehicle taxation. The exemption from vehicle duty seems to be based on the car being classed as a powered bicycle, or, more precisely, a Quadra cycle. Its 400 or so London owners also escape some car parking charges and some municipal car parks offer free charging.

Small electric city cars are clearly a useful addition to the range of emissions reducing technologies in use in cars. They are not, however, a real replacement for conventional saloon cars. Without some form of incentive, such as severe restrictions on the average emissions of motor vehicles placed on each manufacturer, it seems unlikely that electric cars are going to represent a real alternative to internal combustion engines for at least a decade. But advances in battery technology keep on raising the hope that cheap, light electric cars will replace most liquid fuel-driven cars.

The advertising for electric vehicles often refers to the vehicles as 'zero emission'. They are not. They use electricity, generated by fossil fuel combustion. And if power generation becomes more carbon-intensive as a result of a swing towards coal-fired generation, the relatively small advantages of electric cars over diesel will decrease. This raises a thought: the best way to power an electric domestic car is by installing a small wind turbine on the roof in order to charge the battery. This way, we can be sure that the electricity is genuinely emissions free. Combining a rooftop wind turbine and a car battery would be an exceptionally effective way of using a turbine. It would also mean that the turbine owner would not have to buy the expensive equipment necessary to plug it into the grid. The power could go straight into the car battery.

This would make an electric car truly emission neutral, but would be dependent upon the wind blowing. I suppose that if the wind wasn't turning the blades, the next best alternative would be to only charge the car in the middle of the night, when the emissions from electricity are low because the (relatively) carbon-free nuclear plant is generally the only generating capacity at work.

Car clubs

Finding methods of sharing cars looks a very productive way of reducing total car use. This can be done informally, with neighbours jointly owning and maintaining a car. Or it can be done through commercially operated car clubs. These clubs buy cars and place them in on-street locations, often granted free by the local authority. Local people join as members, usually by paying a fee of £100 or so. Upon joining, members can use the internet to book the cars close to them, or indeed anywhere else in the country. Access is via an electronic key. Use of the car is paid for by an hourly rate and a mileage charge, with the car automatically transmitting details of use back to the owner via a data-only mobile phone. Members pay for petrol when needed through a company fuel card – that is, they don't themselves pay directly because the fuel cost is included in the mileage charge.

Table 10.9 gives some details of the pricing of two UK firms operating in this market.

Car clubs seem to work best in London, with its high parking charges, astronomical insurance rates and – I suspect – relatively low mileage users. As of September 2006, Streetcar says that it has 150 cars and 5000 members. Its coverage of central London and the immediate suburbs is good, including (to pick one example out of the air) five locations in Clapham.

Outside London, the coverage only includes Brighton and Southampton. Streetcar received considerable coverage in my local area, Oxford, a year ago by publicizing an imminent launch; but no cars have yet appeared on the streets. I emailed the company with

Table 10.9 *Some pricing details of two UK car clubs*

Club	Fixed fee	Hourly rate	Weekend rate	Mileage charge
Streetcar	£25 joining fee	£4.95	£99	Free 30 miles a day, then 19 pence a mile
CityCarClub	£15 a month	£2.80	£72	17 pence a mile

Source: www.streetcar.co.uk and www.citycarclub.co.uk, accessed September 2006

some suggestions for good locations in Oxford; but the response suggested little interest in the city. Expanding out of London seems tricky. Recent contact with CityCarClub suggests a similar reluctance to expand into Oxford without active help from the city council (the cars of a precursor scheme in Oxford were frequently given parking tickets by the city council, despite being parked in allocated spaces).

In other countries, the progress of car sharing seems a little quicker, although it is still a tiny fraction of the total market. Car clubs are a successful fixture in countries such as Switzerland. Zipcar in the US has a claimed 65,000 members and 1600 cars. It focuses on large cities on the Eastern seaboard and on areas near major university campuses. The prices are broadly comparable to the UK. The hourly charge in Boston is as low as $8.10, although this does come with free mileage up to 125 miles a day, rather than 30 miles as is the case with the UK's Streetcar.

The operators of car clubs claim major environmental benefits. Streetcar says that its members drive 68 per cent fewer miles than they did before joining (this is a major saving in carbon dioxide – perhaps 0.8 tonnes). Slightly implausibly, Zipcar says that each car that it rents takes at least 20 other vehicles off the road. Members of the scheme say that the car club saves them an average of $435 a month (more than £250). In similar fashion, Streetcar claims that an Automobile Association (AA) study showed a typical cost of £2749 a year for two trips a week in a car you own, compared to a Streetcar cost of £707 for the same journeys.

Are the cost savings advertised by the car clubs reasonable? Table 10.10 shows that Streetcar would appear to be very much cheaper than a leased car for ranges of mileage from 5000 to 15,000 miles a year. The table compares the monthly cost of using a leased car and expresses it per mile (from 90 pence down to 36 pence), with the Streetcar costs below (25 to 28 pence a mile). The assumptions behind the figures are simple, but reasonable. Because the first 30 miles a day are free, the Streetcar club member is assumed to pay no mileage charges at the lowest usage level, rising to being charged for 200 miles a month at the highest. These Streetcar figures may *overestimate* the car club costs because some of the trips might well be more cost effective if paid for on the daily, rather than the hourly, rate; or they might *underestimate* the costs if the user actually took a huge number of short trips, each lasting a fraction of the hour. For a large number of very short trips, a little electric runabout might be the best option, rather than a car club.

These figures show that the full cost of using a car appears to be much lower for Streetcar, although the advantage falls as the mileage increases. At 10,000 miles a year, the cost per mile is 27 pence for Streetcar and 50 pence for a new leased car. This is assuming that the driver travels the same number of miles even though car club members generally drive vehicles less than owners. This disparity suggests that, eventually, we all ought to be using car clubs.

Table 10.10 *Comparison of costs of leasing a car and using a car club*

		Monthly Cost		
		for 5000 miles per year	for 10,000 miles per year	for 15,000 miles per year
FLEXXilease	Car lease	270	270	270
	Insurance	45	45	45
	Maintenance	25	25	25
	Duty	Included	Included	Included
	Roadside assistance	Included	Included	Included
	Total fixed (£)	340	340	340
	Petrol (£)	36	73	109
	Total monthly cost (£)	376	413	449
	Cost per mile (pence) fixed	82	41	27
	variable	9	9	9
	total	90	50	36
Streetcar	Hours of use (assumes 20mph)	21	42	63
	Hourly price (£)	4.95	4.95	4.95
	Mileage charge (estimate) (£)	0	19	38
	Total monthly cost (£)	103	225	347
	Cost per mile (pence)	25	27	28

Source: www.streetcar.co.uk and www.flexxilease.co.in

Why do car club users tend to drive fewer miles? Owning or leasing a car obliges the owner to take on a high fixed cost, which does not vary much with the mileage travelled. Once paid for, the user only faces the variable cost (or 'marginal' cost in economists' language). This will tend to be much lower when the car is owned. So if you have a car, travelling the extra mile is cheap, even at today's petrol prices. But car club members face a high charge per mile and almost no fixed costs of ownership.

Human beings sometimes do not act as rational economic actors; but in this case we can see the price mechanism clearly at work. If you have your own car, and have committed to pay the fixed costs, then you will drive even on those occasions when you might walk or not take the trip at all. The cost is tiny. But Streetcar users face a £3.95 bill every time they start the engine. The high charge causes them to ration their use to a fraction of their usual mileage. Therefore, car clubs are good for vehicle emissions and good for the wallets of their members.

Why are they not taking off faster? Why have they actually failed in many UK cities? There are a number of obvious reasons:

- The possession of a private car in the driveway gives total convenience. The user can drive off in a few seconds. The car clubs claim very high levels of availability – more than 95 per cent; but they can never guarantee a vehicle immediately.
- A car is an important symbol of status.
- The economic advantages are perhaps not important enough, or are perhaps difficult to observe and measure.
- Many people run much older cars than the new leased car in the example above. These cars have much lower fixed costs because they are no longer depreciating rapidly and, second, the cost of financing them is low. A car worth £5000 is probably depreciating at less than £1000 a year. If we impute a finance cost of 5 per cent a year on the £5000, the charge is £250. So the truly fixed cost of a £5000 car is probably less than £1250, or £100 a month. In addition, there will be tax, insurance and maintenance costs, and perhaps a parking charge. These will raise the cost by another £100 or so a month. This makes car clubs still worthwhile for motorists doing as much as 10,000 miles (16,000km) a year.
- Last, and possibly most important, people may resist car clubs because of the 'ticking meter'. We all instinctively realize that we are prepared to pay more for the feeling of not paying by the minute. British Telecom (BT), for example, found out before it launched its un-metered telephone calling plans that customers would happily pay 20 per cent more than was strictly rational if they knew that all calls were free once the monthly fixed charge had been paid. Imagine going to pick up a friend at the station in a car club vehicle. In your own car, a train delay would be irritating; but in the club car, the burden might double as a result. To many people, the psychological cost of this would be too great for comfort.

So, car clubs may or may not work in UK urban centres (they are never likely to appeal to those who have to drive to work every day from rural homes with no bus service). Nevertheless, the environmental benefits seem high and the cost savings real. What could policy-makers do? Their aim might be to:

- Increase the variable ('marginal') cost of running a private car. This means increasing the price of petrol in relation to the capital and fixed costs of car ownership. This will make the use of a private car appear to have a cost that is more similar to the car clubs. The problem? It will penalize those in rural areas using a car for travel to work.

- Provide explicit encouragement to car clubs, perhaps by providing free parking spaces in urban areas or by letting users utilize priority lanes.

In the case of increasing the variable costs of private cars, the best way for governments to encourage car clubs is probably to introduce congestion charging – or 'road pricing' in the current parlance – as a means of discouraging private car use at busy times. The most important feature of these schemes is that rural users escape most of the charge; but the urban middle class carting their children to and from school will get hammered. If these latter people could escape road pricing by using car club cars, then the economic incentives for the schemes would increase.

The second economic incentive – encouraging car clubs, rather than discouraging private cars – will probably work best in areas where parking represents a genuine and persistent problem. Obliging developers of new housing to provide no parking except for car club vehicles would be a radical means of encouraging the move away from the two-car household.

Biofuels

In theory, almost all vehicles can run on oils made from plants (biodiesel) or ethanol made from grains and roots (bioethanol, or bio-petrol). Some pioneers are already using used vegetable oils to power diesel cars. Using vegetable oils as the fuel for an engine is not as eccentric as it sounds; Rudolf Diesel's first engine ran on peanut oil when it was exhibited at the Paris World's Fair in 1900.

Vehicle fuels based on processed agricultural crops and oils will attract large amounts of favourable attention over the next few years. Be suspicious. Biofuels look as though they are 'renewable' in the same sense that electricity can be, offering substantial energy without increasing greenhouse gas emissions. But, as is unfortunately often the case in climate change debates, the reality is more complex than the proponents claim. If we substantially increase the volume of biofuel use, we will run into two major problems:

1   Biofuels may use as much fossil fuel in their production as they replace in vehicles.
2   Agricultural land is not particularly good at generating energy for use in fuels. If we were to produce a substantial fraction of our vehicle fuels from crops, most of the land area of the UK would have to be given over to this use. In terms of carbon reduction, we would be far better advised to plant this land with trees.

Before delving into the reasons for scepticism about biofuels made directly from crops, we should acknowledge the efforts of the pioneers of today's biodiesel. Many of these people are not using new agricultural products for fuel, about which there are such fundamental reservations, but are recycling waste products, such as used cooking oil. In such cases, the carbon consequences are exceptionally favourable; but the volume of used vegetable oil is tiny compared to the demand for petrol. Nevertheless, if you ever see a car powered by cooking oil, you know you are watching one of the most nearly carbon neutral vehicles on the planet. The only complaint from their enthusiastic owners is that their exhaust fumes betray the origin of the fuel, whether it is chip shop or school kitchen.

Made in tiny factories – a garage would be big enough to house a small plant – biodiesel from waste oil is a product we could use a lot more of. But the supplies of used oil are highly restricted and could only power just over 100,000 cars even if all of the UK's supply of waste oil was used.[170] Nevertheless, there are already 250 factories churning out diesel that smells ever so slightly like a mobile chip van.

In theory, almost all diesel cars can use processed vegetable oils collected from chip shops, at least as part of their fuel mix. More conventionally, crops such as oilseed rape can be refined to provide oil to power cars and commercial vehicles. Many diesels now run on a 5 per cent biodiesel mixture that is increasingly available at filling stations.

Biodiesel has been used for some time in the UK; but 'bio-petrol' made from ethanol is newer, having been restricted so far to foreign markets such as Brazil and Sweden. This is changing because a number of bioethanol production plants are now planned for the UK. Petrol cars can be modified to accept ethanol – usually made from wheat or sugar beet in temperate countries – as part of a petrol mix, much as biodiesel can be added to fossil diesel. Some vehicles, such as the Saab 9-5 Biopower, can use a much richer mixture of 85 per cent ethanol/15 per cent petrol, though very few filling stations in the UK carry bioethanol yet. So the Saab can also be fuelled with conventional petrol. As with LPG, the first customers will probably be fleets of vehicles that all return regularly to one location, such as delivery vans, where they can fill up with biofuel at a central point.

These fuels, biodiesel from oilseed rape or ethanol from wheat or sugar beet, are probably not cost competitive with petrol using today's technologies. Production costs for agricultural products are greater than for petrol, even at the crude oil prices now being seen. As a result, biofuels can only be a comparable price at the pumps if they are taxed at a lower level. Current biofuel tax is set at about 28 pence per litre, or at least 20 pence less than conventional petrol. Even with this 'subsidy', pure biodiesel – at those few places where it is available – tends to be at least as expensive as conventional diesel. Biodiesel gives approximately the same energy output per litre as fossil fuel, so comparisons can be made litre for litre. One additional and important fact is that cars and vans using biodiesel produce a far more limited range of non-carbon-dioxide pollutants than conventional diesel. For example, exhaust emissions will be completely sulphur free.

The government has provided an additional incentive. From 2010, 5 per cent of all vehicle fuels in the UK must be provided from biomass sources. This will include both ethanol and biodiesel, probably always mixed as a 5 per cent additive to petrol or conventional diesel.

Despite the increasing enthusiasm, manufacturers of diesel cars are frankly equivocal about the biological product. They know that it will probably work on cars constructed since the early 1980s. Made before this date, and biodiesel might corrode some of the fuel pipes and connectors. Today, 100 per cent biodiesel should work in any conventional diesel engine; but manufacturers are reluctant to say this openly for fear that any engine problems will be blamed on the fuel. Indeed, the enthusiasts say that biodiesel, because it is a relatively clean product, helps to keep the engine parts free from the build-up of soot. Manufacturers will, however, support the 5 per cent product, which has now been tested thoroughly, sometimes on cars whose owners may be unaware of the biodiesel additive.

So far, so good. Biodiesel and ethanol are made from agricultural products that can be grown on UK arable land. Properly looked after, this land can produce fuel energy forever. However, this doesn't make the biofuels truly carbon neutral. The agricultural products use substantial volumes of fossil fuels in the forms of oil-based fertilizers, processing energy and road transport.

How much fossil fuel energy is used to make a unit of biodiesel or bioethanol energy? The debate on this question is not always completely even tempered. Some sources suggest that biodiesel and, particularly, bioethanol will generally use more fossil fuel energy than they provide in the car. In other words, there is no net benefit in greenhouse gas emissions from switching a car to biofuels. The leading proponent of the view that biofuels are energy inefficient has been Professor David Pimentel of Cornell University in the US. His work suggests that neither diesel nor ethanol produced from agricultural crops actually reduces the net amount of fossil fuel used.

This is a similar conclusion to the depressing analysis in Table 10.7 that suggested that walking may actually add to climate change if we replace the energy we use by eating foods grown by the Western system of industrial agriculture. Agricultural is, in general, hugely energy inefficient, so it makes little sense to see food products as themselves a source of power. Pimentel recently wrote: 'the United States desperately needs a liquid fuel replacement for oil in the near future; but producing ethanol or biodiesel from plant biomass is going down the wrong road because you use more energy to produce these fuels than you get out from the combustion of these products'.[171] Perhaps with justice, Pimentel sees ethanol production in the US as simply the outcome of the distortion caused by the subsidization of uneconomic agriculture.

This is one view, backed with persuasive science. Others see biodiesel as reasonably good for carbon emissions. Two producer associations have published research that shows that biodiesel has an energy output of 1.44 or 1.78 times the energy input.[172, 173] These figures, showing that 1 litre of biodiesel causes greenhouse gas emissions either 31 per cent or 44 per cent lower than 1 litre of fossil diesel, assume that the waste matter, such as straw, left in the field is not burned for energy (this is currently a reasonable assumption; few farmers are able to take their straw to a plant where it can be burned for electricity production, either here or in the US). Similarly, other waste products, including the glycerol extracted from the oil to stop car engines from gumming up, are assumed to have no residual energy value.

At the optimistic end of the opinion spectrum, biodiesel's proponents see the fuel as being four times as efficient as diesel, in terms of fossil fuel use. Numbers for ethanol are lower, seemingly because of the greater processing necessary to turn wheat, maize or sugar into the end product.

This debate will continue for years. And the future of biofuels is probably more tied to the support system for agriculture than to fundamental economics. As long as biofuels remain much more expensive than fossil fuels, their use is only going to expand significantly because of government support. This support is certainly there today, but may be more to do with the need to maintain agricultural industries than resulting from a concern over global warming. It may not be a coincidence that the UK's first bioethanol plant to use beet sugar as its agricultural input was finally approved soon after the agreement to end the repugnant EU export subsidy that has done so much to harm the sugar farmers of the tropics. The government needed to find an alternative market for beet to replace the lost markets elsewhere, and support for bioethanol does the job. This doesn't make it good for climate change, or even good for the taxpayer.

The latest thinking is actually not to make biodiesel from conventional agricultural crops at all. Algae certainly offer a better ratio of the conversion of input energy to the output of fuel. A pilot plant is operational at the Massachusetts Institute of Technology (MIT). But, of course, agri-business will not be as interested in pushing this technology.

Despite the intense controversy over the precise energy benefit from biodiesel, I thought, nevertheless, that it might be helpful if I estimated the maximum carbon dioxide saving from biodiesel. Perhaps optimistically, I have assumed in Table 10.11 that biodiesel will offer a 50 per cent saving in greenhouse gas emissions. Why is this reasonable if even the producer associations actually offer lower figures than this? My justifications are twofold:

1 Biodiesel manufacturing processes are getting more efficient.
2 Fossil diesel itself requires energy to produce. Extracting, refining, transporting and pumping diesel means that 1 unit of oil extracted from the Earth's crust delivers only about 0.83 units of usable energy in the form of diesel.

But this is a naive analysis and needs to be made more complex. We need to include the impact of land-use change on carbon dioxide emissions. Put simply, if 1 acre (0.4ha) of land is used for crops to produce a biofuel, that land cannot be cropped for food. So if we

Table 10.11 *The carbon dioxide impact of switching to 5 per cent biodiesel*

	Typical CO_2 emissions per kilometre	Average emissions per year, assuming 14,500km (9000 miles) driven
Conventional diesel car	0.150 tonnes	2.18 tonnes
5 per cent biodiesel car	0.146 tonnes	2.12 tonnes
Saving		2.5 per cent

are to make significant quantities of biodiesel or ethanol, we will need to add to the area under arable cultivation. The amounts of land needed are surprisingly large. To replace the current UK demand for diesel with its biological equivalent would require about 12 million to 13 million hectares of arable land if the crop grown was oilseed rape. At the moment, only about 4.5 million hectares are cultivated in the UK. So, to replace fossil diesel, we would need to approximately triple the land under crops. Since this would entail moving onto land that is of marginal fertility, yields would suffer greatly. Since a large fraction of all UK land that can be productively used for arable cultivation is currently already being worked for food, there is little prospect of ever growing enough oilseed rape. Even if biodiesel is sold only in the 5 per cent form, we would still require about 0.6 million hectares. In itself, this seems too much and would more than double the acreage of rape. Seen from the air in May, most of lowland England would glow a bright yellow from the flowers of this impressively bright brassica.

Even if we could convert some extra land to arable cultivation, would this be good for climate change? The answer is almost certainly no because the land would be better used for woodland. One hectare of English oak (*Quercus robur*) captures about 275 tonnes of carbon dioxide over 100 years.[174] At 50 per cent energy efficiency, oilseed rape probably replaces about 225 tonnes of fossil fuel diesel emissions over the same period. In other words, it is slightly better to convert 1ha to the growing of a slowly maturing tree than it is to convert it to oilseed rape for biofuels. Using the land for fast-growing willow, and then coppicing the trees for fuel, would be even better – although this depends upon the percentage efficiency in the power plant burning the wood chippings from the willow.

George Monbiot has made similar arguments about the conversion of tropical forests to palm oil plantations that are intended to produce the feedstock for biodiesel.[175] He points out that the furious rate of planting of tropical plants is largely driven by the EU's imposition of a target for the biological content of vehicle fuels by 2010. Perversely, this apparently benign aim is inflicting huge damage on areas that should be kept as slow-growing forest.

The figures behind biofuels are not as good as are sometimes pretended. Examine, for example, the press release put out by Saab, part of General Motors (GM), when it announced the imminent arrival of the bioethanol car in the UK in late 2005:

> *Unlike petrol and diesel, the consumption of E85 (85 per cent ethanol/ 15 per cent petrol) does not significantly raise atmospheric levels of carbon dioxide (CO_2), which is the greenhouse gas that, according to some scientific research, contributes to global warming. This is because the emissions that are released from the combustion of bioethanol whilst driving are cancelled out by the amount of CO_2 that is removed from the atmosphere, through the natural photosynthesis process, when the crops for conversion to bioethanol are grown. When running on E85, Saab 9–5 BioPower's fossil CO_2 emissions are estimated to be between 50 per cent and 70 per cent cleaner than when running on petrol.*[176]

This marketing literature is remarkable for two reasons: first, the coy statement that carbon dioxide 'contributes' to global warming, at least 'according to some scientific research', and, second, the remarkable assertion that E85 can reduce carbon dioxide emissions by perhaps 70 per cent. E85 is 15 per cent petrol, so this suggestion implies that the 85 per cent ethanol only adds the equivalent of another 15 per cent petrol. In other words, the ethanol only takes about one sixth as much energy to produce as it provides to the car (85 per cent/15 per cent). In hours of research, I've found no source that offers any figures for ethanol energy balance that are remotely as good as Saab/GM suggests.

Perhaps as importantly, the range of cars to which the BioPower technology is added is highly fuel inefficient. The automatic 2.0 litre engine has carbon dioxide emissions of 0.244kg per kilometre, almost 45 per cent above the average for UK new cars. Even if ethanol were the wonder fuel that Saab/GM claims, the car would need most of the magic just to get emissions down to median level for new cars. Perhaps the real reason Saab launched the car is contained in the comment below taken from an internet review:

> *For the 9–5 BioPower Saloon, for example, the zero to 62mph dash can be accomplished in 8.5 seconds, compared to 9.8 seconds when running only on petrol.*[177]

The extra fuel used to accelerate faster will, of course, add to the total emissions of the car. The environmental credentials of the Saab BioPower are thin.

CARBON EMISSIONS FROM CARS: DATA FROM OTHER COUNTRIES

The average UK new car has emissions of about 169g of carbon dioxide per kilometre. This compares with the 15 European Union (EU) member states' average of 164g in 2003. The EU average is lower partly because of the higher percentage of diesel cars in the sales mix of other countries.

Commenting on recent trends, Friends of the Earth said that the UK has the fourth highest average emissions from new cars in the EU15: 'The highest average emissions are in Sweden (193.7g per kilometre of CO_2) and the lowest in Portugal (145.1g per kilometre of CO_2). UK emissions are slightly lower than those in Germany (170.8g per kilometre of CO_2) and substantially higher than those in France (151.9g per kilometre of CO_2).[178] The UK has moved slightly closer to the European average in recent years. The total mileage for surface passenger transport, of which car travel is the predominant form, rose by 30 per cent in the EU15 between 1990 and 2002, and this increase continues.[179] This was almost exactly the same growth rate as European gross domestic product (GDP), suggesting that car use is still closely coupled to economic growth. Germany is the only EU country in which emissions from transport are on a declining path.

FASHION AND FAD

The complicated economic analysis necessary to work out how best to reduce emissions from private cars should not disguise the important requirement to reduce car use in all Western societies. New technologies, such as hybrid cars or oilseed rape for biodiesel, may or may not assist us in cutting vehicle emissions. What will definitely work is getting drivers to cut their annual mileage. Technology, such as the recurrent dream of creating hydrogen cars, may actually impede the search to understand the social levers we might use to cut car mileage. Fantasizing about a hydrogen car may reinforce our optimism that science, rather than behavioural change, will solve our problems. To restate the point made at the beginning of this chapter: moving 1 tonne of metal from standstill to 60mph is an inherently energy-intensive activity. Nothing can gainsay this. And because car travel requires reliably available liquid fuels – gases not being dense enough to store in a conventionally shaped vehicle – the scope for replacing hydrocarbons with renewable energy is limited.

11

. . . .

public transport

All motorized travel is carbon-intensive, but bus and rail are generally far better than cars. Actual carbon emission figures vary according to the type of vehicle and the number of people using it. Intercity coaches are best – as low as 20g of CO_2 per passenger kilometre. These coaches travel long distances and often carry large numbers of passengers. This makes them the best form of travel if one wants to avoid carbon dioxide. On the other hand, empty rural buses are sometimes as bad as cars in terms of emissions per passenger.

The average UK citizen travels about 700km on railways each year. I think the official figures for average emissions are too low, so I use an estimate of 49g per kilometre travelled. The busiest commuter lines will be much better than this, but powerful and heavy long-distance trains may be worse than the average, especially if they are powered by electricity. Total emissions per year average just less than 35kg.

People travel shorter distances by bus – only 400km a year – and the average emissions per year are probably about 30kg at an average of about 70g per kilometre.

The conventional view is that all public transport has relatively low emissions. This belief has considerable truth, but is not a wholly reliable guide to action. A decision today to take the coach rather than drive to London from Birmingham has undeniably positive effects; but across all buses and trains, carbon emissions are more substantial than one imagines. Nevertheless, most people travel very little on public transport. The typical individual accounts for about 35kg of carbon dioxide emissions from rail services, and about the same from bus and coach travel compared to over 1 tonne from car travel.

RAIL

Per kilometre travelled, the government uses a figure of 40g of carbon dioxide per passenger kilometre, or less than one quarter of the typical car[180] (so even having four people in a car means that it would, on average, be better to go by rail). The UK Department for Environment, Food and Rural Affairs' (Defra's) estimate is derived from information about the total diesel and electricity consumption of trains and from knowledge of the number of passenger kilometres. In 2001, the figure used by Defra was very much higher – at 60g per passenger kilometre. This degree of reduction seems highly implausible, although trains have been getting much fuller in the last few years, so the emissions per passenger will certainly be falling (in addition, the swing towards lower-carbon sources of electricity, primarily gas, reduced the emissions from electrically powered trains, at least until the recent swing back to coal).

Individual railway operators produce their own estimates of carbon dioxide per passenger kilometre. National Express says that its rail services average 64g of CO_2 per passenger kilometre.[181] First Group does not appear to give a figure for its own services, but quotes research that suggests an average of 49g of carbon dioxide per passenger kilometre.[182] I prefer to believe this figure rather than Defra's rather optimistic guideline of

40g per kilometre. My suggested figure is about half the figure for British Airways' carbon dioxide emissions per passenger kilometre (or one sixth if one takes into account the other pollutants created by air travel). So, going by train, rather than air, does make a big difference.

What does this mean for the typical rail commuter, with a round trip of 30km carried out 200 times a year? He or she would be responsible for approximately 300kg of emissions, compared to an average of well over 1 tonne from a car with a single passenger.

The typical UK resident travels on a train 17 times a year, for an average of 40km a time. Total journeys over the year amount to about 700km per person, slightly below the European average.[183] This implies carbon dioxide emissions per person of about 35kg, or about 0.3 per cent of the total. The UK rail industry is responsible for 2 million tonnes of carbon dioxide, and increases in travel are likely to push this number up to over 4 million tonnes by early in the next decade. If this is as a result of substitution of car or air travel, then we can be happy. If the travel is, instead, incremental and will arise from further growth of longer-distance commuting into London, then it is another indication of the deleterious carbon impact of the gradual overwhelming of the south-east of England by the gigantic appetite of the capital for people and resources.

The relatively small current emissions of about 2 million tonnes of carbon dioxide for the rail industry disguise two important trends. First, the total amount of rail travel is rising, particularly within the London commuting area. This makes for greater efficiency in fuel consumption. But, second, many of the new long-distance trains are heavier and more aggressively powered than the older diesel commuter trains. The Pendolino train, running at high speed between Manchester and London, weighs as much per passenger seat as half a Landrover Discovery. The exciting new trains can go faster, accelerate more rapidly and weigh far more per passenger seat than old stock. But they use far more fuel. In these respects, they are like modern cars compared to the older generations of automobiles, or big liquid crystal display (LCD) TVs compared to the televisions of five years ago.

Improvements in rail locomotive efficiency have been swallowed up by faster speeds and heavier carriages. This is, of course, a recurring theme.

One example makes this clear. Elderly Class 168 diesels, carrying 278 seats on the regional rail network, are powered by engines with a total output of 1260kW. New 'Adelante' trains, which have made my recent journeys from Oxford to London much more comfortable and reliable, have engines of 2800kW output but only carry 265 passengers. These new trains have well over twice the engine power per seat. Unsurprisingly, Adelante emissions are one third higher per passenger kilometre than the average diesel train in the UK.[184] Trains are losing their advantages, particularly on the less crowded routes.

Very high-speed trains are surprisingly inefficient in terms of carbon, particularly if they are powered by electricity (electricity, a secondary source of energy, is more carbon intensive than fossil fuels such as diesel – or gas at home; electric trains are 30 per cent more polluting than diesel). One interesting study tries to show how car travel from London to Edinburgh can be less polluting than high-speed rail.[185] It relies on some assumptions that can be criticized, such as assuming low thermal efficiency in power stations; but it did demonstrate that long-distance rail travel does not solve the carbon dioxide problem. More particularly, it shows that trying to help rail to compete with air travel by improving track speeds always has a significant penalty in terms of fuel consumption. Faster speeds require heavier, more powerful trains, which reduces the fuel use advantage over air travel.

Those interested in accurately calculating their carbon 'footprint' from rail travel need to make an adjustment if they sit in the bigger seats in first class. First-class carriages have much lower capacity than the crowded standard service. So, as with executive class air travel, we need to apply a premium. Carbon dioxide output from first-class travel will be approximately 50 per cent more than travel in standard seats.

BUS AND COACH

Outside London, bus travel is still falling in most parts of the country. This fact, and the huge differences between empty rural buses and fully occupied intercity coaches, makes data on bus emissions particularly difficult. One figure suggests an average of 76g of carbon dioxide per passenger kilometre, or about 50 per cent more than rail.[186] But break this down, and the huge range becomes apparent. National Express, which operates both buses

---

BUS AND RAIL TRAVEL: DATA FROM OTHER COUNTRIES

Bus travel in other countries is sometimes substantially higher than in the UK. Denmark and Greece have a typical bus mileage of over 5km a day, compared to little more than 1km in the UK. The UK share of bus and coach travel in total surface transport is 6.5 per cent compared to nearly 9 per cent in the 15 European Union (EU) member states as a whole; but France and The Netherlands, for example, are substantially lower than in the UK.

UK rail travel is also a slightly smaller share of total surface travel than in the EU15 as a whole (5.5 per cent versus 6.5 per cent). Unlike the UK, countries such as France and The Netherlands, with low bus travel figures, have substantially higher rail travel at 8.6 per cent and 9.3 per cent, respectively.[188] Emissions from rail vary significantly between countries, depending upon, first, whether the system uses electricity or diesel, and, second, whether the electricity is generated by nuclear power or coal, at the other extreme. The French fast trains (*trains à grande vitesse*, or TGVs) use electricity for power; but most of this is generated by nuclear power.

and coaches, gives figures showing a fourfold difference between its buses and its coaches. Coaches – usually run over long distances – have little more than half the emissions of rail (28g of carbon dioxide per passenger kilometre compared to 49g); but buses are only half as efficient as rail (104g per passenger per kilometre, the same as the best hybrid electric car).

The average number of bus or coach trips per year is about 60, with the distance travelled about 400km, compared to 700km on the railways. For someone travelling in a mixture of bus and coach, the total emissions from this average number of journeys would be about 30kg.

Despite the immediate appearance to the contrary, urban buses are probably very much better for the atmosphere than private cars. It might seem that two people travelling in a car would have lower emissions levels than travelling on a bus.[187] This would probably be mistaken because the car's fuel consumption as it jerked along between endless traffic lights getting in or out of a city will probably be little better than half that of the same car travelling as 60mph on a motorway.

The typical bus produces about 1.3kg of carbon dioxide for each kilometre travelled.[189] The average car, over the mixed cycle used for the standard emissions test, has an output of about 180g per kilometre, or about one seventh of the bus. So, it's very likely that buses are more efficient than cars in all circumstances when they have at least seven times as many occupants as the typical car (1.59 occupants). Many buses, of course, do not achieve this, particularly in rural areas; so the assumption that buses are invariably less polluting is highly arguable.

Coach travel definitely offers very substantial savings over the car. National Express believes that its London to Birmingham coach reduces emissions by over 90 per cent compared to the same trip by a car with a single occupant – if the coach is full.[190] Many coaches do, indeed, operate at near capacity, and for city-to-city travel, they represent a very low-emission type of transport, easily beating rail. Attempts by governments to increase coach use – as long as it is diverting customers from rail, car and air – are particularly to be valued. Comfortable and spacious coaches should be less polluting, and cheaper, than rail travel.

Of course, it is always better not to travel using fossil fuel energy at all.

12

air travel

Travelling by air, in contrast to the train, is an almost unmitigated disaster for the environment. Although an efficient aircraft, travelling fully loaded, can cover miles with less fuel per person than the average car, aircraft travel covers vastly greater distances than cars. The average car goes 9000 miles (14,500km) a year, with an average of about 1.5 people in it at any time. One return flight to the US will probably exceed the per-person emissions of a year's car use.

More importantly, air travel is inherently more polluting than car journeys. As well as carbon dioxide, jet engines emit oxides of nitrogen, which are powerful warming agents. In addition, aircraft put out huge quantities of water vapour at high altitude in the form of condensation trails. These contrails are now thought to worsen global warming, although the science is not yet completely clear. As a result of these two extra emissions, most experts now think that air travel emissions are about three times as bad as the simple carbon dioxide output might suggest. A few flights to remote locations, and we have been responsible for tens of tonnes of global warming gases.

Across the world as a whole, air travel is probably responsible for about 3 per cent of carbon emissions. Multiply this by three to account for the nitrogen oxides and water vapour, and we are almost up to 10 per cent. In the UK, the figure is already 5.5 per cent for carbon dioxide alone and 16.5 per cent after the multiplication. Air travel is growing by 5 per cent a year, and although engines are becoming more efficient, carbon emissions are certainly increasing by around 2.5 per cent a year. No one sees an end to this growth – cheap air travel is immensely popular and many governments are willing to build airports to accommodate the extra travel. The consequence of unconstrained growth of aircraft emissions, even at the relatively modest rate of 2.5 per cent compounded a year, is to double aircraft emissions in the next 30 years. In the UK, that will mean average emissions per person of 3 tonnes just for aircraft travel. This is inconsistent with any aspirations to hold back climate change.

The only really significant change to our lifestyle that we need to make to get our carbon emissions down to 3 tonnes is to cease to travel by air. With this single choice, we can make the most important step to meeting the long-term requirement to cut our contribution to climate change.

To a surprising extent, air transport use drives individual greenhouse gas emissions. Of course, variations in car use are important. But air travel really determines how much carbon dioxide a person generates. A car user who never travelled by air might directly cause the emission of about 3.6 tonnes of carbon dioxide a year.

Table 12.1 *Carbon dioxide emissions by a typical UK individual taking no flights*

Electricity in the home	0.7 tonnes
Gas in the home	1.6 tonnes
Car use	1.2 tonnes
Other ground transport	0.1 tonnes
Total	3.6 tonnes

However much an individual does to minimize his or her impact on the environment, any measures are dwarfed by the impact of taking a few air flights a year. No single step that we could take as individuals to take responsibility for global warming comes close to deciding to stop flying.

What is the impact of adding flying to the total? Table 12.2 includes the three times multiplier applied to properly weight the other greenhouse impacts of flying.

Table 12.2 *The impact on personal carbon dioxide emissions of a small number of flights*

Three return flights within Europe	Average 3000km each(slightly less than thedistance to Rome)	4.5 tonnes
One return flight to the US	10,000km	3.6 tonnes
Total		8.1 tonnes

Many reasonably well-off people take this number of flights every year. The four return flights might include a summer holiday in Greece, a skiing trip at Christmas, a professional conference in Barcelona and a flight to a customer in Chicago.

The total number of flights taken by UK individuals from UK airports is currently about 45 million a year. With 60 million people in the country, the average person takes less than one air trip a year. So, on average, people's greenhouse gas emissions from air travel are significant, but not overwhelming. However, for the increasing number of individuals regularly taking air travel, both for business and leisure, aircraft emissions are the most important contribution to global warming.

THE SCIENCE

No one pretends to be sure about the precise impact of aircraft emissions on the air above us. The complex cocktail of chemicals being added to the atmosphere several kilometres above our heads has effects that are very difficult to accurately assess.

The primary emissions from aircraft engines are carbon dioxide, oxides of nitrogen and water in the form of vapour. The effect of carbon dioxide added to the thin air 10km up is well known. Oxides of nitrogen almost certainly add to global warming because they react with the oxygen in the high atmosphere to form ozone, increasing heat retention.

The most important uncertainty, about which debate rages fiercely, concerns the precise consequences of the emissions of water vapour in the form of condensation trails ('contrails'). If, as is looking reasonably likely, contrails are both warming agents in themselves and significant contributors to the development of high-level cirrus clouds, the net impact of air travel could be many times greater than the impact of carbon dioxide alone. The UK's Royal Commission on Environmental Pollution wrote in 2002:

> *Contrails and cirrus clouds reflect some solar radiation and therefore act to cool the surface. They also absorb some upwelling thermal radiation, re-emitting it both downwards, which acts to warm the surface, and upwards. On average, the latter warming effect is thought to dominate.*[191]

Probably the most important single piece of empirical evidence for the effect of cirrus cloud came in the days immediately after the 11 September 2001 attacks. Civilian aircraft travel ceased for several days. The difference between day and night temperatures in the US increased significantly because, it is thought, some of the effect of the cirrus cloud 'blanket' had been removed. The daytime temperature increased (as more solar radiation got through to the surface), but the night-time temperature fell more.

Today, as more and more aircraft criss-cross the skies, they may be weaving what is, in effect, a denser blanket of cirrus cloud, increasing average temperatures over the day, particularly in regions of dense airline traffic. However, it has to be admitted that the arguments about cirrus clouds are far from settled.

Nevertheless, the consensus assumption across the world is that the Royal Commission is right, and contrails and the consequent cirrus cloud do help to retain the sun's heat in the atmosphere. But few scientists are prepared to guess at the exact impact of these phenomena. So, instead, most people accept the rough estimate that the global warming impact of air travel is about three times that which would be suggested by carbon dioxide alone. This takes into account the effect of carbon dioxide, contrails of nitrogen oxides and other pollutants, but excludes any impact from cirrus clouds seeded by the aircraft contrails. The inclusion of the impact of cirrus clouds would, it seems likely, make this number larger, possibly by a significant amount. It will take several years at least before there is an agreed assessment. In the meantime, most people tend to assess aircraft emissions by working out how much kerosene is burned, calculating how much carbon dioxide results, and then multiplying this number by three.

We should be clear that this is only an estimate and has less precision attached to it than other numbers in the global warming debate. The scientific uncertainty allows some institutions to underestimate the impact of flights. In particular, it allows the airline industry to avoid using any multiplier at all and only calculate the volume of carbon dioxide. I am afraid to say that I think that this is deeply dishonest and reflects badly on the airlines concerned. It also acts further to confuse the public, who are then less likely to take action to reduce their emissions from air travel.

CARBON DIOXIDE EMISSIONS

Internet sites that offer estimates of the global warming impact of air travel are proliferating. Many of them have grown up as institutions working to offset the effect of air travel by 'offsetting' the environmental impact. For example, they run programmes to reforest arable land or to buy energy-efficient light bulbs in developing countries. These sites have little calculators on them that work out the carbon dioxide generated from an individual person's flight – for example, from London to Rome.

These amounts vary from site to site – sometimes by as much as 30 per cent. Three UK sites produced estimates ranging from 1.2 tonnes to 1.54 tonnes of CO_2 for the carbon dioxide output arising from a flight from London to New York and back.[192] These variations arise because we can all make different assessments of the likely distance actually travelled after air traffic re-routings and because different aircraft have varying fuel economy. But all of the ones I have seen only include the carbon dioxide and not the emissions of nitrogen oxides or contrails. So, according to the scientific consensus, the sites offering offset are ignoring the impact of other pollutants and are certainly not taking into account the blanketing effect of high-level cirrus. A far more appropriate measure – and certainly one that is properly cautious – would clearly be to increase these figures by a factor of three.

With this multiplier, the full effect of flying becomes clear. A return flight to New York 'costs' between 3.6 and 4.62 tonnes of carbon dioxide. Put another way, this trip is responsible for 30 per cent or so of the yearly carbon emissions of the typical UK citizen. If we are to reduce average carbon output by 70 per cent, then a trip to the US would use up the whole yearly allowance.

Of course, most flights from the UK are to destinations within Europe. Journeys to the US are relatively unusual. Approximately 65 per cent of all flights from the UK are to European destinations, with 13 per cent to other UK airports, 11 per cent to North America and 12 per cent to the rest of the world.[193] According to the carbon calculator of www.climatecare.org, a round-trip flight from Glasgow to Paris creates 0.22 tonnes of carbon dioxide. Other sites have higher figures. After multiplying by three, the real number is probably between 0.75 tonnes and 1 tonne of carbon dioxide equivalence. Heathrow to Naples and back would be 50 per cent more. Even these short-hop flights are difficult to reconcile with low-carbon lifestyles.

Individuals seeking to estimate the carbon impact of an individual flight can look at one of these calculators and get an estimate of the implications of travel, and then make their own decision as to whether to apply a multiplier to reflect the other pollutants. Another way is use British Airways' published kerosene fuel consumption figures per passenger kilometre and convert this figure to a carbon dioxide equivalent.[194, 195] This produces a figure of about 0.1kg of carbon dioxide per kilometre travelled (perhaps surprisingly, slightly less than the most efficient cars on the road with a single passenger). Other airlines would tend to have somewhat higher emissions, reflecting a higher percentage of inefficient short journeys. The airline industry, beginning to step up its public relations campaign as it sees looming problems ahead, stresses the ability of modern airliners to match the emissions of cars (but a saloon car carrying four passengers is still far more efficient than the most modern of aircraft). The most important difference, however, is the distances travelled by air. A flight to New York and back is not far short of the average distance driven by a car in the UK each year.[196]

Very approximately, UK citizens are now responsible for over 35 million tonnes of carbon dioxide pollution through aircraft travel each year. (Why is the figure 'very approximate'? We cannot be sure about the number of non-UK citizens travelling to and from the UK, and UK citizens travelling between other countries.) Multiplied by three and the number becomes almost 1.8 tonnes per head, or 15 per cent of the total.

Fuel efficiency is improving as engines become better and aeroplanes lighter. Planes are flying fuller, with fewer wasted seats, and small improvements in routing and in air traffic control means less wasted kerosene. But, taken together, these improvements are probably reducing fuel costs per passenger kilometre by less than 2 per cent per year. British Airways fuel efficiency improvements, for example, have been running at about 1.8 per cent per year.[197] On the other hand, traffic growth was about 7 per cent per year in the period of 1993 to 2004.[198] Slowly improving fuel efficiency does not compensate for rapid increases in the numbers of flights. The UK airline industry has increased its consumption of kerosene at about 6 per cent per year, and there is no reasonable expectation that this growth will slacken significantly.[199] As Friends of the Earth puts it: 'any benefits gained by building more fuel-efficient aircraft will be swamped by the rapid growth in air travel'.[200] Increasing fuel efficiency will simply result in cheaper travel and, thus, more demand from UK residents.

This conclusion – energy efficiencies usually result in more consumption – is highly important and appears to be true with respect to travel, home heating and some electrical appliances. We should be extremely sceptical of claims by politicians that improved technology will ultimately reduce carbon emissions.

The policy failures

The UK government's 2003 White Paper on air travel saw passenger volumes through UK airports rising to between 400 million and 600 million people a year by 2030. As the White Paper put it, this means that total numbers of travellers will be between two and three times what they were in 2003. The government's policy has largely been to accommodate this growth by planning to build new runways. It plans no attempt to restrict demand.

Despite its relatively small importance in the national carbon account, air travel represents a hugely significant part of our emissions inventory. It is the only source of emissions that is growing rapidly. Even the optimistic forecasts from government see it increasing, and at a disturbingly rapid rate, until 2040. Independent researchers, such as the scientists at the Tyndall Centre, project that emissions will be as high as 47 million tonnes of carbon dioxide by 2010, or well over 2 tonnes per head after including the tripling effect of including other pollutants.[201] As the Tyndall Centre has appropriately put it, the growth of air travel is likely to mean that total emissions from other sources will have to fall almost to zero if we are meet our long-run goal of cutting UK greenhouse gas output to less than 3 tonnes a head. This is clearly an unbelievably challenging task.

This is why we see a tone of unadulterated panic in the writings of many of the scientific experts in the field. Alice Bows of the Tyndall Centre wrote: 'if we are serious about climate change we must act now to curb aviation growth'.[202] The growth of aviation is so clearly incompatible with temperature stability that scientists working in this area simply cannot understand why the government is failing to act to hold back the growth. It could, for example, refuse to allow new runways to be built; but its policy seems to be to 'predict and provide' the new capacity at airports to meet the growth in UK demand. The lack of interest from governments, both in the UK and elsewhere, in holding down the rate of growth of aviation is deeply frightening and provides the clearest example of the need for individual citizens to exercise self-restraint. Flights from UK airports are probably not going to get any more expensive, and we need to decide to stop flying even though it means fewer winter holidays in the sun, enjoyable city breaks in foreign capitals or trips to far-off island paradises.

What would happen if the same rate of tax were applied to kerosene as it is to petrol? Using British Airways' fuel consumption figures, a flight from London to Rome and back would incur fuel taxes of about £60. This would be significant, I agree, but by itself is unlikely to hold air travel volumes at or below current levels, even if the tax were applied across the world. Of course, it wouldn't be. Taxation, unless at unprecedented levels, is unlikely to be sufficient to deal with the enormous problem of aviation's impact on the atmosphere.

Putative technological fixes

The last refuge of those wanting us all to keep flying is a blind faith in technology. Speaking to a committee of the House of Commons in early 2006, Prime Minister Tony Blair said:

> I just think it is unrealistic to think that you will get some restriction on air travel at an international level, and therefore I think necessarily the best way to go is to recognize that that is just the reality and instead see how you can develop the technology that is able to reduce the harmful emissions as a result of aviation travel.[203]

The government's reluctance to intervene in the largely untaxed world of international aviation is not shared by many of its own constituent parts. Government agencies and individual scientists have taken a more robust stance.

The Royal Commission on Environmental Pollution, for example, in response to the last major government pronouncement on aviation, said that the document:

> ... fails to take account of the serious impacts that the projected increase in air travel will have on the environment. Earlier this year the government published an Energy White Paper setting out its strategy for tackling global climate change, and set challenging but necessary targets for greenhouse gas emissions. Today's Aviation White Paper undermines those targets and continues to favour commerce over vital carbon dioxide reduction measures.[204]

Sir David King, the government's chief scientific adviser, was reported as saying that the impact of aviation on global climate change was 'an issue of enormous concern'.[205] Even Labour party backbenchers – a group usually reluctant to criticize its leaders – have joined in the criticism. Paul Flynn, the MP for Newport West, wrote in his blog that 'we cannot tax aircraft fuel; but we can and must tax their emissions as the greatest single source of pollution'.[206] Later in the comment, he says: 'Our donkey-brained leaders could take us over the precipice. We need a paradigm shift to change our fundamental assumption on the way we live and how we run our economies. Action should be massive and swift.'

The government's independent adviser, the Sustainable Development Commission, was almost as forthright about the issue of aviation. In a June 2004 report, it wrote: 'Governments around the world have failed completely to confront this problem so far. On the contrary, they have done everything they can to encourage further growth in order to promote short-term economic growth and development.'[207]

Think-tanks have weighed in to the issue. The Institute for Public Policy Research, often described as close to the Labour party, published a volume on aviation and climate change in which it concluded 'that unfettered growth would not comply with the objectives of sustainable development'.[208] In fact, it is rare to find anyone, other than people who dissent from all the concerns over climate change, who thinks that air travel can continue growing as fast as it is. This is depressing: we have a high degree of consensus on the problem; but political leaders are frightened of taking any action that might shave emissions by more than a few percentage points of growth.

The unfortunate fact is that there are no technological fixes that will solve the aviation problem within the next 30 years. Aeroplanes will get lighter and engines will get more efficient; but there are no thrilling breakthroughs on the horizon. This is not just because technological progress is relatively slow; it is also because today's stock of aircraft will continue circling the globe for decades to come. These jets are simply not going to disappear. British Airways keeps its aeroplanes for approximately 20 years. The low-cost airlines tend to use newer aeroplanes and buy them fresh from the factory. These aircraft are still going to be in use in 2030. Better technology will not reduce the emissions from these planes.

New concept aircraft, such as the blended wing design that merges the wing with the fuselage, will eventually come to reduce the carbon effect of new aircraft. But just as today's electric hybrid cars are not reducing total emissions, these new aeroplanes will simply add slightly less to global emissions than a plane of the current generation. Other madcap suggestions, such as replacing the entire world aircraft fleet with planes that burn hydrogen, fall down because nobody has yet worked out how to store the gas in a dense enough form to transport in a civil airliner. Hydrogen simply does not carry enough energy for each unit of volume, meaning that the fuel tanks need to be four times the size of those for kerosene. As one might imagine, the illustrative drawings make the resulting aircraft look strange and ungainly. But looks apart, a project to build a hydrogen airliner is decades away.

That's it – blended wing designs and hydrogen – the only even remotely feasible ways of generating significant improvements in greenhouse gas emissions from aircraft. Neither is on the drawing board, and both will take several decades to start to reduce overall emissions. However, UK politicians hang on these remote hopes as a way of avoiding the unthinkable – obliging people to fly less.

The amount of air travel in which a person engages is the primary determinant of how much carbon he or she is responsible for. Frequent flyers can generate hundreds of tonnes of damaging emissions per year. In a study carried out by Oxford's Transport Studies Unit, the 10 per cent of the population with the highest output of greenhouse gases had a carbon burden of 19.2 tonnes a year from flying, or not far from twice the average UK emissions from all sources.[209] These people had emissions over ten times the UK average from flying.[210]

The Oxford study demonstrates the very high percentage of all transport emissions that come from the top 10 per cent of travellers. This group was responsible for about 42 per cent of all transport-related emissions. Most of their carbon came from flying. Amazingly, the lowest 20 per cent of people emitted only 1 per cent of the total transport carbon in the survey. People in the top 10 per cent were responsible for 100 times more carbon that the people in the lowest 20 per cent.

These numbers are extraordinary. Although over half the UK population now travels by air at least once a year – though almost half do not – a very small percentage of people travel many times as often. The pollution from aircraft is overwhelmingly the responsibility of a small number of people. And the Oxford study points to the disproportionate impact of those on high income. Cheap air travel may seem to be a great leveller, making long-distance travel available to all; but its most important impact has probably been to allow the richest few per cent of the population almost unlimited freedom to pollute as much as they want, barely thinking about the financial impact.

Air travel poses the greatest threat to the climate of any single source of carbon. The rich and the powerful are those most tied – sometimes against their will – to the use of the rapid movement between remote cities. It is difficult to think of a high-income occupation that does not push its practitioners towards the frequent use of aeroplanes.

Those most sensitive to the threat from aviation to the long-term prospects for the world's poorest billion people have begun, albeit only in very small numbers, to 'offset' their emissions by paying companies to plant trees or engage in other carbon-reducing actions to compensate for their flights. Is this enough? I suggest not: it may salve the guilt, but it does not assist in changing society's behaviour or attitudes. Offsetting has serious problems: the promised carbon reduction is less certain than many of its proponents claim. But, more important, buying a few pounds of carbon offset for a trip to New York is sending a signal to governments and companies that expansion of air travel is compatible with a stable climate. This proposition needs to be attacked wherever it is found.

This means that the only morally responsible course of action is to avoid flying except in emergencies. People need to accept that this action may reduce chances of promotion and opportunities to see new parts of the world. The unhappy truth is that the arrival of rapid climate change is going to curtail human freedom – we cannot do everything that we want. The particular virulence of aviation's impact on eventual global temperatures means that severe and uncompromising self-restraint is an obligation. Those of us who seek to change the behaviour of others must stop flying. If we do not, we are fatally undermining our own campaign. Perhaps like many others, I am appalled by the international conferences on climate change that involve thousands of delegates travelling many miles by air.

For many people, giving up flying is simply a step too far. Attendees at the talks that I give on climate change often say that they can adjust all the main aspects of their lifestyle except this one. Avoiding all air travel is an uncrossable bridge: at a rational level, they know that flying is the biggest single part of the world's most important problem; but they do not want to change their own behaviour. Of course, this is in some ways an intelligent response – their own actions are not going to reduce the pace of temperature change one iota. But I sometimes sense that behind the slightly aggressive statements starting something like 'I'm sorry, but I'm not going to give up my skiing holiday' is a different sort of calculation. People are discounting the future. Some smokers are similar – they are happy to shorten their life expectancy in return for the immediate pleasures of nicotine. Those who admit the impact of flying, but continue to argue for their own freedom to fly, are similar. The benefits now are greater than the future costs. Governments instinctively recognize this – hence, the lack of any substantive action on aviation growth rates.

The free-market idealists are an even more difficult group to deal with. In their view, the problems of climate change can all be addressed by proper pricing of carbon dioxide emissions. Once what economists call 'externalities' have been priced into air travel, we should travel as much as we want to – there can be no moral difficulties if we simply follow the signals provided by the price of air travel. So, in the free-market economist's view, as long as the true cost of carbon dioxide pollution has been incorporated into the price, it is perfectly OK to fly or to drive a sports utility vehicle (SUV).

INTERNATIONAL AIR TRAVEL: DATA FROM OTHER COUNTRIES

Information on international travel is not reliable because of the difficulty of dealing with flights by passengers coming from abroad and transferring to other aeroplanes. Eurostat data suggests that the number of passenger journeys to or from UK airports was about 143 million in 2001, compared to 97 million in Germany and 66 million in France. UK journeys were almost one quarter of all 15 European Union (EU) member state journeys, though per inhabitant, the figures for Ireland and The Netherlands are at least as high.

Many of the most intelligent economists know that this is not a tenable position. For example, they realize that market pricing is not going to work sufficiently fast to protect the glaciers feeding the water supplies of much of Asia and Latin America. So, instead, they deny the reality of climate change, but then gradually shift into saying that even if it does exist, we should simply get used to higher temperatures. Ruth Lea, a very effective free-market apologist, typically suggested in a letter to the *Financial Times* that international bodies should focus on helping poorer countries adapt to higher temperatures rather than trying to control the causes of climate change.[211] Other reputable bodies say similar things.[212] These people think that it is acceptable to continue to fly.

I don't want to live in a world in which mankind seeks to manage its relationship with the planet in this way. Rather than being constantly at war with nature, contesting its authority over the planet, I would prefer to live at peace. If this means taking less of the world's beneficence, and adjusting my style of life to avoid borrowing from future generations, I am content. This means no air travel.

13

food

The food industry, one of the most carbon-intensive in the world, is by far the largest indirect contributor to UK emissions. The figures in this chapter suggest that producing and distributing food creates over five times the volume of the most energy-intensive manufacturing industry: iron and steel.[213] This isn't just about the carbon costs of transporting foodstuffs. The issue of 'food miles' is now becoming well understood; but it is only a small portion of the problem. The whole chain of supply is a huge user of fossil fuel from fertilizer on the fields to customers' cars going to supermarkets.

This chapter suggests that the food industry adds over 2 tonnes of greenhouse gases to the individual's total emissions every year, or about one sixth of the total. This figure may actually be too low, since it excludes the carbon dioxide and methane emitted by the soil in intensive agricultural systems. This is still higher than some estimates: a recent UK government study put the total at 8 per cent of the UK's energy needs, but omitted consideration of fertilizer production, packaging costs and methane from cows, though it does include the costs of running supermarkets.[214] The energy used to provide the food on our tables is about nine times greater than the calorific value of the food itself.

Changing food purchase habits can dramatically alter the climate change impact of our lifestyle. In its implications, it is comparable to the decision to abandon air travel. The three most important rules are these: buy organic where possible, local when available, and keep away from processed and packaged food.

P revious chapters have concentrated on how our actions directly cause emissions, whether by travelling, heating our own homes or running electric appliances. The rest of this book looks at indirect emissions and, lastly, at how we can counteract the carbon dioxide that we cannot otherwise eliminate from our lives.

The food supply chain is by far the most important source of indirect carbon emissions. Unlike many other indirect emissions, our choices of what to purchase can significantly affect the greenhouse gases for which we are responsible. So this chapter has two purposes: to provide an estimate of the greenhouse gas emissions resulting from the major steps in the UK food supply chain; and to identify how changes in the purchasing habits of a household might affect the food industry's carbon emissions. What do people need to do to reduce the impact of their food consumption on climate change?

I show that by changing eating habits, an individual could – at least in theory – reduce greenhouse gas emissions resulting from food consumption by 85 per cent. This would require very substantial changes in diet for all but those who already eat organic, unpackaged whole foods and who are completely, or almost, vegan.

On the other hand, an individual pursuing a more limited programme to reduce carbon emissions from the food chain could still cut his or her emissions by over two-thirds. I think that many households would find the necessary changes in food consumption acceptable.

THE FOOD SUPPLY CHAIN

Various commentators have given estimates of the impact of the food supply industry on greenhouse gas emissions. Lawrence Woodward of the Elm Farm Research Centre, for example, reported in 2002: [215]

> It has been estimated that the CO_2 emissions attributable to producing, processing, packaging and distributing the food consumed by a family of four is about 8 tonnes a year.

I have found it impossible to find a source which provides a justification for this figure or – even more helpfully – which breaks down the estimate into its constituent parts in order to identify the impact of each part of the food supply chain. This is my aim here; but I am aware that the lack of published research may mean that some of my estimates are inaccurate. With this caveat, my conclusion is that the figure of 2 tonnes per person is likely to be a slight underestimate. Food production and distribution is, indeed, the single most significant source of greenhouse gases in the UK.

Getting food to the home is a complicated task:

- In an advanced economy using intensive agriculture, the process starts with the manufacture of fertilizer. The fertilizer, alongside other agrochemicals, is shipped to the farm.
- The farmer uses fossil fuels to carry out activities on the farm, such as ploughing, sowing and harvesting. Farm animals produce methane, a significant greenhouse gas. Nitrogen fertilizer breaks down in the soil and gives off nitrous oxide, which contributes even more (per kilogram) than methane to global warming.
- The supply chain takes the food, both animal products and plant materials (for example, grain and vegetables), to processing companies. Such companies include heavy energy users, such as sugar beet processors. Primary processors turn farm products into materials that can be further processed by food manufacturing companies. For example, millers grind wheat, which is then sent to factories for the manufacture of biscuits.
- Most food in the UK is sold in a packaged form. It has been cooked or otherwise prepared and is then encased in materials to protect and preserve it, and to allow it to be displayed attractively in shops. Once packaged, it is sent to the huge distribution warehouses of the supermarket chains and, thence, to individual shops.
- The food shop – usually now a large supermarket – uses energy to run its operations. The store is heated, lit and uses electricity to run its food chillers and freezers.
- Most food purchases are made by customers who drive to the retailer. They bring home their food, prepare and eat it, and dispose of the packaging and kitchen waste. Only a small proportion of this material is composted; instead, it is put into landfill where it produces greenhouse gases as it rots in the ground. Some of this gas will escape to the atmosphere and add to global warming.

The greenhouse gas consequences of each of these stages can be calculated. There is a degree of imprecision, sometimes substantial, in each of the calculations. Nevertheless, I believe that the numbers in this chapter are reasonably robust and are usually supported by two or more different sources or calculations.

TOTAL GREENHOUSE GAS EMISSIONS

Emissions are calculated using the standard yardstick of carbon dioxide equivalence. The food supply chain emits large quantities of methane – generally assessed as 21 times as powerful a warming gas as carbon dioxide – and nitrous oxide, thought to be about 310 times as powerful as CO_2.[216]

Table 13.1 summarizes the emissions from each of the main activities in the supply chain. It does not deal adequately with two additional important sources of climate changing gases:

1   The first is the gradual loss of soil carbon as a result of intensive agriculture.
2   Second is the greenhouse gas emissions incurred in other countries as a result of growing food for use in the UK. The UK is a net food importer: if we took into account the carbon costs entailed by other countries in growing our food, our own figures for carbon consumption would look a great deal higher. But calculating or, indeed, reliably estimating, this figure is extremely difficult (I do, however, assess the costs of transporting food from other countries to the UK).

Table 13.1 *The main sources of greenhouse gas emissions in the UK food chain*

Activity	Million tonnes per year (CO$_2$ equivalent)
Fertilizer manufacture and transport	9
Methane from animals and slurry	19
Methane from tilling and soil management practices	4
CO_2 from farm operations	6
Fertilizer use generating nitrous oxide (N_2O)	27
Road transport in the UK	7
Road/sea transport outside the UK	7
Air freight	2
Food and drink manufacturing and processing	11
Manufacture of packaging	10
Operation of retail stores	4
Consumers driving to shops	3
Landfill gas from rotting food: methane (CH_4) + CO_2	13
Landfill gas from rotting packaging: CH_4 + CO_2	4
Approximate total	126 million tonnes per year (or about 2.1 tonnes per person per year)

Source: various sources as cited in main chapter text (see notes 217 to 246)

The estimates in Table 13.1 are provided for the UK, rather than per person as I have tried to do in the rest of the book. This is because many of the numbers are individually quite small and it seems better to provide the UK total. At the foot of the table, I give the figure for the typical individual.

Fertilizer manufacture

Fertilizer manufacture uses natural gas as a raw material and results in substantial emissions of carbon dioxide from the manufacturing process.

Fertilizer use is probably not growing in the UK. The gradual and painful reform of the Common Agricultural Policy (CAP) is tending to slowly decrease the acreage of land under intensive cultivation in the UK. The rapid growth in the acreage under organic cultivation, albeit from a very low base, also tends to reduce fertilizer use.[217]

The UK imports substantial quantities of nitrogenous fertilizer, and the carbon implications of the use of imported material is included in the estimate of about 9 million tonnes of carbon dioxide. I have calculated this figure from data provided by the Soil Association.[218, 219]

I have not included an emissions figure for the production and transportation cost of agricultural liming products necessary to restore the correct acidity to the soil after application of nitrogen fertilizer. Lime will eventually add carbon dioxide to the atmosphere as it breaks down in the soil (the percentage of all liming materials added to UK soils as a direct result of the need to reduce the acidity arising from previous use of nitrogen fertilizer does not appear to be known).

Ruminant animals and slurry

As coal mining has declined, agricultural animals are now the main source of methane (CH_4) in the UK. Ruminant animals, such as cows and sheep, produce methane as a result of the digestive process (the breaking down of organic compounds in the stomachs of these animals creates methane, which is then largely emitted from the animal's mouth and nose). Dairy cows are particularly important sources of methane because of the volume of food, both grass and processed material, that they eat. Animals kept in organic systems actually produce more methane per litre of milk because organic cows give less milk per unit of food eaten. Other, non-ruminant, animals also produce methane, but in much smaller quantities.

In intensive farming systems, particularly those in which cows are kept indoors for most, or all, of the year, additional methane is created by the anaerobic breaking down of manures in slurry heaps. When animal wastes rot in the presence of air, they largely produce carbon dioxide as a waste product. Without air, manure rots to give off methane and some carbon dioxide. In intensive animal husbandry, manures are collected and stored without air, thereby emitting methane. Methane is also emitted to the atmosphere from soil disturbance, the drying out of wetlands and other agricultural practices.[220]

Figures for the amount of methane from UK agriculture come from the *UK Climate Change Programme 2006*, which estimated that the carbon dioxide equivalent UK output of methane from agriculture was 19.1 million tonnes in 2004.[221]

I have checked this number by multiplying the number of methane-producing farm animals by the average methane output per head. This produces a figure of 18.9 million tonnes of carbon dioxide equivalent, excluding the contribution of goats and hens, which would increase the figures slightly.

Carbon dioxide from farm operations

Farms use significant quantities of fossil fuels to keep animal sheds at the right temperature and with the appropriate amount of light. Farm machinery needs diesel fuel to carry out tasks such as ploughing, sowing and fertilizer application.

The UK government estimated the carbon output from farm operations at about 5.5 million tonnes of carbon dioxide for 2004.[222] The UK Environmental Accounts give a figure of 5.6 million tonnes of carbon dioxide for 2004.[223]

Methane from tilling and soil management practices

The soil contains methane as a result of the breakdown of organic matter, such as roots, in the absence of air. Tilling the soil allows this gas to escape. In pasture, much of the methane would be captured by organisms able to digest the gas.

In addition, intensive agriculture seems to result in loss of carbon from the soil. The volume of carbon in world soils is far greater than in the atmosphere.[224] However, the estimates of the volume of carbon dioxide being emitted from UK soils differ greatly from source to source, and I have included a low figure for this loss. Recent work seems to suggest that the carbon losses from UK soils are more significant, which may be a result of higher temperatures arising from climate change or of changes in agricultural methods.[225]

Fertilizer use generating nitrous oxide

When nitrogenous fertilizer is applied to the soil, some nitrous oxide (N_2O) is emitted to the atmosphere. Nitrous oxide is a particularly powerful global warming gas. In terms of its effect on climate change, this source is the single most important element of the food chain. Organic agriculture avoids artificial fertilizers, of course, and this is the prime reason why this form of agriculture is much less harmful to the global atmosphere. This fact is not well recognized and needs to be better understood. Buying organic food is good for the global atmosphere.

Road transport in the UK

Food produced in this country is shipped long and increasing distances.[226] Food manufacturing plants are becoming larger, taking raw materials from wider catchments. Processors are shipping to the regional distribution centres of the supermarket chains. The supermarkets are hauling huge volumes to their stores.

Studies now say that 25 per cent of all UK heavy lorries on the roads carry foodstuffs and raw materials for the food processing industries.[227] I have used the calculations of the direct carbon dioxide cost of this traffic in Table 13.1; but a full costing should probably also include the increased congestion (and therefore higher carbon dioxide emissions) of all other road users as a result of the food-related traffic.

In Table 13.1, I have used figures taken from an extremely detailed 2005 study carried out for the UK Department for Environment, Food and Rural Affairs (Defra) for all transport emissions, including air freight, which estimated that all of these processes caused emissions of about 7 million tonnes.[228]

The movement of food includes the transportation of raw materials, semi-finished goods and final products to the supermarket distribution centres, as well as food retailers' distribution from their warehouses to shops. This figure does not include the emissions costs from private cars travelling to and from shops.

Road and sea transport abroad

Food shipped from abroad generally comes by road or sea. Increasing volumes of imported foods means a larger carbon dioxide cost. The UK is gradually getting less self-sufficient in food, so we can expect the 'food miles' that we generate as a nation to increase.[229] Table 13.1 shows that the food miles in foreign countries, excluding air freight, already amount to the same as the total for UK transport.

Air freight

The shipment of fresh foods into the UK by air is growing rapidly.[230] The consequences are made more severe because of the greater global warming impact of air travel compared to carbon emissions from surface transportation, and the 2005 Defra study includes an estimate of this effect.

Food and drink manufacturing and processing

Food is increasingly processed. According to the figures from their environmental reports, the big manufacturers of packaged foods, such as Nestlé and Unilever, appear to be making substantial strides in reducing the emissions resulting from manufacturing processes.[231] Nevertheless, overall food manufacturing energy requirements are not decreasing rapidly, possibly because of compensating increases in the energy needed for manufacturing the increasing amounts of chilled food sold to UK supermarkets.[232] Chilled food manufacture involves a large number of energy-intensive processes compared to the production of the 'ambient' foods that are typically produced by the largest global food conglomerates. Visiting a bottled sauce factory a few months ago, I was struck by the energy efficiency and simplicity of the process. This would not be the case in a ready-meals factory, a fact that the industry itself increasingly recognizes and seeks to correct.

The Food and Drink Federation estimates that the carbon dioxide emissions of the food production sector were about 11.5 million tonnes in 2003.[233] Per household, this is about 0.45 tonnes, compared to no more than 0.15 tonnes for all the cooking done in a home using a gas cooker. This is a surprising comparison for most people assume that cooking would be done more efficiently in large volumes. Unfortunately, this gain is more than counterbalanced by the energy costs during food processing, such as the quick chilling of cooked food.

The manufacture of packaging

Almost all food is now heavily packaged. Although customers often complain about the excessive packaging protecting many foods, they still seem to show a preference for buying wrapped rather than loose foodstuffs.[234] One of the packaging industry trade associations did detailed work in 1996 on the energy contained in food packaging.[235] It estimated that each UK individual was responsible for 1.9GJ/year of energy used to make food packaging. This equates to about 526kWh/year. If 50 per cent of the industrial use of energy was electricity and 50 per cent gas, this would produce emissions of about 10 million tonnes of carbon dioxide, which is the figure that I have used.

The energy costs to make the packaging used for food are about two-thirds of the energy value of the food itself.

Operation of retail stores

Large supermarkets are major users of energy. Tesco reports that it takes over 100kWh to operate 1 square foot of its retail space for a year. Interestingly, the German chain Metro produces much lower estimates of its own energy use, which may possibly be explained by the greater emphasis on chilled and frozen products in UK supermarkets, which require prodigious refrigeration costs. Tesco's energy use is approximately four times the energy cost to run the same area of the average UK home.

Tesco's 2005 *Annual Report* gives a figure of 24 million square feet for its UK selling space. The company's *Corporate Responsibility Report* for the same year says that its UK selling space had an average energy use of 113kWh per square foot. This produces a figure of 2.7 million kWh for the UK operations. If this was all purchased as electricity, it would create about 1.2 million tonnes of carbon dioxide. If 20 per cent were gas, then the figure would be about 1.1 million tonnes. This is equivalent to the carbon output from heating over 350,000 UK homes.

Sainsbury's 2005 *Corporate Responsibility Report* indicates a figure of somewhat more than 0.6 million tonnes of carbon dioxide from its stores.[236] This figure is consistent with that produced by Tesco because Sainsbury is about half the size of Tesco in the UK. In 2005, the combined share of Tesco and Sainsbury's in the market for groceries was approximately 45 per cent. Assuming that all other retailers had about the same volume of carbon dioxide emissions per UK pound of revenue, the total for UK food retailing would be about 4 million tonnes.

Consumers driving to shops

As grocery retailing becomes more and more concentrated in larger out-of-town shops, the distances travelled by customers have risen and the use of the car has increased. The average householder drives almost 600km a year for food shopping.[237] This is consistent with the government's figure of 3 million tonnes of carbon dioxide arising from shopping for food by car and bus.[238, 239]

Landfill gas from rotting food

Waste food from the home and from catering establishments is still largely taken to landfill sites. Once incarcerated, it produces methane and carbon dioxide. The methane is now largely captured and burned; but some still escapes to the atmosphere.

The average person throws away about 500kg of waste a year. Seventeen per cent is kitchen waste, or about 85kg a person.[240] In addition, people are responsible for catering waste, but this figure is not included. About 88 per cent of all food waste goes to landfill; but the small percentage that is composted almost all comes from catering establishments.

Eighty-five kilograms of food waste (plus some water) will turn into about 27kg of methane and 71kg of carbon dioxide.[241] Landfill operators in the UK now capture almost 75 per cent of the methane from the sites.[242] So each person's food waste will produce about 8kg of methane a year, or about 144kg of carbon dioxide equivalence. The methane and carbon dioxide will therefore equal about 215kg of greenhouse gas (144kg + 71kg).

Multiplied by the 60 million people in the UK, the figure is about 13 million tonnes of carbon dioxide equivalent.

Landfill gas from rotting packaging

The same issue arises from the disposal of putrescible packaging, such as paper and cardboard. Cardboard and paper packaging will rot away to methane, water and carbon dioxide in landfill. The UK produces about 9.3 million tonnes of packaging waste a year.[243] About 4 million tonnes are paper and board, of which about 2.2 million tonnes are recycled. A total of 1.8 million tonnes go to landfill. This will produce about 145,000 tonnes of un-combusted methane and 1.5 million tonnes of carbon dioxide, with a total impact of well over 4 million tonnes after taking into account the greater global warming effect of methane. In fact, the strong preference that many people express for cardboard and paper packaging, rather than plastic, is not strictly rational. Plastic is light, embodies relatively little energy and, most importantly, doesn't rot. The honourable souls who press for biodegradable plastic bags are helping to add to carbon emissions, not to reduce them.

OTHER SOURCES OF CARBON FROM THE UK FOOD CHAIN

I haven't been able to include estimates of the carbon implications of:

- food cultivation overseas;
- food manufacture and packaging overseas.

The UK is a net importer of food products. The country spent £10 billion more on food imports in 2003 than it earned from food exports.[244] This deficit has increased rapidly and will probably continue to rise. There is, therefore, good reason to suppose that the foreign portion of our food chain is increasing in size. So, its emissions of greenhouse gases as a result of goods supplied to the UK market are probably rising as well. I have found no estimates of how much the UK's declining self-sufficiency is increasing carbon emissions elsewhere in the world; but the inclusion of estimates for the global carbon dioxide emissions resulting from UK food consumption would increase the per-person figure for carbon dioxide to well over the figure of 2.1 tonnes used in this chapter.

This chapter has also used low estimates for the impact of intensive cultivation on the level of carbon trapped in the soil. The actual numbers may be very significantly higher. It may also be – although this appears not be known with certainty – that organic methods of cultivation reduce the rate of carbon loss. My hunch is that organic techniques may well make a big difference to the retention of carbon in the soil. If true, this fact would increase the importance of switching to the consumption of organic foods, particularly those produced by smaller-scale farmers carefully looking after the long-term health of their land.

WHAT THESE FIGURES MEAN

A figure of 2.1 tonnes per year for the food production chain is larger than the typical individual's emissions from car use (1.2 tonnes), home heating (1.2 tonnes) or home electricity use (0.7 tonnes). Therefore, an individual can productively focus on food purchasing as a means of decreasing personal responsibility for carbon emissions.

The typical UK adult consumes about 1900 kilocalories a day. Over the course of the year, this means that the individual needs about 800kWh of energy in the form of food.[245] It is illuminating to compare this figure with the global warming cost of the whole food chain. Natural gas that generated 800kWh of energy would result in the emission of about 0.15 tonnes of carbon dioxide, or less than 7 per cent of the global warming cost per person of the UK food chain. It doesn't have to be this way. The UK food chain is very carbon-intensive; it requires massive inputs of fossil fuel to sustain itself. But individuals could choose to consume their daily foods in ways that avoid most of this carbon. The main options for those seeking to reduce their impact on the planet's atmosphere are:

- Eat organic food. Organic food doesn't require fossil fuel-based fertilizer, saving the energy needed to produce the fertilizer and the greenhouse gases that result from its application to the field.
- Buy local food. Locally produced foodstuffs, bought directly from the producer or via a local shop, save transport. It will also probably save in packaging and manufacturing.
- Eat less meat and dairy. Farm animals, particularly dairy cows, produce methane. But organic dairy products probably don't save any carbon emissions and may actually increase methane production. Eating a vegan diet is a reliable way of reducing carbon, supplemented, perhaps, by (non-vegan, of course) local eggs, honey and other wonderful foods.
- Buying minimally packaged foods makes a difference both to the amount of energy used in the packaging and in the methane resulting from packaging materials sent to landfill.
- Avoid processed food and cook the raw ingredients at home. The gas used per person for cooking in UK homes generates one third of the amount of carbon dioxide used in food manufacturing. Large industrial cooking processes may be efficient; but the manufactured foods need chilling and storing after cooking.
- Compost all organic materials, including food packaging.

- Where possible, buy simple foods, sold at ambient temperature, rather than chilled. Avoid supermarkets for their obvious wastes of energy.
- Does being a vegetarian help? By itself, probably not much. All other things being equal, simply stopping eating meat will not reduce emissions very much, particularly if consumption of dairy products rises to compensate for eating less meat. Dairy cows produce over twice as much methane as beef cattle. Becoming a vegan would definitely help.

BY HOW MUCH CAN THESE MEASURES CUT GREENHOUSE GAS EMISSIONS?

Each of the preceding steps reduces emissions by cutting one or more of the sources of greenhouse gases given in Table 13.1. Table 13.2 shows the ways in which these actions could reduce the greenhouse gas emissions from the food chain.

The only portion of the food chain not directly affected by at least one of these actions would be the methane impact of tilling and soil management. And it is certainly possible that good organic agriculture cuts methane emissions from the topsoil, so the benefit of switching to organic agriculture is even greater.

If farmers used renewable electricity, then the emissions from the operation of farms would be reduced. An individual growing some of his or her own food could also expect to reduce these carbon costs as well.

To reduce the carbon costs from food purchasing to as close to zero as possible would oblige the consumer to switch to an entirely organic, vegan diet, bought locally from a small shop selling unprocessed and unpackaged goods at ambient temperatures (much of the energy cost of operating supermarkets seems to come from operating freezers and chillers).

This would mean largely buying whole foods, such as nuts, grains, seeds, dried legumes and fruit, sold at room temperature. Fresh fruit and vegetables and preserves should be bought from local sources. Items such as bread should be made at home if they cannot be bought locally. Of course, it would be even better if the fresh foods were produced on an allotment close to home (for those unable to be vegan, meat, eggs, milk and honey would be best bought locally).

What carbon dioxide costs would remain if everybody adopted a vegan, organic diet, bought their food locally as far as possible, and largely used unprocessed and unpackaged food? Table 13.3 provides an estimate. Of course, the numbers are necessarily extremely approximate, but give a good indication of how much emissions could be cut by radical changes in food purchase habits.

These changes would reduce national emissions from 126 million tonnes to about 19.75 million tonnes or, seen at the level of the individual, from about 2.1 tonnes to below

Table 13.2 *Ways of reducing greenhouse gas emissions from the food chain*

Action	Completely, or almost completely, removes the following	Partly removes the following
Switch to organic food	Fertilizer manufacture Fertilizer use generating nitrous oxide	
Buy local food	Air freight	Road transport in the UK and abroad (only a small percentage of UK residents can buy all food locally) May also result in a reduction in the carbon costs of operating retail stores
Eat less meat and dairy		Methane from ruminant animals Carbon dioxide from farm operations since arable farming will be less energy-intensive
Buy minimally packaged foods	Manufacture of packaging Landfill gas from rotting of packaging	
Avoid processed food		Food manufacturing Road transport in the UK Packaging
Compost all organic materials	Landfill gas from rotting food Landfill gas from rotting of packaging	
Avoid supermarkets		Operation of retail stores

0.35 tonnes per person. This result is supported by Swedish research that compared the total greenhouse gas emissions from four different meals with the same energy and protein content. The paper showed a range from 190g of carbon dioxide equivalent for a vegetarian meal with local ingredients to 1800g for a meal containing meat, with most ingredients imported – a ratio of almost ten to one.[246]

This mixture of unprocessed and local organic vegan foods is clearly unacceptable to a very large fraction of the people in the UK. So, what is a reasonably attainable target that at least some people might accept? Table 13.4 estimates the saving if all UK residents changed their food procurement habits in order to minimize greenhouse gas emissions, but did not radically diverge from their current pattern of consumption. Once again, these are estimates that seek to show the extent of the carbon reductions that might be possible if we changed our food consumption habits. They can only be illustrations because each different type of food is grown and processed in a different way. We cannot accurately estimate the gains in lower emissions from changing our consumption patterns.

Table 13.3 *Remaining greenhouse gas emissions after major switches to purchasing behaviour*

Remaining sources of greenhouse gases after changes to purchasing behaviour	Comments	Greenhouse gas emissions remaining (million tonnes of CO_2 equivalent per year)
CO_2 costs from farm operations		3
Methane from tilling and soil management practice		4
Food transport in the UK and abroad	Cut by three-quarters as a result of purchasing mostly local food	3.5
Food manufacturing	Cut by three-quarters as a result of the move away from packaged food	2.75
Operation of retail stores	Cut by half as a result of a switch to ambient food sold in small shops	2
Consumers driving to shops	Cut by half	1.5
Landfill gas from food and packaging	Cut by almost 90% as a result of lower waste, smaller amounts of packaging and composting (note that rotting food will produce CO_2 in a compost bin, so there are still some greenhouse gas impacts from composting)	2
Packaging costs	Cut by 90% to cover the costs of simple polythene or other containers, reused where possible	1
Total		Approximately 19.75 million tonnes

The reductions in Table 13.4 require us to switch almost entirely to organic cultivation, reduce methane output by buying less milk and meat, and move to a largely whole food diet with minimal packaging, bought and produced locally, and not sold through the supermarket system. This is a long way from the way in which most families today buy and consume their food; nevertheless, it is within the capacity of many of us to alter our behaviour to achieve this result.

These figures suggest that substantial but manageable changes to food purchase behaviour could result in a two-thirds reduction in emissions, with total UK output of greenhouse gases falling from 126 million to 41 million tonnes. This reduces the individual's emissions to less than 0.7 tonnes, down from 2.1 tonnes.

Table 13.4 *Remaining greenhouse gas emissions after moderate switches to purchasing behaviour*

Action	Main exceptions	Reduction opportunity	Greenhouse gas emissions remaining*
Purchase organic food for all meat, dairy, vegetables and most packaged goods	Imported fruit and some types of packaged goods	Perhaps three-quarters of emissions from fertilizer manufacture and use	9
Buy local food (sold by local retailers) Possible for vegetables, some fruit, eggs, meat, honey, bread and some packaged goods in large areas of the UK	Almost everything not bought locally has gone long distances via the supermarket distribution system	If all food were bought locally (and without using freight transport), the saving would be 16 million tonnes a year Perhaps 50% of this is possible	8
Eat less meat and dairy products		Perhaps possible to cut methane emissions from cows and sheep in half by reducing meat purchases and dairy consumption	9
Buy minimally packaged foods (probably by concentrating on whole foods)	Difficult to buy some staples without packaging	Probably possible to avoid at least half the carbon costs of packaging	5
Avoid processed foods More home cooking and more purchase of ingredients, rather than prepared foods		Almost certainly possible to reduce carbon costs of food manufacturing by 75%	3
Avoid supermarkets		May be possible to avoid half the cost of operating shops by shopping in small stores and buying ambient goods	2
Compost		Possible to avoid the methane costs of rotting food and packaging by composting (combined with less waste and less use of packaging)	5
Total			41 million tonnes

Note: * million tonnes of CO_2 equivalent

THE CARBON COST OF SPINACH

Increasing interest in eating a healthy range of fruits and vegetables means a larger number of aircraft lumbering across the oceans carrying fresh produce in the hold. We can argue about the nutritional benefits of eating exotic foods all year; some say that the availability of these fruits has helped to improve healthy eating habits, while others point to easy access to substitutes from the UK. A stalk of broccoli from Lincolnshire in February may not be as appetizing as South African grapes, but it does have many of the same beneficial effects.

However, whether we worry about 'food miles' or not, an increasing amount of freight is shipped into the UK by air. About 1.2 million tonnes of cargo comes into the UK this way each year. Much of this is perishable foodstuffs, and the percentage will probably grow. It varies from South African grapes to Asian prawns and Kenyan cut flowers. Anything quickly perishable from outside Europe brought to your supermarket probably came by air. The key exceptions are likely to be long-lived fruit, such as bananas, which are sent by ship. The energy cost of sea transport is very much lower than airfreight, although not as insignificant as some people claim.

Some time before writing this section of the book, I looked at a bag of anaemic-looking fresh spinach that had just been delivered as part of our weekly shop. The country of origin was the US. This ordinary leafy vegetable, grown in Northern Europe for at least seven months of the year – and reasonably hardy in the cold frame on my allotment – was being shipped from somewhere in the southern states of the US to Heathrow to feed the customers of UK supermarkets.

The energy cost of getting the spinach from (perhaps) southern California was not recorded on the packet. We shouldn't be surprised, for the figures are truly extraordinary. The food value of this 225g bag of spinach was about 60 kilocalories. The carbon dioxide created in order to get it here weighed about 1 kilo, or four times the weight of the food. The typical UK power station would have generated almost 2.5 units (kilowatt hours) of electricity for this amount of carbon dioxide. This makes shipping the calories contained in the spinach about 35 times less efficient than generating electricity.

This figure is before taking into account the especially destructive effects of carbon dioxide and other emissions when released high in the atmosphere. Include this in the calculation, and a bag of spinach weighing less than 0.25 kilos is responsible for a global warming effect equivalent to over 3 kilos of carbon dioxide. It only takes 15 of these bags for the purchaser to exceed the total fossil fuel use of a typical Afghani. And until I looked at the packet, I wasn't aware that the food came by air.

Another way of thinking about this is to compare the spinach to the effect of an energy-saving light bulb. One of these light bulbs in your house might typically save enough electricity to avoid 6 or 7 kilos of carbon dioxide a year. Two bags of midwinter spinach, bought casually off a supermarket website, completely wipe out the virtuous effect of another energy-efficient bulb.

The typical person is responsible for about 20kg of air freight coming into the country each year (some of this will be industrial goods, of course; but much is fruit, vegetables, flowers and fish). In a typical nutrition-conscious middle-class household, the average person might easily consume the produce outlined in Table 13.5 over a year.

Table 13.5 *Produce consumed in a typical middle-class UK household throughout the year*

10 bags of winter vegetables	2.25kg
10 kilos of Southern hemisphere fruit	10kg
2kg of exotic fish (including shellfish)	2kg
2kg of Southern hemisphere cut flowers	2kg
Total	16.25kg

After taking into account the greater destructiveness of aircraft emissions, this menu of goods brought from faraway places accounts for about 200kg of global warming effect. This is well over half the emissions resulting from all the lighting in the home.

14

· ·

other indirect sources
of greenhouse gas emissions

W hile the food supply chain is by far the most important source of indirect emissions of greenhouse gases, other sources should not be neglected. For most of us, the next most important source of indirect emissions is the workplace.

THE WORKPLACE

According the Carbon Trust, the average office creates about 131kg of carbon dioxide per square metre each year. This includes gas or oil for heating and electricity for office machinery and air-conditioning. Typically, offices allocate 10 to 12 square metres of space per person, meaning a figure of about 1.3 to 1.5 tonnes for each employee. Poor performers might be as high as 4 tonnes. The *Guardian*'s office building, for example, has a figure of about 400kg per square metre, and although the work practices in newspapers – such as the need to labour well into the night – mean high emissions, this performance is extraordinarily bad.[247] Per occupant, the average office building uses more electricity than the typical home, even though our home might give us typically eight times as much space. The Carbon Trust suggests that the average office building uses about 226kWh of electric power per year per square metre of space.[248] For a person with about 10 square metres to work in, this means emissions of about 1 tonne just from electricity. However, even the worst offices, such as the *Guardian*'s, still use less electricity than a typical UK supermarket.

Of course, for most people, there is no choice about where to work. However, for those who have the opportunity, working at home is preferable. The extra emissions might seem high, and the cost of keeping the heat all day in the winter may be a couple of hundred UK pounds; but almost all homes are better than an air-conditioned office. If you are obliged to work in a glassy office building with high heating and air-conditioning bills, it makes the best sense to put pressure on the employer to commit to buying electricity that comes from new renewable sources (see 'Green electricity' in Chapter 16) or thoughtfully to offset the emissions by planting trees. Or, perhaps even more productively, it might be possible to get your employer to do an audit of electricity consumption and then take measures to control it. The Carbon

Trust's figure for the average UK office of 226kWh/year per square metre is nearly twice their 'good practice' target of 128kWh/year. Today's electricity prices may mean it makes sense for an employer to work on reducing the most egregious source of waste. Simple steps can include:

- heating the building to a lower temperature in winter and air-conditioning it to a higher temperature in summer;
- buying energy-efficient computers and peripherals (this will reduce air-conditioning needs in summer, as well);
- turning off lights and office equipment at night and on weekends; and
- ensuring that light levels are high in the right areas, but reducing them elsewhere.

It is, of course, not just offices that need to be managed in this way. Many public buildings need to work on cutting their emissions. One busy church that I know has energy costs of almost £8000 and emissions from gas and electricity of perhaps 50 tonnes a year. When I did an audit, total standby energy consumption was about 1.5kW, or the equivalent of 15 large conventional light bulbs on all the time. This costs the parish about £500 and adds over 2 tonnes of carbon dioxide to the atmosphere every year.

The buildings in which we work and engage in our social activities are important users of energy. In most workplaces, I suspect that massive amounts could be done to reduce consumption with absolutely minimal effort. Generally, employers have simply never concerned themselves with this issue, and active work from a few concerned employees can have a huge effect with minimum inconvenience.

OTHER SOURCES OF EMISSIONS

So far, we have focused on cutting indirect emissions from altering food consumption habits and from better energy use in offices. The third and final recommendation is, unfortunately, the most general and unspecific: it is simply to consume less of the material things of life. Even a small new car might embody 3 tonnes of carbon dioxide. A total of 120 beverage cans – the average UK consumption – produce 20kg of emissions if not recycled. One tonne of cement forming the base of a patio gives off 1 tonne of carbon dioxide when setting. Supplying water to the average home creates about 80kg of carbon dioxide per person per year at the pumping stations.[249]

Where do most emissions come from? The UK Environmental Accounts provide a breakdown by industry.[250] As reported, these numbers are suspiciously precise: can we really know that the soaps and detergents industry produced 1,512,000 tonnes of greenhouse gases in 2004? However, as general indications of the relative importance of various sectors of the economy, I think they are very useful. I have rounded the numbers to the nearest 0.1 tonne per person for the most polluting industries (see Table 14.1).

Table 14.1 *Greenhouse gas emissions from industry*

Industrial or service sector	Greenhouse gas outputs per person (tonnes)
Oil and gas extraction and processing	0.7
Metal manufacture and metal processing	0.5
Cement, limestone and plaster	0.2
Chemicals	0.2
Construction	0.1
Plastics*	0.1
Pulp, paper, print and publishing*	0.1
Coal mining	0.1
Timber	0.05
Textiles and clothing	0.05
Motor vehicle manufacture	0.05
Rubber	0.05
Glass*	0.05
Recycling	0.05
Public services	0.3
Retail and wholesale*	0.3
Water transport (fuel for ships)	0.5
Freight transport (lorries and vans)*	0.3
Total across these sectors	3.7 tonnes per person

Note: * These figures will include some greenhouse gas emissions that I have already counted under food.
Source: UK Office for National Statistics, London, www.statistics.gov.uk/focuson/environmental/, accessed May 2006

These figures give us some useful clues about what we need to do to minimize our own responsibility for indirect emissions. But they are only clues. Looking at Table 14.1, one might think that avoiding buying metal products would save 0.5 tonnes per person. However, many metal goods are intermediate products; for example, they might be food processing equipment, rather than being sold directly to us.

Nevertheless, some broad themes can be taken from the table. Freight transport is important, even before considering the impact of air travel. Sea transport is by no means as innocuous as we sometime assume. At nearly 0.5 tonnes per person, sea freight is growing and is now almost one sixth of the total emissions that we can allow ourselves

(3 tonnes). Perhaps the data is a little untrustworthy; but emissions from this source are said to have risen 50 per cent since 2000. Freight transport is partly carriage of food, but is also important if we hope to control emissions from other sources. Moving things around to sustain our lifestyle uses up over 25 per cent of the carbon ration that we can eventually allow ourselves. This point is not talked about frequently, partly because the activity is so dispersed and apparently unimportant. But just as air travel cannot be made harmless by an easy technological fix, neither can the tens of thousands of freighters and tankers be removed from the oceans or inefficient lorries taken from our roads.

By contrast, the financial sector, often said to be one quarter of the UK economy, is reported as being responsible for less than 1 million tonnes of greenhouse gases (though it is not allocated the cost of the electricity it uses). Similarly, the whole – or certainly the majority – of the public sector only accounts for 0.3 tonnes per head. But public service emissions are also disproportionately from electrity use and the real consequences of our grossly inefficient schools, hospitals and council buildings are much more severe than this number indicates. Many large employers, such as banks and other service companies, have total emissions of three or four tonnes per person employed.

The extraction of oil and gas (and excluding its processing into petrol or other products) is almost as important as the whole of the service sector of the economy (though, of course, the service sector does use petrol and other hydrocarbons in its activities).

Plastics are not particularly important in the overall total. At about 7 million tonnes overall, or 0.1 tonnes per person, the industry does not figure substantially in total emissions. It may seem unconventional to say this, but it may not make sense to devote attention to recycling domestic plastics, rather than simply discouraging their use in the home. For example, if lightweight plastics containers are washed after use, the carbon cost of heating hot water may be greater than the benefit of recycling.[251] Plastic bags are absolutely hateful, I know, but weigh so little that their impact on carbon emissions is not of the highest importance. One source (albeit a partial one) estimates that 100,000 plastic bags weigh less than 1 tonne.[252] Replacing these bags with paper – much heavier and greater in volume – would be unlikely to save any greenhouse gases, particularly since some fraction of the paper bags is likely to end up in landfill, where they will eventually rot and produce methane. Don't focus on light plastic packaging – it is not a huge part of the greenhouse gas problem despite the irritating tendency of various types of plastic to litter our streets and our parks.

Reducing consumption of life's newest and most interesting products is not usually considered an appealing option; but one way to avoid adding to emissions would certainly be to try to buy all of our requirements from local sources (avoiding transport and retail costs) and to minimize the consumption of anything with a high fossil fuel content. Where second-hand goods are available, they are clearly superior.

To minimize emissions, we would need not just to avoid buying new cars or other lumps of metal, but also anything that has been through an energy-intensive process, or a process which creates carbon dioxide, such as cement manufacture. This is not a particularly helpful piece of advice; but without careful analysis of the individual steps involved in making a product and then disposing of it (usually called 'life-cycle analysis'), it is virtually impossible to tell how much carbon has gone into the atmosphere as a result of manufacturing processes. Increasing numbers of good analyses of the life-cycle costs of manufactured goods are being carried out; but their results are almost always controversial or disputed. I suspect that the only worthwhile rule is, therefore, to avoid buying anything with a substantial weight of metal or plastics. Even paper creates substantial emissions. A ream of copier paper has almost certainly been responsible for 3kg of greenhouse gases in the process of its production.

This is not an easy rule to follow, or one that will be particularly effective since so much energy is used in the intermediate stages of manufacturing rather than in the final product. The rest of this book therefore looks at how to cancel out emissions for which we are indirectly responsible.

15

**domestic use
of renewable energy**

Wind turbines, solar electricity and solar hot water are all possibilities for avoiding emissions at home (or, indeed, at work). Precise figures depend upon location and upon the orientation of the house. The first generation of home wind turbines have not proved as reliable or as trouble free as their manufacturers expected, but may still eventually produce enough electricity per year to offset at least 1 tonne of emissions – although at a much higher cost per tonne than investing in a large-scale commercial wind farm. Solar hot water is now a well-established technology, particularly in sunnier countries, and even in the UK can cut household emissions by 0.5 tonnes or more a year. Savings from solar photovoltaics can be greater than this, although the amount depends crucially upon the area of panels that are installed.

Using a wood-burning stove as a means of heating the house will also provide a reduction in fossil fuel use. In some circumstances, a wood burner can completely replace gas for heating and hot water.

Table 15.1 on page 258 summarizes the costs and savings of the various technologies.

T his chapter looks at the ways in which domestic households can currently use renewable energy to reduce carbon emissions. It addresses five types of technology:

1   Solar hot water.
2   Wind turbines.
3   Solar photovoltaics.
4   Ground-source heat pumps.
5   Biomass, primarily wood for stoves.

It does not deal with other technologies that may become available in the next few years, such as domestic fuel cells or very small combined heat and power plants (usually known as 'micro-CHP'). Although these technologies may eventually make inroads into the domestic market, and are often written about as though they are similar to wind and sun, they do not actually capture renewable energy. They are simply efficient replacements for existing domestic heating systems, but are some years away from widespread commercial sale. Micro-CHP plants are probably the more interesting and a few houses already have demonstration models. Domestic CHP uses gas to heat the house and to generate electricity. Field trials have shown some savings in carbon dioxide output; but these were small when compared to buying a new high-efficiency boiler.[253]

SOLAR HOT WATER

About 100,000 homes in the UK have some form of solar hot water heater and this number is growing by several thousand a year. Most solar water heaters take the form of a flat metal plate or a set of vacuum tubes on the roof of the house. These devices can provide hot water for the household for most of the year, but will only supplement conventional water heating in the winter months. They don't replace central heating in any way.

Table 15.1 *Summary of the costs and benefits of renewable energy*

Technology	Context	CO_2 savings per year (tonnes)	Cash savings per year	Cost of installation (after grant)	Cost per tonne of CO_2 averted	Comments
Solar hot water – evacuated tubes	Small house, small system	0.2	£23	£3000	£600	
	Large house, large system	0.8	£94	£3500	£170	
Wind turbine (Renewable Devices)	Central southern England location	1.0	£224	£4800	£185	The cost should fall significantly
	Windy location	1.9	£393	£4800	£100	
Solar photovoltaics	2kW peak installation	0.8	£180	£5000	£250	
Ground-source heat pump		–	–	Likely to be substantial compared to electric heating		
Wood-burning stove	Living room heating in Oxford	2.0	Cost of £70	£1500	£65	£35, if only wood is costed
	Whole house, using automatic wood-pellet feed	4.0	Depends upon local price of wood	£2900	May be as low as zero; unlikely to be more than £80	

The advertisements for these products claim that they can replace 50 to 70 per cent of the energy used for heating water. The truth of this statement depends upon the relationship between the size of the installation on the roof and the total hot water demand of the household (if you never wash, then the solar system will, indeed, provide most of your hot water). Later in this section, I show that the figure of 50 per cent is probably achievable, but that 70 per cent is only attainable if the daily hot water needs of the house are restricted to providing one person a shower. The underlying difficulty is that only six months of the year give us enough solar energy to get water anywhere close to a high enough temperature to avoid using the boiler.

The installation

How does solar water heating work? Solar energy falling on a plate or a glass tube heats up the fluid passing through it. This hot liquid, usually water with anti-freeze in it, is pumped through a coil inside the hot water tank, heating the water. Having transferred its energy to the water in the tank, the now cooler liquid is pumped back to the roof. The technology is simple and reliable, and primitive versions have been used for centuries, particularly in countries where sunshine is plentiful. Efficient solar hot water panels – sometimes just called collectors – will work well in strong sunshine, even when air temperatures are low. However, collectors in cold climates will tend to lose a greater part of the energy that they collect. More heat is conducted or radiated to the air or to the surroundings of the solar thermal panels.

Solar collectors will heat water from mains temperature of about 10 degrees Celsius up to 60 degrees Celsius or more. Depending upon the time of year and the number of hours of sunshine, the energy transferred from the collectors will either provide all of the water heating needed or will preheat the water so that it requires less fossil fuel energy to get it to the correct temperature.

How much water will the sun heat?

The savings in gas or electricity both depend upon the amount of the sun's energy falling on the plates and the efficiency with which the energy is collected. In southern England, 1 square metre of surface receives about 1200kWh/year in solar energy. The number is lower in the north. Of course, it is also unequally distributed between the months. The total energy received in December is about one tenth of the June level. On a typical day in June, a 4 square metre solar collector in England and Wales south of the Mersey will receive about 20kWh to 24kWh, compared to no more than 2kWh in December. People often ask me whether one can use solar systems for central heating. The answer, unfortunately, is that when we need heating, there is so little solar energy reaching the UK that it would require a huge collector plate to capture more than a fraction of the heat energy we would need. The typical house requires 65kWh a day of heating (see Chapter 6), and 2kWh is only a small percentage of this.

The most efficient solar collectors are evacuated tubes, which turn about 70 per cent of this energy into useful heat, provided that the installation is facing reasonably close to south at an angle of tilt of about 30 degrees. Evacuated tubes not facing approximately south, or placed horizontally or vertically, will receive less energy. Provided that it is correctly oriented, in an average year 1 square metre of evacuated tubes will carry about 840kWh to the hot water tank in the south of England. Typical domestic installations are between 2 and 4 square metres, giving 1680–3360kWh/year, or an average of up to 9kWh per day for a larger collector (for reference, this compares to a figure of about 19,000kWh for the annual gas consumption of a typical house on the mains gas network).

The average daily figure will vary by a factor of more than 30 between a long sunny day in a summer month and a short overcast period of daylight in the depth of winter. On a sunny day in late June, the figure from a 4 square metre installation might be as much as 30kWh. How much water will this heat (see Table 15.2)?

Table 15.2 *Number of litres of water heated by the sun in late June*

Energy needed to heat 1 litre of water by 100°C	0.11kWh
Typical UK mains temperature	10°C
Typical temperature of heated water in a shower*	60°C
Increase needed	50°C
Energy needed to heat 1 litre of water by 50°C	0.055kWh
Number of litres of water that can be heated by 50°C by 30kWh solar energy	545 litres

Note: * This figure may be somewhat high. It is difficult to measure accurately without highly intrusive research.

Is 545 litres per day enough for a typical house? The rule of thumb is that hot water demand in the UK averages about 50 litres a day per person. So, a household with two people will be hugely overprovided for in June. But this also depends upon how the household does its bathing. Eighty litres will provide a full bath, so a sunny day should deliver almost seven baths. On the other hand, a quick gravity-fed shower might take only 30 litres.

The real question is whether the house has pumped showers, usually called power showers. These water guzzlers use up to 16 litres or more per minute, so the June solar energy will give a maximum of about 34 minutes of hot water.

I have not been able to find a reliable statistic on the average length of time spent in a luxurious power shower. Most sources give a figure of about five minutes, meaning that the water should last for six or seven people even if they are all using a pumped shower. In a household of two adults and two children, a sunny day in June should give enough hot water for all bathing needs, whether the family uses baths, power showers or the gravity-fed variety.

Actually, it is not quite as simple as this. When solar collectors are installed, the household usually gets a new hot water tank of about 300 litres capacity. So unless family members spread their showers throughout the day and give the hot water tank a chance to reheat, there won't be enough water. Or the 300 litre tank needs to get to a hotter temperature so that it can be diluted with cold water. The summer temperature of hot water from solar collectors can rise well above 80 degrees Celsius, meaning that the hot water has to be diluted with at least one part cold for two parts hot. The 300 litre tank delivers hot showers of at least 450 litres (28 minutes in a powerful shower), enough for five or six people.

What percentage of the water heating bill will be saved?

These calculations are complex and somewhat tedious. This section can be easily skipped if you are only interested in the main conclusions, which are summarized at the end.

First of all, we need to estimate how much solar energy is captured and used in comparison to the energy needed to heat a household's water. In this calculation, we must guess at the amount of energy that is not productively used because residents are away, or the system actually produces more energy (on a sunny summer day) than the water users actually use.

From Table 15.3, we can then go on to estimate the savings that this generates. The first row in Table 15.4 shows the amount of water heating that the house still requires. The next row estimates what this costs in terms of gas use (assuming the household uses gas for water heating) by multiplying up the raw energy need by a factor to reflect the inefficiency of the boiler (to get 100kWh of water heating, the typical fairly modern boiler has to burn 133kWh of gas because it is only about 75 per cent efficient).

The likely saving in fossil fuel is given in the penultimate line, and the percentage this figure represents of the required gas expenditure is shown at the bottom. A house using

Table 15.3 *Standard data for a small solar hot water collector of 2 square metres*

	Litres of hot water needed per day			
	50	100	200	400
Yearly energy required to heat water	1004	2008	4015	8030
Energy collected by 2 square metres (tubes)	1680	1680	1680	1680
Amount of solar energy productively used*	800	1200	1600	1680
Remaining energy required	204	808	2415	6350

Notes: Units for energy figures are kWh/year.

* The solar collectors may heat more water than is actually needed by the household. This heat therefore does not replace heat that would otherwise have been provided by gas.

Table 15.4 *Savings from use of solar hot water*

	Litres of hot water needed per day			
	50	100	200	400
Remaining energy need (kWh/year)	204	808	2415	6350
Fossil fuel use at 75% boiler efficiency (kWh/year)	272	1077	3220	8467
Fossil fuel use without solar collector, at 75% efficiency (kWh/year)	1338	2677	5353	10,707
Saving in kWh/year	1067	1600	2133	2240
Fossil fuel saving (percentage)	80	60	40	21

50 litres a day (two quick showers, or a very small bath, and limited use for dish or hand washing) will typically see 80 per cent of its hot water need provided by a 2 square metre collector. On the other hand, the percentage is no more than about 21 per cent for a house that uses 400 litres a day.

As we might expect, the percentage of hot water heating carried out by the sun depends crucially upon the relationship between the size of the solar collectors and the household demand. Table 15.5 shows – at one extreme – a profligate five-person household with a need for 400 litres will only save 41 per cent of their gas use by installing a 4 square metre collector. On the other hand, a more restrained one-person household with a 50 litre a day need will avoid 90 per cent of the energy bills for water heating with a large set of solar hot water panels on the roof.

What does all of this mean in terms of carbon dioxide savings (see Table 15.6)?

The benefits in terms of reduced carbon dioxide emissions will be between 0.2 and over 0.8 tonnes, depending upon the size of the installation and the hot water needs of the household. What about the cost savings?

Table 15.5 *Savings from a 4 square metre collector*

		Litres of hot water needed per day			
		50	100	200	400
Saving in fossil fuel	kWh/year	1200	2133	3533	4400
	Percentage	90	80	66	41

Table 15.6 *Savings in carbon dioxide from using a solar hot water collector*

		Litres hot water per day per house			
		50	100	200	400
Energy savings	2 square metre collector	1067	1600	2133	2240
(kWh/year)	4 square metre collector	1200	2133	3533	4400
CO_2 savings	2 square metre collector	0.20	0.30	0.41	0.43
(tonnes/year)	4 square metre collector	0.23	0.41	0.67	0.84

Table 15.7 shows that the savings from a 2 square metre evacuated tubes collector will be between £32 and £67, depending upon the amount of hot water used. For the larger collector, the figure is as much as £132.

The costs of solar hot water installations are falling. Very simple installations of flat-plate collectors now cost about £2500 for 4 square metres, including 5 per cent value added tax (VAT). A 4 square metre evacuated tube system will be more – probably costing between £3600 and £3900 before a grant. A 2 square metre installation will be cheaper, but only by a few hundred pounds (nevertheless, most installations do seem to be less than 4 square metres or its equivalent for flat plates; many households may have gone for false economy). A government subvention of £400 is available for most domestic installations, bringing the cost down to just over £2000 for the very simplest, smallest installations. And, of course, for new houses, or for houses that need to replace roofs, the costs are much lower.

Collectors are generally thought to have a life of over 25 years, so the cost per tonne of carbon dioxide saved for a 4 square metre evacuated tube system ranges from about £375 down to less than £200, depending upon the household's use of water, before grants. The grant will reduce the cost by £20 to £70 per tonne. The direct financial benefits will, however, be unlikely to repay the cost of installation on an existing house unless

Table 15.7 *Typical savings per year from installing a solar hot water collector*

	Litres hot water per day per house			
	50	100	200	400
2 square metre collector	£32	£48	£64	£67
4 square metre collector	£36	£64	£106	£132

Note: These figures all assume evacuated tube installations, rather than flat plates. To give equivalent performance, the flat plat would have to be 40 per cent larger. In other words, to match the heat generation of a 2 square metre evacuated tube array, the flat plate installation would have to be 2.8 square metres.

the price of gas continues to rise. The payback periods for solar technologies in the UK are long.

However, as I say elsewhere, the impact of having an energy-saving device such as a solar collector on the roof is largely felt in changed family behaviour. The actual savings from a solar collector will be much larger because of the increased awareness of the costs and consequences of fossil fuel use.

One cautionary point needs to be made. Solar hot water is becoming interesting to large numbers of householders in the UK. Inevitably, perhaps, some unscrupulous firms are using aggressive sales tactics and are hugely over-promising the benefits from installing solar collectors. They are also greatly overcharging – one household I know was charged £12,000 for solar collectors and a new condensing boiler. Typically, the salespeople will say that their system will save '50 to 70 per cent of energy costs'. Please treat this claim with huge scepticism:

- Remember that the solar collectors only heat water for your baths and showers and do not heat the house.
- Keep in mind that water heating is generally less than 30 per cent of your gas bill.
- Finally, even a large collector will probably only replace 50 per cent of your water heating needs.

Some issues with solar thermal

Most users of solar thermal systems are very happy with their systems. The apparently free supply of copious hot water during summer gives people particular satisfaction. The owners I know are all enthusiastic advocates of solar collectors.

But it is worth mentioning a few quibbles:

- The water can get very hot in some systems. Of course, it can be mixed with cold water to achieve the right temperature; but the risk of scalding is ever present in high summer unless a temperature controller is installed.
- Second, the effectiveness of solar thermal hot water in the summer months means that the boiler is very rarely on. Many households use the boiler cupboard or room as a place in which to dry clothes. From April to September, clothes won't get dry because the room isn't being heated by the operation of the boiler.

WIND TURBINES

As is particularly well understood by anybody living on the coastline of the British Isles, the UK is a windy place. The wind blows here on more days per year and at greater force than almost anywhere else in Europe. Across the UK, we are reckoned to have about 40 per cent of the European Union's wind energy (Scotland alone has 25 per cent).[254] Against stiff opposition from local interests, large numbers of new commercial wind farms are being built in the exposed quarters of the UK. The number of large turbines – now about 1400 – may even eventually exceed the number of windmills (over 10,000) that flourished during the 18th century before the advent of steam power.

Large domestic wind turbines have been available for several decades. UK companies such as Proven Engineering supply systems on masts specially erected for the purpose. These windmills offered a good supply of electricity to farms and other places with no connection to the power grid, but there are only a few hundreds installed in the UK. Now, at today's electricity prices, these large turbines are close to making financial sense for buildings already attached to the grid. When I looked at a possible installation on the windy south Cornish coast, the payback period seemed about ten years. A large turbine would have provided the electricity needs for a complex of three holiday cottages.

The grail for turbine manufacturers has been a small turbine that can be put onto the gable of a domestic house, supplying power that supplements the existing electricity supply. The challenges have been substantial: domestic turbines must not shake the building excessively and must be nearly completely quiet.

Two small Scottish companies have been promising domestic wind turbines that meet these requirements for the last two or three years. Very low prices were mentioned – and at least one business promised a figure of less than £1500 to eager potential customers three years ago. It hasn't yet turned out quite like this, though the retailers B&Q are finally selling a simple device for this amount.

Renewable Devices Ltd has a very elegant machine that now (September 2006) sells for about £6100, including a very costly fee of about £2600 for installation.[255] As far as I can tell, this machine is handcrafted by skilled labour in Scotland. Eventually, it needs to be manufactured in a low-cost location from standardized components to deliver a much lower price to the purchaser. The turbine delivers a maximum of about 1.5kW from its 2.1m wide five-bladed rotor when the wind is blowing hard (but not too hard; the windmill will stop turning temporarily as a safety measure when the wind speed rises much above 15 metres per second).

The turbines are intended to be connected to the electricity grid. When the house is using a lot of electricity, the power from the turbine is used first in the house. If the turbine is generating more electricity than the house needs, the power is put into the grid, or 'exported'.

When it first began to advertise the turbine, Renewable Devices advertised that its machine generated about 4000kWh/year, or more than the typical household's electricity consumption. Experience has scaled back the optimism for the heavily populated areas of southern England. When I contacted the company's installers, I was told that on the western boundary of Oxford, we could expect about 2300kWh/year, or about two-thirds of the average household's power use. So, for a house in lowland central England, the device will produce just over 6kWh a day, or about one sixth of its potential generation, which would be 36kWh if the wind blew hard all day. Many sceptics have doubted these figures, pointing to the lower wind speeds in city centres and the loss of power from turbulent wind flow.

What do the economics look like for this sort of installation? I will look at two examples (see Table 15.8):

1   The wind speed at our house averages 4.5 metres per second (about 10mph, but please note that we live on the western edge of a huge meadow and not in the centre of a town). A house in an exposed location in northern England or Scotland might see average speeds of over 6 metres per second (13mph).
2   The energy contained in wind goes up by the cube of the speed. So a house getting average winds of 6 metres per second should be able to generate roughly twice as much as our house in Oxford; but, to be conservative, I have used a figure of 4200kWh/year (the windier location is likely to see more hours a year when the turbine isn't working because its blades are furled due to excessive wind speed.)

Table 15.8 *Estimated annual savings from installing a Renewable Devices turbine*

	Oxford, a typical inland, lowland site in southern England on the edge of a town	A more exposed upland house, probably in northern England, Scotland or on the Cornish coast
Total generation per year	2300kWh	4200kWh
Renewables payment (on all generation*) (A)	£92	£168
Estimate of total used in home, remembering that the house doesn't use much at night	1400kWh	2200kWh**
Savings on electricity bill at 10 pence per kilowatt hour (B)	£140	£220
Estimate of total 'exported'	900kWh	2000kWh
Export payment (C)	£36	£80
Total (A + B + C) per year	£268	£468

Notes: * Assumes a Renewable Certificate payment of £40 per megawatt hour.
** The percentage of energy used in the windy location is lower than in Oxford because much of the extra generation will simply spill into the grid at night and when the house is unoccupied during the day.

The owner of a turbine sees three separate financial benefits. First, the electricity bill is reduced. A large portion of the power created will be used in the house, replacing grid power. At current electricity prices, this is about 10 pence per kilowatt hour. Second, the owner will receive a payment for the current delivered to the grid and not used in the house. I expect this to be about 4 pence per kilowatt hour. Third, as a legitimate, though small, generator of renewable energy, turbines are eligible for Renewable Certificates. This might be worth 4 pence a kilowatt hour to the householder for the total annual generation, and not just for the units exported.

Table 15.8 shows that the savings vary by almost a factor of 2, depending upon the windiness of the location. The cost, however, is the same. After a government grant of £1500, the cost of the machine is £4800. The yield on this expenditure is over 5 per cent in Oxford and over 9 per cent in a windy location. The manufacturers say that the expected life of the machine is 20 years, so the turbine is unlikely to pay for itself in Oxford with current energy prices. At a windy site, the payback will be in about 12 years.

What about carbon savings? The total yearly generation in Oxford will save a bit over 1 tonne of carbon dioxide; the windier site will avoid 1.8 tonnes. If the turbine lasts 20 years, the cost per tonne of carbon is reasonably low at the house with more wind at about £127. In Oxford, the number is higher, and comparable to solar thermal, at about £232.

The future is going to be better. The price of grid-connected domestic 1.5kW wind turbines will almost certainly slip below £3000, including installation, in the next few years. At this level, the return will provide an attractive investment, particularly in windy locations. It is also reasonably likely that the government's subsidy scheme for renewable generation will become more generous to micro-power stations, such as wind turbines. The price of power may rise further, making the savings in electricity more valuable.

If my guesses about the evolution of the costs of a small wind turbine are correct, it will eventually be one of the two or three sources of renewable energy of choice for homes in exposed locations, particularly in areas where the sun is less strong. But wind micro-technology is still unproven and we will only need one story about a house being shaken to pieces for the appeal to wear off. The judgement of planning departments is also still uncertain. Although turbines such as those produced by Renewable Devices are barely larger than the first generation of satellite dishes and, at least to some eyes, are elegant and inoffensive, planners may well take an aggressive line. After all, it is only recently that solar panels laid flat on roofs have become acceptable adjuncts to houses. Wind turbines are of a magnitude greater in visual significance; but the government may well change planning laws to allow wind turbines of up to a reasonable size to be added to houses without planning applications.[256] Renewable Devices has a smaller turbine in development that will probably not require planning permission after the rules have been changed. We can expect many other manufacturers to follow suit.

Wind speeds in city centres are, however, generally much lower than the official UK wind speed database would suggest. The increased turbulence also reduces the effective power. As time goes on, these problems may be solved – possibly by the use of rotating vertical turbines – but householders should currently be cautious about some of the claims for domestic wind power.

SOLAR PHOTOVOLTAICS (PV)

Solar photovoltaic (PV) panels generate electricity through the action of the sun's rays falling upon a silicon layer and causing the passage of electrons. Now 30 or 40 years old, the technology has always slightly disappointed. Expectations of rapid improvement have come to little, and the most efficient panels still convert no more than about 20 per cent of the energy falling upon them. Typical figures are lower than this, and the average installation in the UK today will probably turn no more than 15 per cent of solar energy into electricity.

Solar PV installations on the roofs of UK homes are few in number – probably less than 3000. The cost is daunting, with an array that generates 2kW in bright sunshine possibly costing more than £10,000.[257] Grants of 50 per cent can reduce this to about £5000 or so. No one seems to be certain about whether solar PV grants will continue into the foreseeable future, not least because of the considerable scepticism that seems to exist in official quarters about the underlying rationality of pushing PV technology in the cloudy UK. Indeed, it does make far more sense to try to capture wind energy here, rather than the sun.

As with solar hot water, the orientation of the roof and its degree of tilt towards the sun are important for solar electricity, although perhaps not as vital as one might think. A roof facing due east will probably capture about 80 per cent of the energy of panels facing due south. Similar degrees of attenuation accompany roofs that are either flat or very steep.

The amount of solar radiation reaching England and Scotland varies greatly by latitude. The tip of Cornwall gets as much as 30 per cent more than northern England. As a result, a PV installation in the south-west, where electricity costs are generally higher as well, is more economically rational than in the north of England or Scotland (in September 2006, the price of electricity is about 12 per cent higher in Cornwall than it is in London, based on the British Gas price list, so the saving from PV panels might be as much as 50 per cent greater in the far south-west of England).

As with wind turbines, solar PV installations are generally connected to the grid. The house uses the electricity first, if necessary, and any surplus spills over to the grid. The panels generate direct current that needs to be converted into alternating current, synchronized to the 50 cycles per second pattern of the electricity network. Output from the roof has to go through expensive electronics, a meter that registers how much is generated and, possibly, a meter that says how much is exported to the grid, rather than being used in the home. These all add to the cost.

The finances of domestic PV

PV installations are rated like wind turbines in terms of the amount of electricity they can generate under optimum conditions of sunshine or wind speed. In the case of PV panels, they will generally capture most at about midday during the summer months. The maximum solar radiation reaching the panels will be about 1kW per square metre at this time. At about 15 per cent efficiency, it therefore takes about 12 square metres to provide 2 'kilowatt peak', or 2kWp.

Under typical southern England conditions, such an installation will gather about 1800kWh/year (the equivalent of about 900 hours operating at peak potential). The figure might be 1500kWh/year for an installation facing due west, rather than directly to the south.

In financial terms, solar PV attached to the grid offers two benefits to the owner: first, a reduction in bills and, second, a payment for the renewable energy generated. As with turbines, the major electricity companies are prepared to pay for the energy from the sun because it helps, however minimally, to meet their obligations to generate renewable energy. In the case of solar PV, house-owners get the same three benefits as they do from wind:

1   a reduction in their own electricity bills from the units they consume themselves;
2   a payment for units exported to the grid;
3   a payment for all the electricity they generate in the form of money for the Renewables Obligation Certificate (usually known as the ROC).

Assume that one third of the electricity generated is exported to the grid. This seems to be the assumption used by most installers. Generating 1800kWh/year will therefore reduce a household's electricity bill by 1200kWh/year. This will save approximately £120 at today's prices. In addition, generators may pay 4 pence for every unit exported. This means another £24. Finally, the ROC payment might be £72. So the net income from investing £5000, after grants, is about £216 a year, or just over 4 per cent. The life of such systems is probably about 25 years or perhaps more, although the efficiency will slowly fall over the last years of life. To put it bluntly, the system will therefore probably just about pay back its cost.

Given the poor economics, it is not surprising that the UK has only a tiny number of domestic solar PV systems. In some other countries, solar PV has had a much more rapid take-off. In Germany, for example, the number of domestic solar electricity homes is now well over 100,000. An extremely favourable public policy regime means guaranteed high prices for the electricity produced and low-interest loans to reduce the barriers to install the equipment.

OUR EXPERIENCE: A SOLAR PV AND A SOLAR HOT WATER SYSTEM

We installed a solar PV and solar hot water system in December 2004. The search for an installer was not simple; prices varied widely and most companies were reluctant to come to Oxford. In the end, the installation was done by a firm almost two hours' drive away. Except in the most eco-friendly areas, such as around Machynlleth in north Wales, there is no proper infrastructure of local firms ready to do solar installations, although the position is undeniably getting better.

Our installer provided a quote for both systems separately and offered a substantial discount if we bought both at once. The firm would only have to pay for one set of scaffolding, and a lot of the work on the roof would not need to be duplicated. After grants of 50 per cent for the PV and £400 for the solar hot water, the cost was just over £8000.

The installation itself was trouble free, but took the best part of a week. Both systems have worked perfectly since being inaugurated, except for a short period when one of the two sets of PV electronics mysteriously failed. It was replaced under guarantee without any quibble. The meters recording the electricity generated tell us every second of the day how much electricity is coming into the house. For those of us with an interest in the economics of renewable energy, this is endlessly fascinating. More conventional people in the household do not have the same tendency as me to go to look at the meters whenever the sun starts shining.

The track record of the system has been slightly better than we thought. 2005 was a sunny year and the installers are forced to be conservative in their sales promises by the conditions of the grant-making bodies. The total amount of electricity generated was about 1430kWh. (This figure would, perhaps, be 20 per cent higher if we had a roof that was south facing. One of our sets of panels faces east, the other west, so we don't get as much solar radiation as many other houses.) The pattern is shown in Figure 15.1.

The pattern is not quite what statisticians call a normal distribution, symmetrical around a peak. The generation faded fast after the second week of September after five months at a rate of about 6kWh a day.

The solar thermal collectors worked very well indeed in their first year. For the six months when the sun was highest in the sky, the collectors gave us a reliably large tank of hot water, except on the cloudiest days. Even in early February, when the sun is strong the tank will be heated to over 45 degrees Celsius, and possibly reach 50 degrees, after being only 10 degrees after the morning showers. The water is scalding in summer and care needs to be taken to ensure that children don't ever use our mixer taps fully set to hot. The profligate

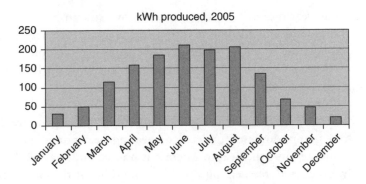

kWh produced, 2005

Figure 15.1 *Monthly energy output from a solar photovoltaic (PV) system in Oxford*

nature of our water use means that we still use a small amount of gas in the summer to heat up part of a tank of hot water for morning washing before the sun starts really shining.

The total savings from our investment in solar energy of £8300 are about £300 a year at current prices. As we say to ourselves when justifying the expense, it's better than having money in a taxed savings account. We saved about 1.5 tonnes of carbon dioxide in the first year.

This is the rational side of the analysis. Something more significant went on when we installed the solar equipment, and this goes on in most solar homes. Suddenly, energy conservation becomes more important. Wasteful appliances are turned off at the wall, the thermostat gets turned down and the microwave is used instead of the gas oven. So, for example, our gas consumption fell by about 35 per cent, even though the solar water heating was probably responsible for no more than one third of the reduction. The visible economic benefits of using domestic renewables may be small; but the psychological impacts are noticeable and sometimes even dramatic.

GROUND-SOURCE HEAT PUMPS

For domestic use, solar and wind installations are relatively well understood, even though micro-turbines are some years away from being widely used. Ground-source heat pumps are less well known, although the technology is simple and reliable. They can be used to provide relatively low-cost space heating – not water heating – in homes with large gardens in which the fairly long pipe work can run to collect the energy from the ground.

Modern domestic heat pumps rarely use geothermal energy, or the warmth that can be found several hundred metres below ground. Instead, their energy source is the fairly constant temperature of the ground 2m or 3m below the surface. This is normally about

10 degrees Celsius all year round. A heat pump works by extracting some of the low-level heat energy in the ground and turning it into a higher grade of energy, perhaps at 35 degrees Celsius, to heat the water for under-floor heating. Having done its work, colder fluid, at perhaps 5 degrees Celsius, is then sent back out to run through the ground again, picking up more low-level heat to use.

Heat pumps do not produce free energy – for example, they need electricity to power the compressor that squeezes the internal gas and thus raises its temperature. Like a fridge, also a form of heat pump, domestic under-floor heating heat pumps need electricity to separate hot and cold, sending the heat to where it is wanted and the cold back outside.[258]

Very roughly, ground-source heat pumps need one third of the energy they put into a house's heating in the form of electricity to run themselves. This means that they make no financial sense for houses with access to gas for heating, even though under-floor heating is less wasteful of heat than radiators. Gas at 3 pence a kilowatt hour is less than one third of the price of electricity at 10 pence per kilowatt hour.

In addition, heat pumps are only well suited to under-floor heating. Getting the heated water to the higher temperatures needed for successful radiator heating, or for domestic hot water, would mean that the pumps would lose significant amounts of efficiency. In the UK, this means, in effect, that ground-source heat pumps are only really valuable for reconstructions of houses or for the building of new houses in which under-floor heating pipes are put in place. In this instance, the carbon savings can be noticeable, although not as overwhelming as their proponents sometimes claim. The enthusiasts tend to forget that households will still have to have a boiler for heating high-temperature water for washing use.

BIOMASS, PRIMARILY WOOD FOR STOVES

A wide variety of agricultural crops can be used for combustion and heat generation. In the next decade we may well see an enhanced role for woods, grasses and straws as a source of energy for commercial electricity and heat generation, particularly in community schemes covering all of the housing in a new development. This is certainly the case in other countries in Northern Europe, such as Sweden. At the moment, wood is the only real option for burning biomass in the home in the UK.

Is wood truly renewable? In the UK, at least, the answer is yes. Despite most people's impression to the contrary, the area under woodland is growing year on year, particularly in areas where arable agriculture is of marginal financial viability. Using wood from trees that are grown, cut down and then replaced by more saplings means no net emission of carbon dioxide to the atmosphere. As wood is burned, of course, it emits carbon; but the next generation of trees grown on the same land will naturally take up an equivalent amount from the atmosphere as they grow. In other countries in Europe, the position is broadly the same; but in some tropical countries wood should not be considered renewable, since the area under forest is tending to fall, in some places, very rapidly.

A wood-burning stove sitting in a niche in the centre of a living room is an attractive thing, and a good fire has a visual value, as well as providing a replacement to fossil fuel heating. Open fires do not provide anywhere near as much useful heat to the room as a wood stove, which operates at 70 per cent efficiency or more. These stoves need flues and must exhaust to a chimney. Well-designed stoves can provide heat for less than peak electricity costs, but almost certainly more than gas, even at today's prices. A hot stove, working efficiently, emits very low levels of non-carbon-dioxide pollution; nevertheless, it will normally be prohibited in the clean air zones of large cities. Some people, rightly noting the low emissions of their stoves, choose to ignore this rule.

Typical stoves of reasonable size (500mm wide, 600mm high and 500mm deep) might deliver 5kW to 6kW of heat. This will typically provide enough heat to warm a large and well-insulated room of 35 or so square metres (100 square feet). The average home in the UK is little more than 80 square metres, so a stove can replace a significant fraction of all gas or electricity heating. You can also buy large stoves that provide the space and water heating needs of an entire house.

How much wood is required? A full load of logs might be 800kg, but probably contains 30 to 40 per cent moisture. If left to dry for a year, this could fall to 20 per cent, and the weight of the wood would be reduced to as little as 640kg. Dry wood of this type generally provides just under 2000kWh per tonne, so a load like this might offer almost 1300kWh. From our domestic wood supplier, a pick-up van's load of this weight costs £65; therefore, the cost per kilowatt hour is about 5 pence, almost twice the price of gas, but much less than standard electricity costs.

This is not the full story. An efficient wood-burning stove delivers a very large fraction of its energy directly into the room or to the chimney. A well-insulated house will capture perhaps 80 per cent of a stove's output. A modern boiler might achieve 75 per cent (more if it is a condensing gas boiler); but some of the heat will be lost taking the hot water to the radiators in a living room. And these radiators will also often sit in exposed places, such as beneath windows, where their heat is easily lost. Precise calculations are difficult because they depend upon individual houses; but wood is still likely to cost more than gas.

A 5kW stove working eight hours a day for 180 heating days a year will put out 7200kWh/year. If a stove is 50 per cent more efficient than a gas boiler at delivering effective heat where it is wanted, the use of a stove might replace as much as 2 tonnes of carbon dioxide a year. This is clearly significant. Our domestic wood supplier would need to deliver almost six loads of logs to achieve this, costing £370, compared to less than £300 for gas.

Therefore, saving 2 tonnes of carbon dioxide costs a little more than £70. In comparison to other ways of reducing emissions, a wood-burning stove is an excellent idea and delivers good reductions at a reasonable price per tonne. Of course, installing the fire is quite costly – a figure of £1500 to £2000 should be budgeted; but wood-burning stoves look so nice and last forever that I don't count this. If you did, it might add another £30 to the incremental cost per tonne.

The lazy among us would want to incorporate the cost of the labour to stack and store the wood. I resist this; it is one of the true pleasures of life, and you will find that a neat pile of well-ordered logs stacked against the house is much admired by the neighbours.

Living room stoves like ours are all very well; but real savings can be had from installing a large stove, fuelled by pellets with the capacity to heat hot water as well. The wood for these monsters is cheaper than from the gentleman who delivers logs to us. Some studies show that wood pellets can cost no more than the current price of gas, particularly if you live close to the source of the wood. If you have a big house and plenty of room for a pelleted wood burner, buy one. The cost of £3500 or so can be partly offset by a government grant of £600, or 30 per cent for homes in Scotland.

16

cancelling out emissions

Choices about consumption levels, patterns of food purchase and where one is employed are the crucial determinants of indirect emissions. For those things we can't do anything about, the best choice is to offset our emissions. Offsetting means reducing the greenhouse gases from another source of emission to compensate for our own actions.

The easiest ways to do this are purchasing green electricity, investing in new renewable power plants, planting trees or buying into other 'offset' schemes.

GREEN ELECTRICITY

We said earlier in the book that electricity generation is not the UK's main source of carbon emissions. Out of the total greenhouse gas emissions of 12.5 tonnes per year, less than 1 tonne results from electricity use in the home. Gas for heating and cooking is far more important. Nevertheless, it is worth cancelling out the carbon dioxide from electricity. Each kilowatt hour of electricity (about as much as it takes to run a dishwasher) generates nearly 0.5kg of carbon dioxide.

The UK electricity system does not, of course, separate out electricity created from renewable and fossil fuel sources. The thousands of different generating plants around the country – ranging from Sizewell B nuclear power station, supplying about 2 per cent of the UK's electricity, to the 1500kWh generated on our roof each year – all put their output into the transmission system. The big plants insert it into the main network, usually called 'the grid'. Our solar panels put surplus power into the local network in our street. Both Sizewell B and our panels help to keep the whole network across the country 'pumped up' to 240V. On a sunny day, our panels mean that a power station somewhere else in the country is having to work very slightly less hard than it otherwise would have. This will generally be a fossil fuel-generating plant. So, our solar photovoltaic panels are reducing the total amount of carbon dioxide in the atmosphere.

It would therefore seem quite obvious that buying your electricity from a supplier that produces renewable energy would 'save' carbon dioxide. In the UK, this means electricity companies operating wind turbines, hydroelectric schemes and less important sources, such as burning biomass or solar panels. Actually, this is a very complex issue and many 'green' tariffs do not reduce the UK's carbon dioxide emissions.

Great care is needed – if I buy my electricity from a green supplier that has owned the same wind farm for ten years and is not investing in new generating capacity, my decision to switch to this supplier has no impact whatsoever on carbon dioxide emissions. On the other hand, if I buy power from a company that is currently entirely fossil fuel based but which has committed to buying renewable energy to cover the needs of all new customers, it might well be that emissions would go down if I switched to this firm.

Ideally, I want my purchases to influence the electricity market into providing new renewable generation as a direct result of my custom. Given that renewables generation is rising already (albeit at a much slower rate than the government wants), how can I be sure that my decision results in more supply than would otherwise have come into operation? I think the honest answer is that you can't, and anybody who says anything different is probably trying to sell you something.

In 2004, Friends of the Earth produced a document that estimated that green tariffs had only achieved a market share of 0.2 per cent of UK homes in 2001.[259] But the total percentage of electricity generated from renewable sources now exceeds 4 per cent. Domestic consumers of renewable energy are not significant enough in number to force generators to substantially increase their production of green electricity.

The best green tariffs are, I think, provided by those companies investing most heavily in new renewables. At the very worst, your decision to buy from them is helping them to grow their business and provides a signal that the market wants more renewable electricity generation. As of June 2006, probably the most effective green tariff is that provided by Ecotricity, which claims to be investing far more per customer in new renewable plants than other suppliers. Its website quoted approvingly a figure from the *Ecologist* journal, suggesting it made an investment of over £900 in new carbon-free capacity for every customer in the UK during 2004.[260] Ecotricity is building several new wind farms around the UK, and when people ask me to recommend a green tariff, I always mention this company's name.

Don't assume, however, that all Ecotricity's electricity is from renewable sources – only 23 per cent is. Nevertheless, as one of the most important backers of new wind projects, customers do appear to get some carbon reduction in return for their patronage. On the other hand, Good Energy, a small supplier with an excellent reputation and its own wind farms and hydroelectric plants, sells only renewable energy. But it is not systematically growing the number or size of the locations at which it captures renewable electricity. Therefore, we can argue that switching to this supplier does not actually reduce emissions. This is a controversial conclusion with which many would disagree.

Many of the other so-called green tariffs have a rather thin veneer of environmental respectability. Take, for example, the current London Electricity scheme.[261] It adds 0.42

pence to the price of the conventional tariff and uses this – matched by an equivalent amount from the company – to invest in community renewables schemes. Very approximately, 10 per cent of the customer's bill goes to small-scale carbon-neutral energy production from new sources. This is insignificant, both because of the small sums involved and because the investments are in very small ventures (a £2000 wind turbine on a school roof generates far less electricity than £2000 in a large wind farm).

Do green tariffs add to household electricity bills?

The price comparison in Table 16.1 shows a price difference of about £65 between Good Energy's all-renewables prices and those of Scottish and Southern, a mainstream company with a relatively large renewables component in its electricity supply (roughly 10 per cent). This difference is clearly significant, but not an enormous figure in the context of a household's total expenditure on goods and services. It might be as little as the price of a family meal in a good restaurant. Ecotricity matches the price charged by the electricity companies in their home regions.

Ensuring that your purchases do genuinely signal to the electricity market that more renewable capacity should be built is a tough challenge. Suppliers such as Ecotricity are probably the best way of doing this, and I think it is fair to estimate that electricity bought from such companies will, indeed, cancel out carbon emissions.

Increasingly, large manufacturing or office sites are putting up their own renewable capacity or getting a generator to do it for them. These companies let electricity suppliers construct wind turbines on their land and then buy some or all of the output at a reduced rate. The financial services division of the Co-op has 19 small wind turbines on its office building in Manchester, with estimated generation of 44,000kWh/year. The Michelin tyre factory in Dundee has two large turbines, owned and operated by Ecotricity, that provide an estimated output of 8 million kWh/year. Clearly, persuading an employer to build or sponsor a wind turbine is an exceptionally efficient means of increasing the total amount of renewable electricity capacity in the UK.

Table 16.1 *Electricity prices for a home in Oxford*

Supplier for a home in Oxford	Yearly electricity bill for 4500 kilowatt hours (kWh)	Comment
Scottish and Southern	£470.99	
Ecotricity	£470.99	Matches Scottish and Southern
Good Energy	£536.17	Assumes 4.25% discount for quarterly payment in advance

Source: UK electricity tariffs in September 2006.

But at a household level, buying from Ecotricity, or a company with similar credentials, will 'offset' about 1.6 tonnes of carbon dioxide, or about 0.7 tonnes per head.

ZERO-EMISSIONS POWER GENERATION

A second way of definitely neutralizing carbon emissions is to invest personally in zero-carbon emissions power generation. There are already a small number of cooperative ventures in electricity production that would be perfect for offsetting emissions. The recent projections for a community-owned wind farm in west Oxfordshire showed that the investment needed from shareholders (£3.75 million) could be expected to generate 13.8 million kWh/year for the 25 years of the farm's operation.[262]

These figures suggest that the average individual's total carbon dioxide emissions for the whole life of the turbines would be offset by an investment of about £7500. The cost per tonne of carbon dioxide cancelled is less than £40, and makes mutually owned wind farms an exceptionally cheap way of neutralizing emissions. Compare this, for example, to installing a solar hot water system that costs at least £170 per tonne of carbon dioxide avoided. The wind investment will, if the projections turn out to be accurate, earn a return of over 12 per cent a year over the life of the project.[263] The site at Westmill near Faringdon in Oxfordshire is also not particularly windy. Turbines elsewhere will be even better at turning cash from individuals into substantial emissions reductions. I think that cooperatively owned wind farms are a very good way of neutralizing the carbon dioxide for which we are all indirectly responsible.

Westmill announced that it had successfully raised its capital in March 2006, and by May another wind co-op was trying to tap private money in Scotland. In the Scottish case, the co-op investors will only acquire a small share in the farm, which will mostly be owned by a commercial developer. The ceding of a small share to the cooperative members, who will probably primarily be local residents, will provide an element of good neighbourliness to the project. This will surely help other wind energy proposals move more rapidly to successful local planning permission and eventual implementation. (The last few sentences can be summarized by saying that commercial wind developers should sensibly bribe local communities by offering a share in the projected profits and thus getting their turbines up and running more quickly.)

By providing a portion of the capital to build new renewable power stations such as this, individuals can be reasonably certain that their money actually diminishes global emissions. Of course, the number of such opportunities is not unlimited but the demand from investors for these opportunities is now clear. In Denmark, over 100,000 people own a share in a wind farm and in Germany the figure is almost 200,000. We can expect a larger and larger number of renewables ventures to tap these willing, and relatively cheap, sources of finance.

TREE PLANTING

Other than turning your neighbour's lights off or giving her low-energy light bulbs, the ways of directly cancelling out emissions are few (commercial 'offsetting' is discussed in the next section). But it is possible to buy 1 acre (0.4ha) of land currently used for agriculture and plant it with permanent trees, or a biomass crop such as willow which can be used for fuelling central heating stoves.

In this case, the idea is that a fully grown tree planted on an area of land that would otherwise be cultivated (and therefore not store carbon from the atmosphere) will offset substantial amounts of greenhouse gas emitted elsewhere in the economy. One source says that 1 acre of broadleaf trees will eventually capture up to 2.6 tonnes of carbon a year, enough to compensate for slightly less than half our share of annual indirect emissions of 6.5 tonnes.[264] So it needs about 2.5 acres (or about 1ha) to capture all of our share of indirect emissions. If one bought 1ha of land and put trees on it, how much would it cost? For maximum effect, this would need about 1000 trees (see Table 16.2).

The figures in Table 16.2 are drawn from a source that details the cost of planting woodland at lower density so that sheep may productively graze as well, and I have adjusted the numbers appropriately.[265]

Table 16.2 *Cost of establishing 1 hectare of woodland*

Item	Cost
1000 saplings at £0.50 apiece	£500
Good tree guards at £0.65 apiece	£650
Post and tie at £1.50 each	£1500
Three applications of herbicide around the trees	£120
Total	£2770

Before costing the labour, or the value of the land, 1ha of woodland will save around 600 tonnes of carbon over a 100-year period. The cost per tonne is less than £5. So, even if the full cost were twice the cost of saplings and materials, the cost per tonne of carbon dioxide is below £10. Unsurprisingly, planting trees that would otherwise remain unplanted is one of the most effective and cheapest ways of cutting back carbon.

'OFFSET'

Most people won't be able to buy 1ha of land for planting trees and will be thinking about handing the obligation over to a commercial firm that specializes in the neutralizing of carbon dioxide. The seductive promise of carbon offset is that by planting a tree, or some other such carbon-reducing act, one's greenhouse gas emissions can be counter-balanced, or 'offset'. The thought is that the Western consumer's lifestyle can be made carbon neutral by careful investment in reducing carbon emissions elsewhere. Other than tree planting, typical offset projects include handing out free low-energy light bulbs or providing efficient cooking stoves that reduce the need for cutting down firewood.

In theory, the idea is useful. A single energy-efficient light bulb that replaces a conventional incandescent may save over 200kg of carbon dioxide. A return flight to New York can be offset by installing 20 bulbs for apartment owners who wouldn't otherwise have bothered.[266] If we can find projects that genuinely reduce emissions, we can diminish our own responsibility for climate change. One person I know does, indeed, take light bulbs in his suitcase when he makes a flight to the US, though I fear he is running out of places to install them in his friends' houses.

These schemes are good. They increase awareness of climate change issues and bring home the point that travel has real consequences for carbon emissions. Whether they actually achieve genuine reductions in greenhouse gases is much less clear.

Is carbon offsetting the right way forward? Emotions are now running high in the discussions of this question. The proponents, who are usually very thoughtful people concerned about the future of the planet, think that offsetting can neutralize the impact of Western lifestyle choices, such as the desire to fly for business and pleasure. These people think that we cannot do much about the levels of emissions from advanced societies, and paying for offset projects provides a valuable example of how individuals can take some steps to recognize their own responsibilities. The critics say that offsetting is both ineffective in reducing emissions and allows modern society to avoid any consideration of how to achieve a sustained diminution in overall emission levels.

Offsetting is also suspiciously cheap. One UK offset company offers a price of about £7.50 per tonne of carbon dioxide, less than the cost we calculated for planting trees in the UK that neutralized this amount of greenhouse gas. We should also understand what this means: it implies that an individual's yearly carbon dioxide output – direct and indirect – could be abated by a payment of less than £90. Scaled up to the whole UK population, the payments would be less than £5 billion. If it is really so cheap, why doesn't the government do it?

More formal mechanisms for trading emissions, such as through the various European carbon exchanges, suggest a cost of cutting emissions of about 15 to 25 Euros (£10 to £17) per tonne, or about twice as much. Carbon exchanges match companies who do not need their full emissions allowance with those who do. Generally, emissions caps in the European Union (EU) scheme are not hard to achieve for most polluters, so we see quite low levels of pricing per tonne. The long-run price of proper offsetting will be much higher and may, perhaps, reach several times the current price of 16 Euros or so.

One Witney-based retail gas supply company offers a scheme that allows households to buy EU emissions trading certificates to compensate for household use of fossil fuels. Ebico is an unusual supplier that charges no premium for those customers obliged to pay in advance for its gas and electricity, but, nevertheless, in September 2006 was charging a very attractive price for household gas. The customer can ask the company to buy emissions certificates and then retire them from the market. This means that an industrial power user or electricity generator somewhere in the EU will be obliged to produce slightly less carbon dioxide than otherwise would have been the case. In my view, this is the simplest and most effective way of ensuring that our payment results in genuine net emissions reduction.

Nevertheless, on balance, I think the critics of offsetting are partly right. I don't think offset offers a full alternative to the systematic reduction of emissions. Let's look first at whether offsetting is effective in neutralizing greenhouse gases. If I plant a tree that eventually grows to contain 1 tonne of carbon, does that counter-balance those activities of mine that result in the release of 1 tonne of carbon to the atmosphere? This depends upon many things. First, and most importantly, the tree must be planted on land that otherwise would not be forested. In other words, planting a tree in my garden that I would have done anyway, or which simply replaces an existing dead tree, is not sequestering any new carbon. In the UK, guaranteeing that a new tree is genuinely additional is tricky. Forest cover is growing anyway as we take land out of intensive agriculture. The land now under tree cover is over twice as much as it was in 1900.[267] How can we be sure that our payment to the offset company does not go towards planting a tree in a plantation that would have been introduced anyway? Next, we have to be sure that the area we have planted with trees remains as woodland for centuries to come, otherwise the carbon that the tree has captured will be returned to the atmosphere.

These are relatively easy questions compared to those arising with other types of projects used by offsetting companies. One good example of the problems ensuring that emissions are genuinely balanced by offset schemes has been recently provided by ClimateCare's project to give energy-efficient light bulbs to South Africans. The idea is that if one gives low-wattage bulbs to households, power consumption will be reduced below what it would have been. Of course, it is difficult to measure whether households increase their usage of electric light if it becomes cheaper, or whether they would simply add a new light fixture in the house (UK households are typically adding one new lamp to the home every year).

But the situation has recently been made even more complicated by the fact that the South African power generation company Eskom was recently having problems guaranteeing electricity availability because of maintenance at one of its largest plants. So, it has been giving out free low-energy bulbs to householders. Newspaper reports say that Eskom has bought 5 million energy-efficient bulbs from China for handing out to any homeowner who wants one.[268] It is, I suspect, totally impossible to say whether the 50,000 bulbs given out in 2005 (1 per cent of Eskom's number) by ClimateCare have actually resulted in any net reduction in emissions above what will be achieved by Eskom's much bigger campaign to flood the Western Cape area with free bulbs.

The critics of offsetting have much stronger attacks on the principle of letting people buy themselves out of responsibility for emissions. One writer says: 'the overall effect of the industry is to make it even harder to persuade people to actually "reduce" their emissions from source'.[269] He goes on to say that offsets 'send the wrong signals to high polluters', as well as working with projects that are sometimes 'highly contentious' in the countries that they are meant to help.

Carefully chosen and well-managed offset schemes can work to neutralize the odd emergency flight to see relatives; but they are not a long-run solution to the need to reduce greenhouse gases across the world. So, if you need to pay into offset schemes, do plenty of research. The main question is: does this project stand a good chance of genuinely reducing overall carbon dioxide emissions? A vague promise by the offset company to plant some trees or to 'work with a community to improve the techniques used to cook food so as to use less wood and reduce deforestation' is not sufficient. The best way of offsetting is probably to use small gas supplier Ebico's scheme for buying and retiring European emissions certificates.

17

conclusions

The biggest sources of emissions matter most. Getting down to 3 tonnes per year isn't easy; but neither is it impossible.

For the UK homeowner, the best steps for cutting direct emissions are as follows:

- Run a good new central heating boiler, insulate the house properly and turn down the thermostat.
- When the time comes to change the car, buy a small diesel with manual transmission. If you can, join a car club instead and travel fewer miles.
- Only fly when absolutely necessary (this probably means never).
- Buy small, highly efficient electric appliances, such as refrigerators and TVs. Don't use tumble dryers.

Other important steps to indirectly reduce emissions are:

- Buy food from local organic sources. Use unpackaged and unprocessed foods. Reduce meat and dairy.
- Install solar hot water heating.
- Put up a wind turbine when you are convinced that they work, are reasonably priced and don't cause unpleasant vibrations to the house.
- In addition, use a carefully researched electricity supplier who will use your custom to build new renewable sources of energy.
- Where possible, invest yourself in new renewable energy projects, such as community wind farms.
- Avoid buying items that contain large amounts of metal or weight of plastic.
- Persuade your employer to let you work from home, or get it systematically to reduce its energy use.
- Research offset schemes when nothing else is possible and buy into the projects that seem genuinely to reduce emissions.

Carefully thought through and implemented, almost everybody's emissions can be reduced by 50 per cent or more. Moving to 3 tonnes of carbon dioxide or less is perfectly attainable. By themselves, your actions are insignificant. But by showing others that it is possible, and by showing governments and companies that you and others like you are genuinely concerned, you can make a substantial contribution. Every important social movement has started with a few thoughtful individuals deciding that they are compelled to take action. Your decision to reduce your emissions to 3 tonnes will be an early part of the movement to turn back what is arguably the greatest threat the planet has ever faced. I wish you all success.

Afterword

I n the months since this book was submitted to the publisher, the amount of coverage of climate change has continued to increase. The news from scientists seems to suggest a slightly higher likelihood of extremely severe temperature changes during the next half century than we thought a year ago. Data on global emissions continue to provide evidence that no country is yet taking the actions necessary to stabilize, and then reduce, the use of fossil fuels. The European Union's Emissions Trading Scheme (ETS), about which I express scepticism in several chapters of this book, still demonstrates all too clearly the huge difficulties faced by liberal democracies when dealing with a problem as difficult as climate change. Most European countries have requested allocations of CO_2 allowances that are almost blatantly in excess of what they need. The ETS simply isn't working as was intended, and its main impact so far has been to increase the profits of electricity generators.

The policy failures continue to demonstrate the vital role of individuals. By our actions we need to show governments that we will accept significant restraints on fossil fuel use. Similarly, we can demonstrate to commercial companies that we will buy low-carbon goods, even at a higher price. Encouraging news is hard to come by in the global warming debate but a poll in the *Daily Telegraph* in November 2006 showed that 19 per cent of Britons accepted that living standards will have to fall in order to curb global warming.[270] 27 per cent of the respondents said that they would fly less frequently as a contribution to slowing the speed of temperature change. These are high figures and they demonstrate that individuals are beginning to get the message, even if government isn't.

Two important documents have been published in the last two months. Sir Nicholas Stern's review of the economics of climate change appears finally to have turned many members of the economics profession into active participants in discussions of how best to avert the worst impacts of global warming.[271] As someone trained as an economist and who briefly taught the subject at university, I have often in the past felt ashamed of my choice of academic subject. I hope Sir Nicholas's extraordinary depth of analysis convinces economics practitioners that the problem of climate change is not amenable to the conventional policy tools we might use to deal with other social issues. Frankly, I'm not optimistic that he will make much real difference in other ways. The recommendations in his report seem likely to be very limited in their effect. His proposals – more investment in research and development, better consumer education and a well-defined price for carbon – are little more than extensions to the existing policies of European governments. I hope that anyone reading this book will have seen that heavy and profligate use of fossil fuels is so ingrained into the fabric of modern life that real reductions are hugely difficult and Sir Nicholas's prescriptions are not enough.

George Monbiot's exciting and influential book *Heat* [272] shows that radical measures to reduce our emissions are completely compatible with the Western way of life. He recognizes that many of his suggestions are difficult to implement. Nevertheless, and surprisingly for a book of this sort, I've heard people discussing Monbiot's proposals approvingly over a cup of coffee or while chatting in the bus queue. Perhaps there is hope. *Heat* suggests that we will need to reduce our emissions by far more than I have suggested in this book, saying that a 90 per cent cut is necessary. Monbiot's figures differ from the conventional analysis used, for example, by Nicholas Stern or other writers in the past. He may well turn out to be right, and the emissions reductions I have identified in this book may turn out to be insufficient.

Some of George Monbiot's examples are similar to those I use to make my points. I didn't copy him – my book was submitted a few days before his book got into the shops – but I apologize if you notice some similarities. I am particularly proud of using one quotation that Monbiot also spotted: a UK government minister describing improvements in the insulation requirements for new buildings as 'unnecessary gold plating'. It was a wonderful example of the struggle we face convincing politicians that climate change is a serious problem.

If I had had a chance I would have wanted to use his persuasive arguments about the unsuitability of wind turbines for domestic houses, and also copy many other points he made. George Monbiot is a wonderful, and unique, commentator on the insanity of the Western world's approach to many of the biggest problems it faces.

I would have also wanted to comment on the increasing evidence that large UK companies are beginning to make real, sustained and successful attempts to reduce emissions. The actions of companies such as Tesco, Carphone Warehouse and Sky are impressive demonstrations of commitment. I think it is no accident that these three firms are among the best in the UK at spotting trends in consumer attitudes and behaviour. They sense that climate change is an issue of great concern to many of their customers and are adjusting their actions accordingly. For example, Tesco reported a 15 per cent reduction in the emissions from its stores in one year. During 2006 there has been very little good news about greenhouse gases and this was an extraordinarily heartening achievement.

Appendix

Sources of the Main Averages

This book uses data for the 'average' UK home. The data is as up-to-date as possible, but readers can check this book's companion website (www.lowcarbonlife.net) for latest figures.

This home is assumed to have access to mains gas and to use it for space and water heating. Electricity is used for lighting and appliances. In January 2006, the number of people in the UK was estimated at 60.2 million (the mid-2004 figure from National Statistics was 59.8 million, with the population rising by 250,000 to 300,000 a year) and the number of households was 25.8 million. This means that the average number of people per home is 2.333, which I have rounded to 2.3.

The following estimates are for the main individual elements of a person's direct emissions. None of these figures is perfectly accurate; but I believe all are correct to within 5 to 10 per cent.

CARBON EMISSIONS FROM GAS USE IN THE HOME

Total gas use by domestic users in the UK is about 400,000GWh/year.[273] About 80 per cent of UK homes have mains gas. Therefore, these homes typically consume about 19,000kWh/year. This is rising by about 1 per cent a year; but the pattern depends upon winter temperatures. Per person, this is about 8500kWh/year, equivalent to about 1.6 tonnes of carbon dioxide (CO_2).

CARBON EMISSIONS FROM ELECTRICITY USE IN THE HOME

The carbon emissions from UK electricity-generating stations were about 47 million tonnes in 2004.[274] This number will have risen in 2005 as a result of the slight swing back to coal-fired generation, and I estimate the 2005 figure was over 48 million tonnes. Multiplied by 3.667 to provide a figure for carbon dioxide, the total is about 176 million tonnes. About 34 per cent of all electricity is used for domestic purposes, meaning that almost 60 million tonnes of emissions were directly due to home consumption (in fact, the figure should be substantially higher since periods of high domestic use – primarily the generated by coal, a much more carbon-intensive fuel than gas). The total emissions per person resulting from electricity were therefore about 1 tonne.

This includes homes that use electricity for heating. Taking out an estimate for heating demand produces a figure of between 0.7 and 0.8 tonnes per person. Why do we exclude heating use? The answer is because our 'average' home is heated by gas.

This is consistent with the other easy way of calculating emissions by applying the standard factor to total domestic electricity demand. Government statistics show that total domestic demand for electricity was about 135 million gigawatt hours in 2005.[275] The standard assumption is that 1kWh of electricity is responsible for about 0.43kg of carbon dioxide. Total emissions resulting from domestic use of electricity were therefore about 58 million to 59 million tonnes, or just under 1 tonne per person. Excluding heating demand, the emissions per person were between 0.7 and 0.8 tonnes.

CARBON EMISSIONS RESULTING FROM TRAVELLING

Cars

A total of 27 million private cars drive an average of 14,500km (9000 miles) a year and, on average, emit 180g (0.18kg) of carbon dioxide per kilometre. This equates to 1.2 tonnes per person per year.

Bus and rail

Total emissions per person are under 0.1 tonnes per year. More detail is in Chapter 11.

Air travel

Various estimates suggest that current aviation emissions are about 10 million tonnes of carbon, or 37 million tonnes of carbon dioxide per year.[276] Using a multiplier of three to reflect the greater warming impact of aviation, the UK total is 111 million tonnes of carbon dioxide, or just over 1.8 tonnes per person.

TOTALS

These figures come to 5.4 tonnes per person per year.
  In addition, we need to add:

- carbon emissions from domestic burning of coal and propane – 0.1 tonnes per person;
- methane output from mining – substantially less than 0.1 tonnes per person;[277]

- carbon emissions resulting from coal mining – substantially less than 0.1 tonnes per person;
- carbon emissions resulting from oil refining – about 0.15 tonnes per person to cover the carbon costs of producing petrol, aviation kerosene, diesel and liquid petroleum gas (LPG) for domestic cars;[278]
- emissions from the process of extracting oil and gas – about 0.2 tonnes per person.[279]

Including other costs, such as the carbon emissions from shipping fuels and emissions generated in other countries, I use an additional figure of 0.6 tonnes of carbon dioxide per person.

Notes

1 This includes an allowance for aviation – usually omitted from government figures – with air travel emissions adjusted to allow for the impact of water vapour and nitrous oxide emitted at high altitude.

2 DETR (Department of Environment, Transport and the Regions) (2000) *UK Climate Change Programme*, DETR, London, November 2000.

3 EIA (US Energy Information Agency) (2006) *International Energy Outlook*, Energy Information Agency, Washington, DC.

4 Nuclear Energy Agency (2006) *Uranium 2005: Resources, Production and Demand*, Nuclear Energy Agency, Issy-les-Moulineaux, France, June 2006. This source estimated known reserves at 85 years at current rates of consumption. The agency indicated that it thought that future exploration would very significantly increase the known reserves. But the proposed future building of nuclear power stations in various parts of the world is likely to substantially increase the rate of consumption.

5 EIA (US Energy Information Agency) (2005) *System for the Analysis of Global Energy Markets*, Energy Information Agency, Washington, DC.

6 EIA (US Energy Information Agency) (2006) *Annual Energy Outlook*, Energy Information Agency, Washington, DC.

7 EIA (US Energy Information Agency) (2006) *International Energy Output*, Energy Information Agency, Washington, DC, June. The EIA sees a 75 per cent rise by 2030.

8 'When carbon dioxide changed there was always an accompanying climate change': comment by Dr Eric Wolff of the British Antarctic Survey (BAS) to the BBC on 5 September 2006, explaining the significance of the BAS's examination of Antarctic ice cores dating back 800,000 years.

9 Estimates are from Hillman, M. and Fawcett, T. (2004) *How We Can Save the Planet*, Penguin, London.

10 The estimate that half the UK population now flies at least once a year appears in *The Future of Air Transport*, published by the UK Department for Transport, 16 December 2003.

11 Easyjet (2005) *Preliminary Results Presentation*, Easyjet, available on the investor relations section of the Easyjet website, www.easyjet.com/en/investor/investorrelations_introduction.html.

12 IEA (2006) *Oil Market Report*, International Energy Agency, Paris, France, 12 April, p4, available for download at http://omrpublic.iea.org/.

13 IEA (2006) *Oil Market Report*, International Energy Agency, Paris, France, 12 April, p4, available for download at http://omrpublic.iea.org/.

14 First Group (2005) *Annual Accounts*, First Group, Aberdeen, Scotland/London, 17 May.

15 Published in the *Scotsman* newspaper, 18 May 2006.

16 As a major industrial customer, Tesco will pay less for its electricity than domestic consumers.

17 Information from a personal conversation with Rudolph Kalveks, the corporate development director of Rexam, one of the world's largest can manufacturers.

18 National Grid Company (2006) *Seven Year Statement*, National Grid Company, Warwick, UK, May.

19 The price of coal in Manchester is said to have fallen by nearly two-thirds within a year of the opening of the Bridgewater Canal.

20 Electricity price obtained from www.econ.cam.ac.uk/dae/repec/cam/pdf/wp0202.pdf.

21 International Air Transport Association (IATA) airlines are targeting a fuel-efficiency improvement of 10 per cent between 2000 and 2010 (see www.iata.org).

22 EIA (US Energy Information Agency) (2003) *Office Buildings: Consumption Tables*, Energy Information Agency, Washington, DC, available at www.eia.doe.gov/emeu/cbecs/pba99/office/officeconstable.html.

23 Office of Fair Trading (2006) *The Grocery Market: The OFT's Reasons for Making a Reference to the Competition Commission*, Office of Fair Trading, London, May.

24 Office for National Statistics (2006), *Family Spending 2004/5*, Office for National Statistics, London.

25 Guardian Unlimited website, http://politics.guardian.co.uk/, 11 April 2006.

26 Bernard Mandeville (1714) *The Fable of the Bees* (current edition by Hackett, Indianapolis, IN); and, from a very different perspective, Thorstein Veblen (1899) *Theory of the Leisure Class* (current edition by Penguin, London).

27 UK Department for Transport (2005) *National Travel Survey 2004*, Department for Transport, London, July.

28 Estimate provided by Freescale Semiconductor, a maker of components for electric, rather than hydraulic, power steering: see www.freescale.com.

29 ICM Research (2006) 'BBC environment poll', report, ICM Research, London, March.

30 Populus (2006) 'SN environment poll', survey, Populus, London, July.

31 HM Treasury (2006) *What is the Economics of Climate Change?* HM Treasury, London, 31 January.

32 Commission of the European Communities (2000) *Taxation of Aviation Fuel*, Commission of the European Communities, London, 2 March.

33 A short summary of this case can be found in Can Makers (2005) *UK Market Report*, www.canmakers.co.uk.

34 First Group (2005) *Corporate Responsibility Report 2004*, First Group, Aberdeen, Scotland/London.

35 Reported in the Point Carbon newsletter, *Carbon Market News*, 12 April 2006.

36 Information taken from the Point Carbon newsletter, *Carbon Market News*, 12 April 2006.

37 Gas-fired stations generate about 0.19kg of carbon dioxide per kilowatt hour. UK wholesale electricity prices are over 4 pence a kilowatt hour, and the price of permits is about 0.4 Euro cents per kilowatt hour.

38 European Environment Agency (2006) 'EU greenhouse gas emissions increase for second year in a row', report, European Environment Agency, Copenhagen, 22 June.

39 Energy Review (2006) *The Energy Challenge*, Department of Trade and Industry, London, July, p99.

40 National Grid (2006) *Seven Year Statement*, National Grid, Warwick, UK.

41 Both figures are published by the National Grid in its formal *Seven Year Statement* and confirmed in a personal email exchange in June 2006.

42 World Wide Fund for Nature, Scotland (2004) *Submissions to the Enterprise and Culture Committee Enquiry into Renewable Energy*, Scottish Parliament, January.

43 BBC News website, www.bbc.co.uk, 12 April 2006.

44 AECB (2006) *Minimising Emissions from New Homes*, Association for Environment Conscious Building, Llandysul, Wales, February.

45 *Guardian* (2005) 'Energy saving targets scrapped', *Guardian*, 18 July.

46 Estimate from British Airways in a newsletter entitled *Environment Matters* sent to its staff (no date, but available at www.ba.com).

47 UK Department for Transport (2003) *The Future of Air Transport*, Department for Transport, London, December, Chapter 2, p6.

48 Response to a question from Tim Yeo, MP, at a meeting of the House of Commons Liaison Committee of 7 February 2006.

49 Government White Paper (2003) *The Future of Air Transport*, December.

50 ICM Research (2006) *Environment Survey*, fieldwork 23–25 March, ICM Research, London.

51 Assumes duty of just under 50 pence a litre, 11,000km round trip and fuel consumption of 4 litres per 100 passenger kilometres. If VAT were included as well, the cost would have to rise by a further £60 or so.

52 Press release from the European Commission (2005) *Climate Change: Commission Proposes Strategy to Curb Greenhouse Gas Emissions from Air Travel*, 27 September 2005.

53 UK Department for Transport (2003) *The Future of Air Transport*, Department for Transport, London, 16 December.

54 UK Department for Transport (2004) *The Future of Transport*, Department for Transport, London, 20 July.

55 Transport 2000 website, www.transport2000.org.uk, accessed 23 May 2006.

56 Transport 2000 website, www.transport2000.org.uk, accessed 23 May 2006.

57 These figures are from UK Department for Transport (2004) *The Future of Transport*, Department for Transport, London, 20 July, Chapter 3.

58 See www.ss-philip-and-james.oxon.sch.uk/travel/travelplan2005-09.pdf.

59 Defra (2002) *Government Commits to Sustainable Development*, press release, UK Department for Environment, Food and Rural Affairs, London, 25 July.

60 Sustainable Development Commission (2004) *Annual Report*, Sustainable Development Commission, London.

61 Sustainable Development Commission (2005) *Leading By Example? Not Exactly*, Sustainable Development Commission, London.

62 Sustainable Development Commission (2005) *Leading By Example? Not Exactly*, Sustainable Development Commission, London.

63 Joseph, S. (2006) 'Ending the cult of the car', *Blue Skies* (supplement to *The Parliamentary Monitor*), issue 137, March/April, available at www.epolitix.com/EN/Publications/

Blue+Skies+Monitor/137_1/bfb56eb3-76da-4963-91e9-0254c801486b.htm, accessed November 2006.

64 UK Department for Transport (2003) *The Future of Air Transport*, Department for Transport, London, 16 December.

65 To be found at www.publications.parliament.uk/pa/cm200506/cmselect/cmcumeds/650/5110802.htm.

66 SolarCentury comment posted on its website, www.solarcentury.com, on 13 July 2006 by Oliver Sylvester-Bradley.

67 Friends of the Earth (2006) 'Budget must help tackle climate change', press release, 20 March 2006.

68 HM Treasury (1997) *Statement on Environmental Taxation*, HM Treasury, 2 July 1997.

69 Office for National Statistics (2006), *Family Spending 2004/5*, Office for National Statistics, London.

70 Particularly David Henderson in many articles, such as 'Are the IPCC's global warming forecasts based on faulty economics?' available at www.marshall.org/pdf/materials/275.pdf.

71 Larry Summers, President of Harvard University, said at Morning Prayers at Appleton Chapel, Harvard, 15 September 2003.

72 Professor Paul Klemperer of Oxford University gave me this illustration. I don't mean to suggest that Professor Klemperer would agree or disagree with the main theses of this book.

73 Lomborg, B. (ed) (2004) *Global Crises, Global Solutions*, Cambridge University Press, Cambridge.

74 E.ON UK (2006) 'E.ON UK considers world-leading clean coal technology for new pilot power station in Lincolnshire, calls for government support', press release, E.ON UK, Coventry, UK, 24 May.

75 First Group (2005) *Corporate Responsibility Report 2004*, First Group, Aberdeen, Scotland/London.

76 Figures on BP's renewable energy programme are taken from its 2005 *Corporate Sustainability Report*. Its total 2005 capital investment is taken from the corporation's annual report.

77 E.ON UK (2006) *Corporate Social Responsibility Report 2005*, E.ON UK, Coventry, UK, June, p13.

78 Reported in the Financial Times, 7 June 2006.

79 Lee Raymond of Exxon Mobil was reputed to have this in his back pocket when he left corporate headquarters in 2005.

80 See, for example, the references on www.climatedenial.org.

81 To be found on the Friends of the Earth website at www.foe.co.uk/living/poundsavers/deborah_moggach_pride_prejudice.html.

82 Lexus website, www.lexus.co.uk, accessed January 2006.

83 Wiener, M. J. (2004) *English Culture and the Decline of the Industrial Spirit: 1850–1980*, Cambridge University Press, Cambridge. This is one of the most powerful books on this subject and, although first published in 1981, is still extensively read today.

84 *Health Statistics Quarterly* (2005) 'Live births, stillbirths and infant deaths, 1976–2004', *Health Statistics Quarterly*, vol 27, autumn.

85 See www.statistics.gov.uk/cci/nugget.asp?id=881.

86 But note that Cuba's infant mortality rate is almost as low as in the UK, even though Cuba is materially much less well off.

87 For example, Denmark now gets 25 per cent of its electricity from renewable sources.

88 Dresdner Kleinwort Wasserstein research, quoted by the analyst James Montier on the Investors Insight Publishing website (www.investorsinsight.com), indicates the average holding period for New York Stock Exchange shares is now about 11 months.

89 Brook Lyndhurst/MORI (2001) *Household Waste Behaviour in London*, Resource Recovery Forum, Skipton, UK.

90 John Kay, 'Thinking outside the blue box on recycling', in the *Financial Times*, 25 February 2004.

91 Gross, L. (2005) 'Altruism, fairness and social intelligence: Are economists different?', Stanford University, 1 June 2005. This paper summarizes the research on economists and altruism by saying: 'While the majority of experiments find economists to be more self-interested, not all do.'

92 *Wrap* (2006) 'Environmental benefits of recycling', *Wrap*, May.

93 NEF (New Economics Foundation) (2005) *The Ethical Consumerism Report*, NEF, London.

94 London Renewables (2003) *Attitudes to Renewable Energy in London*, London Renewables, December (available on the Greater London Authority website, www.london.gov.uk).

95 NEF (New Economics Foundation) (2005) *The Ethical Consumerism Report*, NEF, London.

96 Some of this research is analysed in 'Shaping pro-environment behaviors', published at www.pyschologymatters.org.

97 Assumes a three times 'forcing' effect.

98 A figure of 3900kWh is higher than the conventional figure for electricity consumption in homes that have gas heating. Most sources use about 3300kWh; but this is insufficient to explain total UK electricity consumption and is inconsistent with aggregate figures for the UK residential sector.

99 This figure has been multiplied by three to take into account the effect of emissions other than carbon dioxide from jet engines operating at altitude. Prior to this multiplication, the figure would be 0.10kg per kilometre. This figure is lower than used in most analyses, but corresponds to the emissions of British Airways aircraft as reported in the company's most recent environmental reporting. British Airways has a higher proportion of long-haul flights than most world airlines.

100 Such as www.marinewaypoints.com/learn/greatcircle.shtml.

101 AECB (2006) *AECB Consultation response on 2nd Draft E.S.T. Best Practice Standards*, Association for Environment Conscious Building, Llandysul, Wales, January.

102 How can a 1 degree reduction cut use by nearly 15 per cent? The arithmetic is reliant on the fact that homes are also heated by cooking, by electric appliances such as lights and by water heating, as well as by solar gain in spring and autumn. The boiler is topping up a base load of other sources of heat.

103 Data on domestic gas consumption can be found by consulting the UK Department of Trade and Industry's (DTI's) *Digest of UK Energy Statistics*. The first quarter of 2006 was a particularly cold period; but even adjusting for variations in external temperatures, there is no evidence yet of falling gas demand from homes. The National Grid's latest forecast suggests that homes and the smallest businesses will increase their requirements by over 1 per cent a year into the foreseeable future (the recent, August 2006, further spike in domestic gas prices may cause the National Grid to modify downwards future forecasts).

104   The average UK house is about 76 square metres in extent. A figure of 14,000kWh of gas is used to heat the typical property, meaning that the house uses about 184kWh per square metre. This assumes that gas-heated properties are typical of all UK homes. This assumption may slightly bias upward the energy consumption figures.

105   This information is from www.passivhaustagung.de/englisch/Passive_House_E/ step_by _step _towards_passive_houses.html#abb4.

106   These figures are calculated by multiplying the degree of variation of the typical heat loss rate (watts per degree of heating) for the different types of house by the average gas usage of 14,000kWh. These figures should be treated as little better than guesses; but I have included them because many people ask me for an estimate of typical heating bills for different types of houses.

107   Shorrock, L. D. and Utley, J. I. (2003) *Domestic Energy Fact File 2003*, Building Research Establishment, available free on the internet at www.bre.co.uk. Figure 6.1 contains data resulting from manipulations of Figure 35 in Shorrock and Utley.

108   Boilers that are not frequently and well serviced will have efficiencies lower than these figures.

109   Data from Market Transformation Programme (2005) *The Domestic Heating Boiler Energy Model: Methods and Assumptions*, Appendix B, Table 1, p18, Market Transformation Programme, Future Energy Solutions, Didcot, UK (see www.mtprog.com).

110   See www.theyellowhouse.org.uk/themes/heatwat.html.

111   This information may seem unbearably trivial or obvious. However, some recent research has shown that many people think that the thermostat is a simple on/off switch. Many also think that the turning the thermostat up high increases the speed at which a room heats up.

112   WarmWorld Ltd.

113   Information from the National Energy Foundation website, www.nef.org.uk.

114   From a manufacturer (Rockwool) of the insulation materials in a personal communication. For the technically minded, Rockwool says that its product will cut the typical 'U' value, a measure of thermal conductivity, from about 1.5 to about 0.5 for a 60mm cavity.

115   British Gas has offered to increase existing thicknesses to 25cm (10 inches) for £220 for most sizes of house.

116   These products are available from companies such as the Green Building Store.

117   Office of Fair Trading (2004) *Doorstep Selling*, Office of Fair Trading, London, Annexe H, May.

118   'Good' double glazing should use low emissivity glass, such as Pilkington K, and argon filling.

119   See www.oxford.gov.uk/environment/insulation.cfm.

120   Barnet Borough Council's energy advice pages at www.barnet.gov.uk.

121   See www.theyellowhouse.org.uk/themes/ventil.html.

122   Boyle, G. (ed) (2004) *Renewable Energy*, 2nd edition, Oxford University Press, Oxford.

123   Rudge, J. and Winder, R. (2002) *Central Heating Installation for Older, Low Income Households: What Difference Does It Make?* Network for Comfort and Energy Use in Buildings, Proceedings of Indoor Air 2002, Monterey, CA.

124   AECB (2006) *AECB Consultation Response on 2nd Draft E.S.T. Best Practice Standards*, Association for Environmental Conscious Building, Llandysul, Wales, January.

125   Enderdata, www.odyssee-indicators.org/Publication/PDF/households_eu04.pdf, p17.

126   The numbers in this box are taken from a very interesting presentation by Enerdata, available at www.odyssee-indicators.org/Publication/PDF/households_eu04.pdf, p13.

127 The website www.dti.gov.uk/energy/consumers/fuel_poverty/hot_water_consumption.pdf gives estimates for 1998. I have increased these figures slightly to reflect the rise in general water consumption since then.

128 One Australian supplier of this type of shower can be found here at www.ecoshower.com.au.

129 This information can be found on the government's Market Transformation Programme website, www.mtprog.com.

130 Matilde Soregaroli of the market research firm GfK, presentation at Sabaf, May 2006, available at www.sabaf.it.

131 These figures are based on a 70kg freestanding cooker, made mostly of steel with embedded energy of 5500kWh per tonne, made using the electric arc method.

132 Paul Waide, presentation at Sabaf, March 2006, available at www.sabaf.it. I have made this calculation from raw data provided by Mr Waide in this presentation.

133 Dr Tudor Constantinescu, presentation at Sabaf, March 2006, available at www.sabaf.it.

134 Nicola King, Market Transformation Programme, presentation to Sabaf, March 2006, available at www.sabaf.it

135 Paul Waide, presentation at Sabaf, March 2006, available at www.sabaf.it.

136 Paul Waide, presentation at Sabaf, March 2006, available at www.sabaf.it.

137 Assuming that the home doesn't also use electricity for heating.

138 IEA (2006) *Light's Labours Lost*, International Energy Agency, Paris, France, July, p185.

139 People worry about the mercury in CFLs. Mercury is a human and environmental poison. But here's a fact to impress your friends. Well over one third of UK electricity is provided by burning coal. Coal contains mercury. Adding a compact fluorescent to your house reduces electricity production. This reduces mercury emissions by more than the mercury contained in your new light bulb.

140 On 5 March 2006.

141 IEA (2006) *Light's Labours Lost*, International Energy Agency, Paris, France, July, p273, reporting a study by ECODROME in 1998.

142 IEA (2006) *Light's Labours Lost*, International Energy Agency, Paris, France, July, p273, reporting a EURECO 2002 study.

143 These figures are from Table 4.2 in IEA (2006) Light's Labours Lost, International Energy Agency, Paris, France, July, p189.

144 Odysee (2004) *Energy Efficiency Indicators in Europe*, Enerdata, Paris.

145 Ecofys (2004) *Electricity Conservation as Alternative for Building Power Plants*, Ecofys, Utrecht, the Netherlands, July.

146 DTI (2006) *Digest of UK Energy Statistics*, annual tables, UK Department of Trade and Industry, London, updated 27 July.

147 International Energy Agency's Demand Side Management Programme.

148 A number of the headline figures in this chapter are derived from work by Defra's Market Transformation Programme. The detailed reports and commentary from this organization are excellent and deserve the highest praise. The detailed follow-up analysis is generally my own work, and I accept responsibility for errors and omissions.

149 Stamminger, R., Barth, A. and Dörr, S. (2005) *Old Washing Machines Wash Less Efficiently and Consume More Resources*, University of Bonn, Bonn, Germany, www.landtechnik.uni-bonn.de.

150 The John Lewis JLTTC01 appears to be this model with a John Lewis badge on it.

151 Stamminger, R., Badura, R., Broil, G., Doerr, S. and Elschenbroich, A. (2004) *A European Comparison of Cleaning Dishes by Hand*, University of Bonn, Bonn, Germany. Because it compares in intimate detail the dish-washing habits across several European countries, the paper gives us unfettered scope for reinforcing prejudices about national characteristics. I cannot recommend it highly enough as a source for anthropologists.

152 Assumes a ten-year life and a dishwasher cost of £250.

153 For the economists, this is the result of a simple ordinary least squares regression of energy consumption against size.

154 The data in this box is garnered from Enerdata, www.odyssee-indicators.org/ Publication /PDF/households_eu04.pdf, p42.

155 From the Market Transformation Programme, www.mtprog.com.

156 This is an approximate figure. I'm sure a more accurate number exists, but I have had problems finding a good source.

157 See www.smecc.org/litton_-_for_heat,_tune_to_915_or_2450_megacycles.htm.

158 *Fujitsu Siemens E30 Scenic Green PC*, datasheet consulted August 2006.

159 See www.efficientpowersupplies.org/pages/SeptNRDCLaptopSummary_digital.pdf.

160 Data from a paper by the International Energy Agency to be found at www.iea.org/ textbase/papers/2002/globe02.pdf.

161 Energy Saving Trust (2006) *The Rise of the Machines*, Energy Saving Trust, London, July.

162 Energy Saving Trust (2006) *The Rise of the Machines*, Energy Saving Trust, London, July.

163 Data from EEA (2006) *Transport and the Environment: Facing a Dilemma*, European Environment Agency, Copenhagen, March.

164 See www.behrgroup.com/produkte/fahrzeug/klimatipps/text5.php#. But note that the Australian government says that over 50mph, having a window open has more impact on fuel consumption than having the air-conditioning on because of the worsened aerodynamic characteristics of the car.

165 Some sources put the figure lower at around 23 million private cars; but these totals appear to omit private cars used for business.

166 The National Travel Survey (NTS), published by the UK Department for Transport gives copious detail on all these matters. These figures are the most regularly cited in the UK; but they are inconsistent with other estimates, particularly those relating to the average number of miles that the typical car travels in a year. NTS figures suggest that the average car does less than 6000 miles (9700km) a year, whereas this chapter suggests the real figure is about 9000 miles (14,500km).

167 Data from Unander, F. (2004) *Thirty Years of Energy Prices and Taxes*, International Energy Agency, Paris, France.

168 Dual-fuel cars use a sip of petrol to get the engine started.

169 Hivert, L. (1996) 'Dieselisation et nouveaux dieselistes: Les évolutions récentes', *Actes INRETS*, no 59.

170 See www.esru.strath.ac.uk/EandE/Web_sites/02-03/biofuels/quant_waste_fuel.htm. This site estimates that about 110 million litres of waste-oil diesel could be produced. At about 1000 litres a year per typical diesel car, this implies about 110,000 possible users.

171 See www.news.cornell.edu/stories/July05/ethanol.toocostly.ssl.html.

172 See www.biodiesel.co.uk/levington.htm, published in 2000.

173 See www.biodiesel.org/resources/reportsdatabase/reports/gen/19940101_gen-027.pdf, apparently published in 2003.

174 See www.eccm.uk.com/pdfs/TD7.pdf.

175 See www.monbiot.com/archives/2005/12/06/worse-than-fossil-fuel.

176 See www.saab.co.uk/main/GB/en.

177 See www.easier.com/view/News/Motoring/Saab/article-30323.html.

178 Friends of the Earth (2006) 'UK motor industry failing to tackle climate change', press release, 25 April 2006.

179 Data from the European Environment Agency (2006) *Transport and the Environment: Facing a Dilemma*, European Environment Agency, Copenhagen, March.

180 Defra (2005) *Guidelines for Company Reporting on Greenhouse Gas Emissions*, UK Department for Environment, Food and Rural Affairs, London, Annexes, updated July 2005.

181 National Express Group (2005) *Corporate Responsibility Report*, National Express Group, London.

182 First Group (2005) *Corporate Responsibility Report*, First Group, Aberdeen, Scotland/ London, data from AEAT Environment.

183 Association of Train Operating Companies (2005) *Ten Year European Growth Trends*, Association of Train Operating Companies, London, July 2005.

184 The figures on diesel consumption are from AEA Technology's report to the Rail Regulator on the *Environmental Costs of Rail Transport*, August 2005.

185 Kemp, R. (2004) 'Environmental impact of high speed rail', Presentation to the Institution of Mechanical Engineers, London, 21 April 2004.

186 From AEA Technology's report to the Rail Regulator on the *Environmental Costs of Rail Transport*, August 2005.

187 A typical private car with two occupants would produce about 90g of carbon dioxide per person kilometre, somewhat less than a bus.

188 All of these figures are from Eurostat, the European Commission's statistical agency.

189 Data from National Express Group (2005) *Corporate Responsibility Report*, National Express Group, London.

190 National Express Group (2005) *Corporate Responsibility Report*, National Express Group, London.

191 RCEP (Royal Commission on Environmental Pollution) (2002) *Environmental Effects of Civil Aircraft in Flight*, RCEP, London, November 2002.

192 The three sites, www.climatecare.org, www.co2balance.com and www.carbonneutral.com, were accessed on 5 June 2006. On the British Airways offset site, run by www.climatecare.org, the calculator produced a figure of 1.26 tonnes.

193 These figures are from Civil Aviation Authority (2006) 'CAA figures show increased traffic at UK airports in 2005', press release, 19 April 2006. This release is a confusing document because it double counts internal air travel, once as a departure and once as an arrival at UK airports.

194 The figures needed to estimate this number are contained in British Airways (2005) *Corporate Responsibility Report*, British Airways, London.

195 One litre of kerosene produces approximately 2.57kg of carbon dioxide.

196 About 11,000km to New York and back, compared to 14,500km for the average UK car.

197 British Airways (2005) *Corporate Responsibility Report*, British Airways, London, indicates that the airline's fuel efficiency had improved by 25 per cent over the previous 14 years.

198 Quoted in Tyndall Centre for Climate Change (North) (2005) Presentation entitled 'No chance for the climate without tackling aviation'; the figures are for the period of 1993–2004.

199 Quoted in Tyndall Centre for Climate Change (North) (2005) Presentation entitled 'No chance for the climate without tackling aviation'.

200 Friends of the Earth (2006) 'CAA figures show increased traffic at UK airports in 2005', Press release, 17 May.

201 Tyndall Centre for Climate Change (North) (2005) Presentation entitled 'No chance for the climate without tackling aviation'.

202 Tyndall Centre for Climate Change (North) (2005) Presentation entitled 'No chance for the climate without tackling aviation'.

203 Response to a question from John Denham, MP, at a meeting of the House of Commons Liaison Committee meeting of 7 February 2006.

204 Royal Commission on Environmental Pollution (2003) 'Royal Commission disappointed by government white paper', press release, 16 December 2003.

205 Quoted in Friends of the Earth (2004) 'Government must listen to top scientist's warning on aviation', press release, 30 March 2004.

206 See www.paulflynnmp.co.uk/newsdetail.jsp?id=444.

207 Sustainable Development Commission (2004) *Missed Opportunity: Summary Critique of the Air Transport White Paper*, Sustainable Development Commission, London, June.

208 IPPR (2003) *The Sky's the Limit*, Institute for Public Policy Research, London, May.

209 Oxford University Transport Studies Unit (2006) *Counting Your Carbon*, March 2006.

210 Please note the logical problem here, perhaps suggesting some problems with the Oxford data. If 10 per cent of people have over ten times the average, then the net emissions from all the rest of the population must be less than zero.

211 *Financial Times* (2006) 'Letter to the *Financial Times*', *Financial Times*, 7 June 2006.

212 Such as the House of Lords Committee on Economics Affairs in its report *The Economics of Climate Change*, published 6 July 2005.

213 2004 figures from the UK's *Environmental Accounts* suggest that the iron and steel industry had greenhouse gas emissions of about 24 million tonnes of carbon dioxide equivalent, compared to the figure presented in this book of 126 million tonnes for the food supply chain.

214 Defra (2005) *The Validity of Food Miles as an Indicator of Sustainable Development*, UK Department for Environment, Food and Rural Affairs, London, July.

215 Elm Farm Research Centre (2002) 'Eating oil', January 2002. This paper provides a reference to support the figure of 8 tonnes; but documents to which the reference is made do not appear to actually cover the topic.

216 These two figures are used by the European Environment Agency and most climate change bodies around the world, though not the US, which uses a higher figure for methane and a slightly lower figure for nitrous oxide.

217 The Soil Association (one of the organic certifying bodies in the UK) estimates that 4 per cent of UK farmland is in organic use: Soil Association (2005) *Stern Review of the Economics of Climate Change: Soil Association Evidence to HM Treasury*, December, available from www.hm-treasury.gov.uk/media/FCF/4A/climate_change_azeez.pdf. The Soil Association seems to suggest in this document that sales of organic food are growing by about 10 per cent per year.

218 Soil Association (2005) *Stern Review of the Economics of Climate Change: Soil Association Evidence to HM Treasury*, December, available from www.hm-treasury.gov.uk/media/FCF/4A/climate_change_azeez.pdf; see p3 of this document.

219 Soil Association numbers are 1.4 million tonnes of fertilizer at 6.7kg of carbon dioxide equivalent per 1kg of fertilizer. This includes the transport of fertilizer and the energy consumption arising in the manufacture of the raw materials used to make the product.

220 See ftp://.ftp.eia.doe.gov/pub/oiaf/1605/cdrom/pdf/ggrpt/057304.pdf, pxi.

221 Defra (2006) *UK Climate Change Programme 2006*, UK Department for Environment, Food and Rural Affairs, London, March.

222 The *UK Climate Change Programme 2006*.

223 Available from www.statistics.gov.uk as *Environmental Accounts: Emissions, Greenhouse Gases, 93 Industries*.

224 British Association for the Advancement of Science (2005) 'Soil cancels out UK's efforts to reduce CO_2', press release, www.the-ba.net/the-ba/Events/FestivalofScience/FestivalNews/_Soils.htm.

225 British Association for the Advancement of Science (2005) 'Soil cancels out UK's efforts to reduce CO_2', press release, www.the-ba.net/the-ba/Events/FestivalofScience/FestivalNews/_Soils.htm.

226 Defra (2005) *The Validity of Food Miles as an Indicator of Sustainable Development*, UK Department for Environment, Food and Rural Affairs, London, July 2005. The average distance for each trip by heavy goods vehicles carrying food has risen by 50 per cent since 1978.

227 For example, Defra (2005) *The Validity of Food Miles as an Indicator of Sustainable Development*, UK Department for Environment, Food and Rural Affairs, London, July.

228 Defra (2005) The Validity of Food Miles as an Indicator of Sustainable Development, UK Department for Environment, Food and Rural Affairs, London, July.

229 Defra (2005) Agriculture in the United Kingdom, UK Department for Environment, Food and Rural Affairs, London.

230 Defra (2005) The Validity of Food Miles as an Indicator of Sustainable Development, UK Department for Environment, Food and Rural Affairs, London, July.

231 Some of the biggest companies in the food industry provide data to the Carbon Disclosure Project.

232 Page 9 of the Food and Drink Federation's submission to the Food Industry Sustainability Study suggests a figure of about 1 per cent per year; but as the UK is becoming less self-sufficient in food at about the same rate, this reduction is not significant.

233 Food and Drink Federation (2005) *Response to Defra's Public Consultation on Draft Food Industry Sustainability Strategy*, Food and Drink Federation, London, August.

234   An INCPEN (Industry Council for Packaging and the Environment) report said that a major
      grocery retailer had reported that 55 per cent of vegetables were sold loose and 45 per cent
      packaged. INCPEN (undated) *Consumer Attitudes to Packaging*, INCPEN, Reading, UK.

235   INCPEN (1996) *Environmental Impact of Packaging in the UK Food Supply System*, INCPEN,
      Reading, UK.

236   The figure is not stated precisely in the J. Sainsbury (2005) *Corporate Responsibility Report*; but
      I have performed some analysis on data provided by J. Sainsbury.

237   Figure quoted by Transport 2000, www.transport2000.org.uk/factsandfigures/Facts.asp.

238   Defra (2005) *The Validity of Food Miles as an Indicator of Sustainable Development*, UK
      Department for Environment, Food and Rural Affairs, London, July.

239   This is also consistent with National Travel Survey data showing that the average car was
      driven about 600km per year for food shopping, with the typical car producing about 180g
      of carbon dioxide per kilometre, and with about 29 million cars on UK roads.

240   Figures from www.wasteonline.org.uk/resources/informationsheets/wastedisposal.htm.

241   These figures are based on calculations shown at www.greenhousegas.gov.au.

242   Severn Trent published a figure of 71.7 per cent for December 2004.

243   These figures are from www.wasteonline.org.uk/

244   Trade data can be found at www.statistics.defra.gov.uk/esg/reports/afq/afqbriefsup_dec.pdf.

245   1900 kilocalories equals about 2.2kWh.

246   Quoted in the European Environment Agency article on household consumption at
      www.epaedia.eea.europa.eu/page.php?pid=526.

247   Data to be found at www.guardian.co.uk/values/socialaudit/environment/story/0,,130510
      3,00.html.

248   Similarly from www.guardian.co.uk/values/socialaudit/environment/story/0,,1305103,00.html.

249   I calculated this from figures given in Southern Water (2005) Environment Report, Southern
      Water, Worthing, West Sussex.

250   Defra (2006) *Environmental Accounts: Emissions, Greenhouse Gases, 93 Industries*, UK
      Department for Environment, Food and Rural Affairs, London, updated 23 May 2006.

251   *Wrap* (2006) 'Environmental benefits of recycling', *Wrap*, May 2006. This study disagrees
      with the conclusion stated in my text; but its own data suggests that having to wash plastics
      may outweigh the environmental impact of recycling.

252   BPF (2006) *Plastic Bag Tax, – The Full BPF Position*, British Plastics Federation website,
      www.bpf.co.uk, accessed 19 June.

253   E.ON UK (2006) *Performance of Whispergen Micro CHP in UK Homes*, E.ON UK, Coventry,
      UK, May.

254   Data from Energy Saving Trust website, www.est.org.uk/myhome/generating/types/wind/,
      accessed November 2006.

255   Email from Renewable Devices, 1 September 2006.

256   The government is currently (September 2006) consulting on a proposal to remove all
      domestic renewable installations from planning control unless the house is in a sensitive area.

257   The electrical retailer Currys is now advertising a price of about £9000 for a simple 2kW
      system.

258 I hope this non-technical explanation does not offend experts. It seems a good way of explaining it to me.

259 Friends of the Earth (2004) *Guide to Green Electricity Tariffs*, Friends of the Earth, available at www.foe.co.uk/resource/reports/green_electricity_tariffs_2004.pdf (accessed November 2006).

260 Figure is from the *Ecologist* (2005) 'Green Energy – are you being conned?', *Ecologist*, June, and repeated to me on the phone by a company sales representative on 19 June 2005.

261 June 2006.

262 Westmill Wind Farm (2005) *Prospectus*, Westmill Wind Farm, Barrow in Furness, UK, November.

263 I should disclose that my family owns £5000 worth of shares in this wind farm.

264 This data is from www.merseyforest.org.uk/pages/fun_carbon.asp. Figures from Australia (www.greenhouse.gov.au) are somewhat higher.

265 Information from the Macaulay Institute, Aberdeen, www.macaulay.ac.uk/agfor_toolbox/try_it.html.

266 Twenty 20W compact fluorescent bulbs replacing twenty 100W conventional bulbs used for one hour a day for ten years.

267 Forestry Commission (2001) *Forestry Statistics*, Forestry Commission, Edinburgh.

268 *Business Day* (2006) 'The market and energy security', *Business Day*, Johannesburg, 23 May.

269 Adam Ma'anit from Carbon Trade Watch, 10 April 2006, available at www.carbontradewatch.org.

270 YouGov/*Daily Telegraph* survey results available at www.yougov.com/archives/pdf/TEL060101021_1.pdf.

271 Stern, N. (2006) *The Economics of Climate Change: The Stern Review*, report to the Prime Minister and the Chancellor of the Exchequer by the Head of the Government Economics Service and Adviser to the Government, Cambridge University Press, Cambridge, UK, available for download at www.hm-treasury.gov.uk/independent_reviews/stern_review_economics_climate_change/stern_review_report.cfm.

272 Monbiot, G. (2006) *Heat: How to Stop the Planet Burning*, Allen Lane, London.

273 This figure is from DTI (2006) *Digest of UK Energy Statistics*, annual tables, UK Department of Trade and Industry, London, updated 27 July.

274 Association of Electricity Producers (undated) *Frequently Asked Questions about Electricity*, www.aepuk.com/need_info.php#3 (accessed November 2006). The figure on the website should be multiplied by 3.667 to turn it into a carbon dioxide equivalent.

275 DTI (2006) *Digest of UK Energy Statistics*, annual tables, UK Department of Trade and Industry, London, updated 27 July.

276 Including data from Bows, A. (2005) 'No chance for the climate without tackling aviation', Tyndall Centre for Climate Change (North) presentation at the University of Manchester, UK, which estimated 2004 emissions at 9.5 million tonnes of carbon. UK aviation is growing in excess of 5 per cent per year, so I have estimated total emission of carbon in 2005 at 10 million tonnes.

277 Eighty-five per cent of coal output in the UK is used for power stations. About one third of electricity goes to domestic use.

278 About one quarter of the output of UK oil refineries is petrol. About 15 per cent is aviation kerosene. About 25 per cent is motor diesel, of which a small fraction goes into domestic cars.

279 About 40 per cent of the UK gas demand is from private houses. About one third of electricity is for domestic use. About half of the material from oil refineries goes into private cars, aircraft and as LPG for cars. So, I assume that 40 per cent of the energy costs of running refineries should be applied to domestic uses.

List of Acronyms and Abbreviations

AA	Automobile Association
AECB	Association for Environment Conscious Building
BA	British Airways
BRE	Building Research Establishment
BT	British Telecom
BTU	British thermal unit
C	Celsius
CAP	Common Agricultural Policy
CFL	compact fluorescent
CH_4	methane
CHP	combined heat and power
cm	centimetre
CO_2	carbon dioxide
CRI	colour rendering index
CRT	cathode ray tube
dB	decibel
Defra	UK Department for Environment, Food and Rural Affairs
ETS	Emissions Trading Scheme
EU	European Union
EU15	15 European Union member states
g	gram
GDP	gross domestic product
GE	General Electric
GJ	gigajoule
GM	General Motors
GNP	gross national product
GP	general practitioner
GW	gigawatt
GWh	gigawatt hour
ha	hectare
HFC	hydrofluorocarbon
IEA	International Energy Agency

kg	kilogram
km	kilometre
kW	kilowatt
kWh	kilowatt hour
kWp	kilowatt peak
LCD	liquid crystal display
LED	light-emitting diode
LPG	liquid petroleum gas
m	metre
MIT	Massachusetts Institute of Technology
ml	millilitre
mm	millimetre
MP	member of parliament
mph	miles per hour
MTP	Market Transformation Programme
NEF	New Economics Foundation
N_2O	nitrous oxide
OECD	Organisation for Economic Co-operation and Development
OLED	organic light-emitting diode
PV	photovoltaic(s)
ROC	Renewables Obligation Certificate
rpm	revolutions per minute
SUV	sports utility vehicle
TGV	*train à grande vitesse* (high-speed train)
UK	United Kingdom
US	United States
V	volt
VAT	value added tax
VCR	video cassette recorder
W	watt
WTO	World Trade Organization

Index

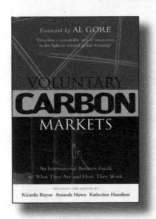
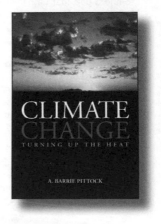

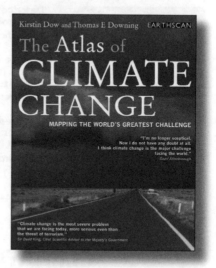